# *REPO*
## the ultimate guide

Daniel Corrigan
Christopher Georgiou
Jonathan Gollow

Pearls of Wisdom Publishing Ltd believe that the sources of information upon which this book is based are reliable and has made every effort to ensure the accuracy of the text. Neither the Publishers nor any of the authors nor their employers accept any responsibility for loss occasioned to any person acting or refraining from acting as a result of the material published in this book. This book should not be relied upon as advice and professional advice should be sought before undertaking any business in the markets which form the subject of this book.

First published in Great Britain 1999 by
**Pearls of Wisdom Publishing Limited**
11 Beaumont Court,
38/40 Beaumont Street
London W1N 1FA

Email: info@repobook.com
Web-site: www.repobook.com


© Pearls of Wisdom Publishing Limited
ISBN 0 9537010 0 X

Printed October 1999.


*Cover Design by: crutes la mar, 0191 230 2444*
*Typesetting by: David Siddall Associates, 01600 740683*
*Printing by: Black Bear Press Limited, 01223 424571*

# About the authors

Daniel Corrigan, Christopher Georgiou and Jonathan Gollow were co-authors and editors of the "NatWest Markets Handbook of International Repo" (IFR Publishing, 1995).

## *Daniel J Corrigan* BA (Econ) (Hons), MBA (Finance)

Daniel Corrigan is currently working as an adviser to the London Clearing House and has been instrumental in the development of and responsible for the marketing of "RepoClear", the first pan-European repo netting service in Europe.

Danny has been involved in the financial markets for twenty years and in the repo markets for 10 years. Prior to this role, he was Director and Head of Treasury Markets for MFK Renaissance Capital in Moscow, Director and Head of Repo Desk for Greenwich NatWest and Bear Stearns International.

Danny is a member of the Giovannini working group advising the EU on changes in the repo markets; he is a member and former secretary of the ISMA repo dealers association Sterling committee; a member of the Examination Committee of the Securities Institute and was a member of the Bank of England Gilt repo working party.

Danny is co-author of "Bunds and Bund Futures" (Macmillan, 1991) and of "Gilts" (IFR Publishing, 1989)

Danny holds a degree in Economics from the University of Liverpool and a Masters in Business Administration from City University.

## *Christopher K Georgiou* LLB (Hons)

Christopher Georgiou is General Counsel at NatWest Global Financial Markets, where he advises the trading floor on repo, derivatives, emerging markets and treasury products. He trained and qualified as a solicitor in 1991 at Allen & Overy specialising in banking and capital markets products, and joined NatWest in 1995.

He is the author of the ISMA-sponsored publication "NatWest Users Guide to the 1995 Global Master Repurchase Agreement".

Chris has participated regularly in ISDA and ISMA documentation meetings and working groups and is a regular speaker at conferences on the legal and documentation aspects of repo and derivatives.

### *Jonathan M Gollow* BSc (Econ) (Hons), MSc

Jonathan is a freelance consultant in the financial markets and has recently been involved in financial markets PR, marketing and market research. He acted as General Manager for European Benchmarks, a financial index provider in Brussels, from November 1997 - March 1999 and has diverse business interests in the areas of Photography, Design & Marketing and the Internet.

Jonathan worked with Chris and Danny at NatWest Markets where he was Head of Marketing for Repo 1994-96. Prior to that, Jonathan was a broker for 7 years in the commodity and interest rate markets.

Jonathan holds a first class honours degree in Accounting and Financial Management from the University of Buckingham and a Master of Science degree in Operational Research from the London School of Economics.

## Dedications

Danny Corrigan

*"To my wonderful Kerrie and my lovable sons James, Ben and Luke. They don't want to know about repo, they just need the money!"*

Chris Georgiou

*"For Patricia and our blue-eyed baby boy".*

Jonathan Gollow

*"To all my family and friends and to the boundless possibilities of possibility".*

Cedelbank, the International Depository, provides clearing, settlement and custody services to more than 2000 customers in 80 countries worldwide. The Bank is assigned short-term and long-term ratings of A1+ and AA+ respectively by Standard and Poors and F1+ and AA respectively by FITCH IBCA.

Currently, securities transactions in 38 currencies are cleared and settled through a network of links spanning 33 markets. Since the beginning of the 1990s, the number of transactions processed has grown to more than 10 million a year and the value of the securities deposited now exceeds USD 2 trillion.

Cedelbank is a subsidiary of Cedel International and is headquartered in Luxembourg. There are Regional Offices in Dubai, Hong Kong, London, New York, São Paulo and Tokyo. Some 32 nationalities work for Cedel International, mirroring the international breadth of the customer base and market know-how. In addition to the core services of clearing, settlement and custody, Cedelbank also provides an asset optimisation suite of services which include the tripartite repo service, securities lending and collateral management.

On 14 May 1999 Cedel International, the parent company of Cedelbank, and Deutsche Börse Clearing, the German central securities depository announced that they would merge to form new Cedel International. Deutsche Börse Clearing is a leading central security depository which offers custody and settlement of domestic and international securities, risk management and related customer services. In 1998, it executed 65.5 million transactions. The custody volume amounts to USD 4.9 trillion with around 87,000 securities in custody. Also on 14 May 1999, ParisBourse SA/SICOVAM SA, the French central securities depository, signed a memorandum of understanding to join new Cedel International. These announcements were the prime movers in creating the ECH. On the 26 May 1999 an invitation was extended to other European national and international central securities depositories to join the European Clearing House (ECH).

For more information and a copy of our annual report or corporate brochure, please contact us by e-mail at: marketing@cedelbank.com.

You can also visit our web site at: www.cedelbank.com

Cedelbank
Luxembourg Head Office
67 Bd Grande-Duchesse Charlotte
L-2967 Luxembourg
Tel + 352 44 99 21
Fax + 352 44 99 28 210

**FRESHFIELDS**

Domestic and international repo markets have grown dramatically over the last few years. This is because of an increasing need to be able to take and hedge short positions in the capital and derivatives markets; growing concern over counterparty credit risk; and the favorable capital adequacy treatment given to repos. Most important of all is the growing awareness among market participants of the flexibility of repos and wide range of markets and circumstances in which they can be of benefit.

Freshfields has been involved in the Repo market for many years and has a wide ranging experience which enables our lawyers to help clients continue to innovate in this fast evolving market.

In particular we have been involved in the preparation of the market standard PSA/ISMA Global Master Repurchase Agreement (GMRA) for ISMA and the Gilt Repo Agreement for the Bank of England. Freshfields participates in ISMA's repo sub-committee and we also act for ISMA in obtaining legal opinions on the GMRA from over thirty jurisdictions. In addition we have lawyers in our network of offices in Europe and Asia who advise on the repo market in their jurisdiction.

Freshfields lawyers are regular contributors to publications and seminars on repos and they provide a repo course which is held twice a year in London for in-house lawyers and other practitioners in repo markets.

For further information on our services in this area, please contact
Guy Morton on +44 (0)20 70936 4000 or for information on Freshfields please visit our
website at www.freshfields.com

**Freshfields** *
Amsterdam;  Bangkok;  Barcelona;  Beijing;  Brussels;
Hanoi;  Ho Chi Minh City;  Hong Kong;  London;
Madrid;  Milan;  Moscow;  New York;  Paris;  Rom;e
Singapore;  Tokyo;  Washington

**Deringer Tessin Herrmann & Sedemund** *
Berlin;  Brussels;  Cologne;  Frankfurt;  Moscow;

Also in association with Wolf Theiss & Partners:
Vienna;  Prague

* *To merge on 1st January 2000.*

# FOREWORD

It is now over three and a half years since the market in gilt repo was established. Just before its introduction, when the previous book by these authors was produced, I said that the development of the market was the most important structural change since Big Bang. Repo has indeed proved to be a huge influence on the sterling capital and money markets, playing a pivotal role between the two, as indeed it does internationally. The fact that the Bank of England, along with the most other central banks, now uses government bond repo as one of the main tools of implementing monetary policy, also adds to the significance of the market. This updated version of the book provides an opportunity both to make a comprehensive survey of the state of the market so far and to look at important future developments.

Repo markets have grown steadily and impressively both in the UK and internationally, but this growth would not have been possible without the elements of a solid framework within which to transact. This book deals in detail with each aspect of the framework, taking account of the latest developments in each area. Tax and accountancy treatments are also analysed in detail, as well as legal considerations and the development of repo documentation. So far the repo market has proved an extremely safe one in which to operate and the awareness of the risks involved in market participation and the weight which the authorities attach to them also have chapters devoted to them.

Of course the financial world never stands still and the book also anticipates some of the important future developments for repo markets. The introduction of netting systems both in Europe and the UK is likely to be an influential factor in the market's growth. This has already been seen to some extent in the US where the liberation of balance sheets which netting provides has already added impetus to repo there. The ability to manage collateral in the most efficient and appropriate way has gained increasing prominence in financial companies in recent years and this aspect of market practice gets its due consideration in the final chapter.

As well as thanking the authors of this authoritative text, I would like to use this opportunity to recognise the achievements of those involved in repo markets internationally and particularly those involved in these first years of the gilt repo market. Whether they have been involved as market practitioners or as part of the market authorities, they have ensured that repo is one of the most widely used and flexible financial instruments, both in the UK and worldwide.

**Ian Plenderleith**
*Executive Director*
*Bank of England*

# Contents

# Acknowledgements

Danny Corrigan, Chris Georgiou and Jonathan Gollow are extremely grateful to the following people for their assistance in the production of this book:

Cedelbank and Freshfields for their sponsorship.

Sincere and respective thanks to Guy Morton, Michael Raffan and Ben Staveley of Freshfields for their work on the Legal, Regulation and Tax chapters. Our gratitude also to Clare Adshead-Grant, Elaine Hawes and Michelle Scott of Freshfields for co-ordinating the sponsorship, project managing the delivery of the chapters and for typing up those chapters.

Boundless appreciation to Saheed Awan of Cedelbank for arranging the sponsorship for this book, for his work on the Tri-party section and for writing the chapter on Collateral Management. Thanks also to Saheed for inspiring the title!

We gratefully acknowledge the work of Lena Fedotova on the Risk chapter. She works in the Russian securities business, and managed the risk of a repo business at MFK Renaissance Capital in Moscow - accordingly she knows a thing or two about repo risk!

Thanks to Andy White of the London Clearing House who read, re-read and commented on the risk chapter and is now acknowledged as the second best risk manager in London. Indeed, Danny wishes to especially acknowledge all LCH's RepoClear team who added their 'pearls of wisdom' directly or indirectly. Thanks to Larry Shearer (who provided a thoughtful insight into the French market) to Peter Meechan for his complicated but welcome netting example and to the team headed by Sara Williams which provided many ideas that were drawn on for this book and who, in RepoClear, produced a great product in double-quick time.

Thanks also to Sarah Best, editor of International Securities Lending magazine at Euromoney Institutional Investor for her work on co-writing the Markets Chapter with Danny, co-editing for consistency with Chris and helping us fine-tune the book into a publishable form!

Thanks and acknowledgement to Phil G Rivett, Andrew D Hawkins and David M Lukach of Pricewaterhouse Coopers for their work on the Accounting for Repo chapter.

Finally, thanks to Marc Beerts of Reuters and to Lisa Gras of Bloomberg for providing the screen prints we needed to make the book complete.

# Chapter 1

# Introduction

The repo markets continue to experience growth in turnover, outstandings and range of participants. New products have been added such as eurobond, corporate bond, emerging-market and equity repo. In mature markets over half of all bonds issued are lent via repo, securities lending or 'sell-buys'.

The mobilization has been driven by traditional forces - dealers' need to finance long and short positions, together with the securities lenders' desire to enhance yield. However, there are many new reasons behind the continued growth.

These include the collateralization of credit and liquidity exposures, the adoption by central banks of repo as their main platform of open market operations, and significant regulatory and fiscal changes. The introduction of favourable capital treatment regimes and the adoption of repo by central clearing counterparties as a viable netting product have been further drivers.

## Benefits of repo

The use of repo generally results in reduced financing costs to market makers, it is a flexible tool for central banks in their open market operations and it offers a reduction in funding costs to issuers, primarily governments. In addition, it increases the liquidity of bonds and their derivatives, enhances the auction process through the ability to pre-place new issues, and allows for improved hedging efficiency as pricing anomalies between the physical and derivative product are eroded. It acts a secured lending product, reducing credit risk by incorporating an outright transfer of legal title to the collateral, close-out netting rights and rights to call for margin. Finally, it extends the range of available money market products and leads to increased return to bond investors via bond lending.

## Disadvantages of repo

The ability to sell short the underlying bond market - that is, to sell a security that is not currently owned in the belief that the price will fall allowing for the bonds to be bought back at a lower price thus ensuring trading profits -- may be seen as a disadvantage. Also reverse repo allows the holder, assuming that the firm has enough of the bond, to 'squeeze' the bond and its repo rate which can force those that are short the bond in the underlying cash bond market or in the term repo market to have to buy it back to cover a position or to effect settlement.

## The nature of repo

Repo may be viewed as a capital market product with demand and supply governed by bond market considerations. But it is also a money-market tool with the money supplied being considered economically as a loan and repo payments as loan interest. In essence it is a hybrid; the purpose for one participant may be to cover a short position, and for their counterparty to borrow cash.

## Matched-book repo

Matched-book trading, where banks and investment banks earn income from the rate difference between the repo and reverse rates on general and specific collateral, is now a major activity. The information available to a repo desk via its 'firm financing' activities led to the development of matched-book trading in which repo dealers trade repos as on-balance sheet risk instruments earning revenues from the difference between the repo rate (the cash 'borrowing' rate) and the reverse repo rate (the cash 'lending' rate) and the difference between these rates for 'general collateral' and 'specials' i.e. those that have value due to the specific characteristics of the bond issue itself rather than its general characteristic as a 'risk free' security.

Collateral switching by which securities lenders lend one security against another, via stock loan or repo markets, and earn a fee for their efforts is also increasing. In many repo markets it is now possible to switch eurobonds and corporate bonds or even equities for government bonds.

## Repo and the bond markets

Liquidity in the major government bond markets - especially in benchmark issues - has increased as repo markets developed. Indeed, the repo markets trade a large multiple of daily settlement value in the underlying bond market and play a crucial role in providing liquidity.

Repo takes place within existing securities markets, and settles via the same settlement depositories, yet it is a distinct and massive market in its own right. Structures that were developed for outright movement of bonds have been commandeered by the repo market to support its product.

The majority of bond market trades that are matched and settled are repo trades and it is generally the case that where active repo markets exist so do active bond markets. The same is true of exchange traded financial futures. Where active futures, repo and reverse repo markets exist, liquid bond markets prevail. Where one or more of these constituents are missing, the underlying bond market is flawed.

## Repo and the money markets

In the money markets, as a result of the risk reduction quality of government bond repo, there is a trend away from unsecured deposit and placements to repo and reverse markets. The regulatory treatment is, as you would expect, favourable. It has further developed as a money-market investment with active participation by the reserve managers of central banks, banks, money funds and corporates alike.

Indeed the repo markets now provide a great deal of liquidity to the money markets which increasingly require Real-Time-Gross-Settlement (RTGS) and intra-day collateral deliveries for limit requirements.

Repo allows for RTGS systems to develop, provides the securities that are included in commercial banks' liquidity ratios and allows Central Banks a route to provide liquidity whilst taking limited counterparty and collateral risk.

## Central banks and the regulators

The Central Banks have adopted repo as their main platform of open market operations and across Europe the repo rate and changes in its level long ago surpassed Lombard and Discount type rates as an indicator of central bank policy.

The banking and securities authorities, often working with securities markets associations, have successfully lobbied for the removal of legal, regulatory and fiscal barriers to trading.

In recent years many uncertainties concerning repo have been removed. The development and extensive use of master repurchase agreements, backed by numerous jurisdictional legal opinions have reduced concerns such as enforceability of close-out netting. Unfavourable tax treatments (e.g. stamp duty and turnover taxes), the application of withholding tax on the underlying security and enforced limitations on foreign ownership of securities have largely been changed.

Regulatory restrictions concerning 'short-selling' have largely been lifted and barriers such as minimum reserve requirements for repo have gone.

The regulators have reacted favourably to market developments and the introduction of the Capital Adequacy Directive (CAD) has allowed significant capital savings to firms engaged in documented repos.

## History and development

The market has its origins in the USA where, from 1918, the Federal Reserve Bank undertook repos in Bankers Acceptances (BAs) known as 'resale agreements. Today, substantial amounts of treasury bond repos are traded by investment and commercial banks and their customers. This has created a market with outstandings of $1.85 trillion or 55.35% of the value of Treasury securities issued and an average turnover of $512bn per day .

The market in international repo was started in the mid-to-late 1980's by the London operations of the largest US investment banks which had come to dominate the mature domestic US market. US firms were joined in the early 1990's by European firms such as Barclays Capital, UBS, Deutsche Bank, CSFB, SBC and Banque Paribas and by Japanese firms such as Nomura and IBJ. Additionally, in many European centres such as Frankfurt, Paris, Milan and Madrid, banks and securities houses run repo desks for firm financing and matched-book purposes.

One of the primary forces driving the international repo market was the demand from securities dealers and smaller commercial banks (institutions with limited access to the interbank deposit market and often with modest credit ratings) for a source of cheaper financing than that provided by commercial banks, to fund proprietary bond trading books. Underlying the need for bond financing are fundamental forces in the form of the securitization of international capital flows, the international diversification of investment portfolios, and the more cyclical force of a bull market in bonds.

The late entry of non-US names into the repo markets reflects the fact that they have had access to other sources of cheap finance. For example, the securities subsidiaries of European universal banks often have access to funds from their parent banks. However, the need to finance bond trading has outstripped the capacity of many such sources of funds, and, of course, the credit rating of the collateral means that financing may often be raised at rates lower than those for unsecured money. This partly reflects the bull market in bonds and the expansion of government/sovereign bond markets.

A second force behind the emergence of international repo has been the cost of borrowing securities from Cedel Bank and Euroclear to cover failed trades (1.875-3.875%, depending on the currency). The settlement depositories also place a limit of 5% on the amount of an issue which can be borrowed by one party.

While financing and securities borrowing initiated the repo market, its subsequent growth has also been encouraged by arbitrage opportunities against bonds, swaps, deposits, futures and options. These opportunities have expanded dramatically in recent years as derivatives markets have become established in more and more countries and instruments. The take-off of the international repo market can be traced back to late 1988, when Liffe launched its Bund future and basis trading began in the Matif Notionel futures contract.

In a number of markets, repo provides the only way of borrowing bonds. In addition, in countries such as Spain and Sweden, bonds are difficult to move between the domestic and international markets.

From the early nineties, 'matched-book' trading in the international market expanded. A substantial number of securities houses in London are estimated to run matched books, with many more in Europe and beyond. The rapid increase in matched-book activities has led to narrower margins but has encouraged greater volumes of transactions.

The international repo market also benefits from central bank repo in domestic repo markets. This is a key source of both cash supply and demand for bonds. Many repo dealers also note the usefulness of repo as a source of information on the bond market. In effect, the repo rate measures the balance between short and long positions in the underlying bond market, and changes in individual repo rates give an early indication of moves in specific bond issues, shifts in particular parts of the yield curve and overall market sentiment. This sort of information is obviously important for proprietary bond, and other forms of, trading. More specialized use of the repo market is made by banks to avoid the capital adequacy requirements imposed on unsecured loans.

The next phase in the development of the international repo market is expected to be a broadening of the range of participants to include more bond investors on one side and more cash investors on the other. Dealers are expending considerable energy selling repo to new counterparties.

Repo can be an incremental source of income for bond investors. It allows a switch into cash without liquidating investments, while retaining the economic benefits of the underlying security, such as coupons and increases in market value. Cross-currency repo also provides investors with additional scope for currency plays and yield enforcement.
The international repo market has recently developed as a secured money market investment

product for cash investors. However, non-financial customers are not yet strongly represented in the international repo market. The development of a truly international market is complicated by fragmentation of legal, regulatory and fiscal frameworks in Europe, as well as different traditions and cultures.

There are eighty members of the ISMA CRD (Council of Reporting Dealers) repo dealer's sub-committee, of which some thirty to forty meet on a regular basis. Ten of these form the RepoClear Steering Committee. It should be noted that the sub-committee operates at arm's length to ISMA and is essentially a very effective lobby group for repo dealers based in London. It successfully lobbied for changes to the CAD and was at the forefront of the development of the gilt repo market. It has informal communications with the various repo lobby groups in Europe including the German foreign exchange and money market committee.

The international repo market started as a wholesale market but is developing on the retail side, particularly as a home for the investment of cash. Increasingly, dealers are targeting smaller banks, funds and corporates in order to expand and diversify their sources of funding.

Repo is being presented to customers as a more flexible alternative to traditional money-market instruments such as deposits, CDs and CP. In particular, stress is being placed on the flexibility (in terms of maturity and amount) and the security provided by collateralization, compared to the outright purchase involved in traditional instruments. In effect, the bank risk usually taken in the money market is substituted by risk on the counterparty for the period of the trade, which risk is limited to the net difference between the value of the cash invested and the value of the collateral. This avoids the problem of utilising unsecured credit lines which may be fully committed for any particular counterparty.

There is also the attraction of higher yield. In theory, repo should pay less than deposits because of their lower credit risk. However, because of the alternative cost of funds to securities houses, they are often willing to pay around LIBOR as they are generally restricted from entering the inter-bank market where cash investors can expect LIBID at best for their deposits.

There are a number of advantages which should draw non-dealers into repo. In some markets, repo is the only liquid short-term investment available to foreign investors. In addition, interest rate volatility, most recently volatility in European bond markets, should also encourage use of this more flexible investment tool. In the US, the early growth of the repo market was driven by high interest rate levels which prevailed from the late 1970s and which encouraged new and more aggressive cash management procedures among corporates.

A major obstacle to broader acceptance of repo seems to be a lack of awareness. This may be reflected in the perceived complexity of repo, in particular confusion about the variety of structures. There are also more mundane problems such as the administrative requirements and the need for documentation in the case of classic repo. Some dealers suggest that corporate treasurers are creatures of habit and that it is hard to wean them from established money-market instruments.

On the securities lending side of the market, some investors are reluctant to lend to those dealers thought to be shorting a specific issue as it might drive down the price of their holdings and, consequently, adversely affect the value of their portfolios. Penetration of the potential lender market for international repo has been limited. The principal disincentives lie with the requirements of the lenders. These often include over-collateralization, i.e. lenders generally do not hold the view that 'cash is king' (as the repo market does) but rather value their bonds as being of greater worth than the ultimate liquid financial instrument, cash, and demand up to 105% of a bond's value in security. Additionally, since many of the securities lenders are based in USA, they often demand dollar cash transfers the day before bonds are delivered and sometimes even through a different settlement exchange.

Some dealers had hoped that the concept of triparty repo would facilitate corporate use of repo by increasing the security of collateral, allowing collateral to be substituted during term repo (which also increases the yield to the lender of cash), delegating administration to the third-party custodian and reducing transactional and operational costs. Apart from the perceived complexity of triparty repo, there is suspicion among some corporates that the need for a custodian adds to rather than reduces costs, even though the dealer (as the borrower of cash) pays the fee for the service provided by the custodian. Another obstacle has been the fact that corporates have not had direct access to custodians such as Euroclear and Cedel Bank, but have had to use clearing banks as intermediaries, making the return on general collateral repo unattractive. Euroclear and, more recently, Cedelbank have opened up to corporates for this purpose.

The development of repo markets is largely dependent on the following conditions:
- the size and structure of the government bond markets
- the nature and ownership of these bonds
- the structure and credit of the counterparty universe
- the manner in which day to day operations are conducted by the central banks
- regulatory, legal, accounting and fiscal treatment of repo.

## Participants

The market in international repo originated as, and remains, an 'over-the-counter' market. Dealing is by telephone, via hybrid systems linking screens and telephones or by messaging for example via Bloomberg's messaging functionality.

Business in the international repo market flows through three main channels:
- the broker-dealer market between market-makers and institutional investors;
- the professional inter-dealer market between market-makers; and
- the brokered professional market between market-makers via inter-dealer brokers (IDBs).

IDBs act on a 'name give-up' basis disclosing the entities to the trade once it has been dealt. At this stage it is subject to credit line availability which in most cases is a foregone conclusion.

6

## Brokers

There are seven brokers in the market: Cantor Fitzgerald, Liberty/Tullets/Sputz, Prebon-Yamane, Garban/ICAP, GFI, Viel /Tradition, Dawney Day, & Monercor/Finacor.

Broking is conducted via telephones and electronic screens. Some firms provide purely a telephone broking service but the majority especially the larger ones provide an electronic system with prices posted to a screen where trades are executed by calling the broker on a direct telephone line who then executes the trade via a keypad. At the time of going to press some of the major brokers were implementing dealer-input automated trading systems.

Brokerage firms employ 200+ repo brokers in London and additional people in continental Europe.

In addition, there are a number of repo brokerage firms across Europe which, with some major exceptions, concentrate on domestic business (ie between two domestic counterparties or one domestic and one international).

## Obstacles

The greatest current obstacle to the growth of the repo business is its on-balance sheet treatment. Whilst capital treatment by the major regulators is favourable for documented repos in firms with adequate credit and risk policies, repo is a balance sheet 'hog' and the return on competing, albeit longer dated products, is by definition often greater. Whilst return on assets long ago lost much of its importance as a measure of financial performance for banks it remains a focus of analysts, especially the ratings agencies.

In recent years, government bond repo has become very competitive and now bears many of the characteristics of a commoditized market. Dealing spreads have been reduced and a 'bid-offer' spread such as that which exists in the unsecured deposit and placement market no longer apply to government repo.

There are low barriers to entry to new firms and latterly margins have been squeezed by new entrants. The market is visible, brokers who are integral to the inter-professional market are not restricted as to whom they transmit prices to. The barriers to entry to new brokers are low; very little capital is required and technology demands are limited.

The cost of settlement and brokerage charges have led many firms to reduce their matched book activities. Brokerage costs which are being reduced often act as a deterrent to trading. Currently, both sides to a deal pay upto 0.01% pa of the nominal value of the trade with discounts for major dealer. Clearly, the larger the trade and the longer the period the greater the brokerage. The major houses have negotiated bilateral brokerage reductions.

The low level of interest rates together with the flat yield curve in most major markets acts as a disincentive to trading in both matched book repo and the underlying product which by definition limits 'firm financing' requirements.

The rash of mergers over the past two years have led to the consolidation and withdrawal from the market of a number of firms and desk sizes are now generally smaller.

## Market trends

One major development in recent years has been the development of central clearing counterparty services including the use of a clearing house in the repo markets. Netting of repo transactions reduces balance sheet footings and overall repo settlements affording its users cost reductions.

Prime brokers, institutions that provide settlement, operational and funding support to customers especially smaller broker dealers, investment managers and hedge funds, have developed their range of products. These institutions do not have the scale of operations to finance and settle their business independently but rather outsource to prime brokers who are generally the larger US investment banks. The prime broker acts as principal in raising finance or borrowing bonds and on-lends to its customer.

There is, however, a possibility of re-regulation. Following the hedge fund crisis in September 1998 there has been a review of margin requirements and risk methodology adopted, at the institution and regulator level. Clients have reacted by holding a cash cushion - which is essentially accessible liquidity - to be used as additional initial margin should haircut requirements be increased when trades roll over.

Increasingly central banks have entered the market to provide a 'last resort' source of bonds should borrowers need it.

## Likely market developments

### Same day settlement

There is a trend towards same day settlement, driven in part by the shortening of the delivery cycle of outright bonds but also by the availability of same day funds by central banks. In July 1999, Cedelbank introduced nine same-day settlement cycles and in September, and Euroclear will shortly launch a real-time settlement platform.

### Multilateral netting

The introduction of multi-lateral netting in the USA, first by Delta and subsequently by GSCC, has led to greatly increased volumes of matched-book trading and many market participants felt this was likely to happen in Europe.

### Technology

The main brokers have already introduced semi-automatic screen based trading and we have been advised that all have the technology available to operate an interactive repo broking system some with settlement and matching functionality. They will supply this to their customers if requested. This will compete directly with other entities such as SWX and MTS.

### Substitution

The increased use of term trading could lead to increased use of trading with multiple rights of substitution.

## Conclusion

Our aim in writing this book was to give a comprehensive and current explanation of the product known as repo. Market experts in the relevant fields have contributed their 'pearls of wisdom' and we hope that this final product provides a true and accurate coverage of repo. However, the markets remain fragmented and opaque and the sources of information limited. Please forgive us for the inevitable errors that may have crept in.

In the first three chapters we define repo and give examples to put it in context; we explain the mechanics of the products; we discuss how the repo markets developed, how repo is used, the characteristics of the major markets, and the events that have brought this product to its present position.

In chapter four we consider repo conventions and methodologies; chapter five explains the concepts of netting and clearing within a clearing house; and chapter six examines the risks inherent in repo and explains how to manage them.

In chapters seven to ten we look at the legal, accounting, taxation and regulatory environments affecting both the product and the market participants.

Chapter eleven considers the principles of collateral management and the final chapter includes a thorough glossary of market terminology.

We have assumed that our readership will have a basic understanding of bond and money markets, but we have tried to keep our explanations as clear and jargon-free as possible with a view towards demystifying repo.

# Chapter 2

# What is Repo?

## Definition of Repo

The term 'repo' is an abbreviation of repurchase and means a sale and repurchase agreement. A repo is a sale of securities for cash with a simultaneous commitment to repurchase them on a future date. Generally, the cash and securities have an equivalent value and the collateral is valued at prevailing market prices including accrued interest.

The seller usually delivers securities on a 'delivery-versus-payment' basis and receives cash from the buyer. This cash is supplied, for the period of the repo, at a predetermined rate (called the 'repo rate') which remains constant throughout the trade.

Securities used as collateral are generally government bonds, but can also include eurobonds, domestic corporate bonds, equities or other assets. The term of a typical repo is from overnight up to one month although it is possible to undertake trades of over one year and to trade with extended forward starts.

The term 'repo' is often used generically to cover three different transaction structures:

- Classic repo: this is essentially a sophisticated form of sell/buy-back, evidenced under a written agreement and is the type of transaction which the US market would tend to recognise as a 'repo'. A classic repo is invariably referred to simply as a 'repo';

- Sell/buy-back: this is the simplest form of repo and involves an outright sale of a bond for value on a nearby date and an outright repurchase of that bond for value on a forward date. A sell/buy-back transaction is often referred to generically as a 'buy/sell'. Buy-sells can now be documented under the Global Master Repurchase Agreement, or GMRA (see Chapter 7) giving them a level of legal protection similar to that afforded by repos; and

- Securities lending: this involves a transfer of securities for a temporary period in exchange for collateral. Securities lending transactions are sometimes called 'bond borrowed' or 'stock lending' transactions. Although securities lending has had a different history from the other types of repo, and has different participants and driving forces, the two co-exist in many markets. It is not true repo, as it does not involve a sale or repurchase of the assets, but is mentioned in this chapter for the sake of completeness and because of its resemblance to the other forms of repo. The rest of this book focuses on true repo.

Each of the above transaction structures is described and illustrated below and a summary comparison is set out in Table 1 at the end of this chapter. It will be seen that there are differences in legal structure but few are of substance and the economics of each form of trading are similar.

The three structures developed for a variety of different reasons. Repo trades are cash-driven transactions: the supplier of bonds needs cash to finance positions. Correspondingly, reverse repos are driven by the need to borrow bonds i.e. to cover a short position. Buy/sells and sell/buys are driven by the same economic incentives but developed as undocumented trades in markets where no master repo agreement had developed and where participants lack the ability to mark to market and call for collateral (see section entitled 'Margin' below), largely because of IT deficiencies. In some countries, buy/sells have become institutionalised and not marking to market or calling margin has become the norm.

## Transaction Structures

### Classic repo

As described above, a classic repo is essentially a sophisticated form of sell/buy-back.

In common with sell/buy-backs:

- classic repo involves a contract to sell securities and repurchase them a a later date;
- the purchased securities are usually bonds, notes or bills;
- the supplier of cash receives a return;
- suppliers of cash are called 'buyers', 'borrowers' (of bonds) or 'investors' (of cash); and
- suppliers of collateral are called 'sellers' or 'lenders' (of bonds).

However, classic repos involve some notable differences from sell/buy-backs:

- classic repos have formal documentation, in addition to the repo confirmations, contractually linking the two legs of the repurchase transaction (see Chapter 7 on 'The Legal Treatment and Documentation of Repo'). As discussed in Chapter 7, this distinction is now being blurred with the possibility of documenting sell/buy-backs under the GMRA, the standard contract used for repo transactions;
- the return for the supplier of cash is quoted separately as a repo rate;
- any coupon paid on the bonds during the term of the transaction must be passed onto the original seller upon receipt;
- classic repos have added contractual rights, including the right to mark the transactions to market and to call for variation margin where necessary (see 'Margin' below), and to terminate transactions and set off in the event of a default (see Chapter 7). However, buy/sells documented under the GMRA will also share some of these protections; and
- the transaction is known as a 'reverse repo' from the viewpoint of the party supplying the cash, and as a 'repo' from the perspective of the collateral supplier.

A typical classic repo structure is illustrated in Diagram 1 overleaf.

## Diagram 1: classic repo

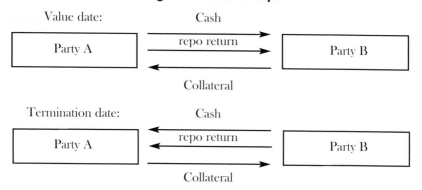

## Diagram 2: repo and reverse repo

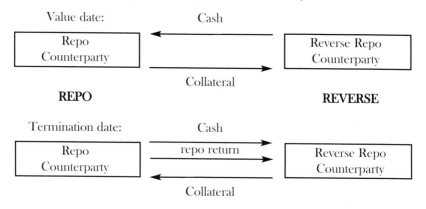

## Example

Consider the following classic repo involving a German government bond.

| | |
|---|---|
| Trade date | June 12 |
| Value date | June 14 |
| Termination date | June 15 |
| Seller | Securities House |
| Buyer | Bank |
| Term | Overnight |
| Security | Bund 3.75% 4th Jan 2009 |
| Nominal amount | Euro 10 million |
| Clean price | 92.00 |
| Accrued interest | 1.65411 |
| Dirty price (rounded) | 93.65 |
| Cash payment (purchase price) | Euro 9,365,000 |
| Repo rate | 2.70%p.a. |

## Diagram 3: repo/reverse repo analysis

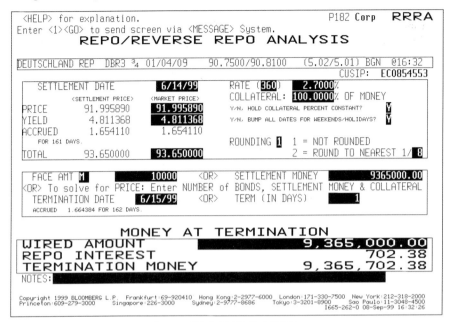

```
<HELP> for explanation.                        P182 Corp   RRRA
Enter <1><GO> to send screen via <MESSAGE> System.
            REPO/REVERSE  REPO  ANALYSIS

DEUTSCHLAND REP  DBR3 ¾ 01/04/09   90.7500/90.8100   (5.02/5.01) BGN  @16:32
                                                           CUSIP:   EC0854553
   SETTLEMENT DATE        6/14/99     RATE (360)   2.7000%
            <SETTLEMENT PRICE>  <MARKET PRICE>   COLLATERAL: 100.0000% OF MONEY
PRICE        91.995890    91.995890  Y/N, HOLD COLLATERAL PERCENT CONSTANT?   Y
YIELD         4.811368     4.811368  Y/N, BUMP ALL DATES FOR WEEKENDS/HOLIDAYS? Y
ACCRUED       1.654110     1.654110
   FOR 161 DAYS.                      ROUNDING 1   1 = NOT ROUNDED
TOTAL        93.650000    93.650000             2 = ROUND TO NEAREST 1/ 8

   FACE AMT M            10000    <OR>   SETTLEMENT MONEY         9365000.00
<OR> To solve for PRICE: Enter NUMBER of BONDS, SETTLEMENT MONEY & COLLATERAL
TERMINATION DATE      6/15/99    <OR>   TERM (IN DAYS)           1
ACCRUED   1.664384 FOR 162 DAYS.

               MONEY  AT  TERMINATION
WIRED  AMOUNT                        9,365,000.00
REPO  INTEREST                              702.38
TERMINATION  MONEY                   9,365,702.38
NOTES:

Copyright 1999 BLOOMBERG L.P.  Frankfurt:69-920410  Hong Kong:2-2977-6000  London:171-330-7500  New York:212-318-2000
Princeton:609-279-3000     Singapore:226-3000     Sydney:2-9777-8686     Tokyo:3-3201-8900     Sao Paulo:11-3048-4500
                                                                         I665-262-0 08-Sep-99 16:32:26
```

*Source: BLOOMBERG RRRA*

In this classic repo, Bank agrees to deliver to Securities House Euro 9,365,000 cash in exchange for collateral in the form of Euro 10 million of a 3.75% coupon Bund maturing 4th January 2009 with accrued interest of Euro 1.654110. The cash amount reflects the market value of the collateral, and a return on the repo monies at a rate of 2.7% per annum on an A/360 day basis (actual over 360 days) will be paid to the cash supplier.

On value date, Bank pays Euro 9,365,000 to Securities House, which in turn transfers Bunds with a nominal value of Euro 10,000,000 to Bank.

The next business day, Bank returns the Bunds to Securities House on a delivery-versus-payment basis and Securities House repays to Bank the original cash amount of DM9,365,000 plus one day's return on that cash at the agreed repo rate of 2.7 % per annum. The return is calculated as:

$$\text{Euro } 9,365,000 \times 2.75/100 \times 1/360 = \text{Euro } 702.38$$

## Sell/buy-back

A sell/buy-back is a contractual commitment between two parties, first to sell securities and then to buy them back at an agreed future date. The securities are typically bonds, notes or bills.

The supplier of cash receives a return, which takes the form of a difference between the repurchase price of the securities and the original sale price. The repurchase price is determined by the difference between the coupon income accrued during the term of the

14

transaction on the nominal quantity of bonds and an implied interest rate or 'repo rate' on the cash advanced.

In many markets, there is still no formal documentation between the parties except for the confirmations of the sales of the securities (see Chapter 7 on 'The Legal Treatment and Documentation of Repo'). In each repo transaction, there are two sides. One party sells and buys back and the other buys and sells back. Thus, a sell/buy-back for one party is a 'buy/sell-back' from the viewpoint of the other party. Suppliers of cash are called 'buyers,' 'borrowers' (of bonds) or 'investors' (of cash), and suppliers of securities are called 'sellers' or 'lenders' (of bonds). For reasons discussed below, the securities are typically referred to as 'collateral'.

With the advent of the 1995 version of the GMRA came a buy-sell annex which may be used to document these kinds of transactions, providing significant extra protection over undocumented sell/buy-backs. The structure of a sell/buy-back is illustrated in Diagram 4 below.

### Diagram 4: sell/buy-back

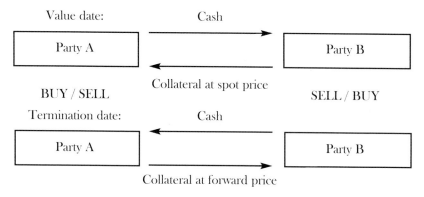

### Example

Consider the following sell/buy-back involving a German government bond as in the earlier repo example:

| | |
|---|---|
| Trade date | June 12 |
| Value date (first leg settlement date) | June 14 |
| Termination date | June 15 |
| Seller | Securities House |
| Buyer | Bank |
| Term | One day |
| Security | Bund 3.75% 4th January 2009 |
| Nominal amount | Euro 10 million |
| 'Clean' price (i.e. excluding accrued interest) | 91.99589* |
| Accrued interest | 1.65411 |
| Cash payment (purchase price) | 9,365,000 |
| Implied repo rate | 2.7% p.a. |

*In reality, this trade would have been dealt at 92.00 but, for the sake of comparison with the classic repo example above, we have priced the trade to an unrealistic six decimal places.

15

# Diagram 5: forward pricing analysis

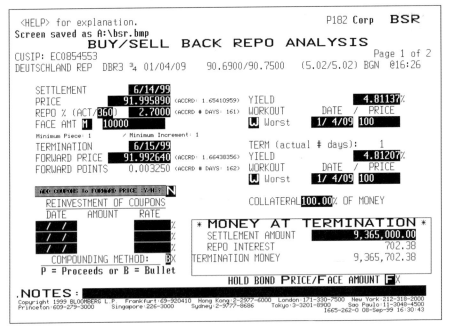

*Source: BLOOMBERG BSR*

The seller (Securities House) contracts to sell a nominal Euro 10 million of the agreed Bunds to the buyer (Bank) against payment of Euro 9,365,000 for spot value. The amount of cash is equivalent to the value of the Bunds at their 'dirty' price (i.e. including accrued interest). The dirty price is calculated as follows:

dirty price = clean price + (nominal amount x coupon percentage x day count fraction)

At the same time, Securities House contracts to buy back the same nominal amount of Bunds from Bank after one day. The repurchase price to be paid by the original seller is determined as follows:

Coupon on bond = 3.75% on 10,000,000 x 1/360     =     1041.67
Repo rate = 2.7% on    9,365,000 x 1/360     =     702.38
Coupon on bond - repo return = 1041.67 - 702.38     =     339.29

Therefore, the original seller buys back the bonds at:
91.99589 - 0.003393     =     91.99264

This represents the forward repurchase clean price.
The accrued interest on that date is 1.664384.

The invoice monies are:
Settlement     =     9,365,000
Termination = {(91.99264 + 1.664384)/100}
    x 10,000,000     =     9,365,702
Difference     =     702

16

It can be seen that the economic benefit of the coupon continues to accrue to the original seller, and the repo rate on the cash is for the benefit of the buyer (the cash 'lender'). Accordingly, the difference represents the net benefit to the seller. The start price of a sell/buy-back is higher than the end price if the coupon on the nominal amount of bonds is greater than the repo rate on the repo monies. However, we will see later that the buyer is entitled to receive any coupon actually paid during the term of a sell/buy-back but is not legally obliged to return it to the seller.

## Securities lending

A securities lending transaction is a contract which commits one party to lend, and the other to borrow, agreed securities for an agreed period. The borrower of the securities is required to deliver collateral in the form of securities or cash to the securities lender and to pay a fee for the use of the borrowed securities. The supplier of securities is called the 'lender' and the supplier of collateral the 'borrower', even if the collateral is cash.

The structure of a securities lending transaction is illustrated in Diagram 7 below.

### *Diagram 6: securities lending*

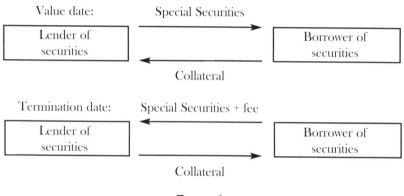

### *Example*

Consider the following international securities lending transaction involving the same Bund as above:

| | |
|---|---|
| Lender | Investor |
| Borrower | Securities House |
| Term | One day |
| Security | Bund 3.75% 4th January 2004 |
| Nominal amount | Euro10 million |
| Market value | Euro 9,365,000 |
| Security II (collateral) | Bund 7.25% 11th November 2004 |
| Nominal amount | Euro 9million |
| Market value | Euro 9,552,300 |
| Fee | 50 basis points (0.50%) |
| Margin | 2% |

17

Investor agrees to lend a nominal Euro 10 million of the Bund 3.75% 4th January 2004 to Securities House against collateral in the form of a nominal Euro 9 million of a different agreed Bund. The loan is for a period of one day. On redelivery of the Bunds on the following day, Securities House pays Investor a fee of 50 basis points on the Euro10 million nominal of Bunds which it borrowed.

This is equivalent to Euro 14 (i.e. 10,000,000 x 0.5/100 x 1/360).

# Uses of repo and economics

## Uses

All forms of repo provide a means to borrow or lend a particular security issue. Classic repos and buy-sells also provide a means to borrow or lend cash.

**Borrowing cash**. For the cash taker:

- the collateralised nature of repo provides a means of reducing the cost of financing, particularly for institutions such as securities houses without access to the interbank deposit market. Costs can be further reduced where cash in the repo market is provided by central banks' open market operations;

- the unsecured financing cost for securities houses is typically at a spread over Libor and the savings available through financing via repo can be large. Additionally, if a bond is scarce, reductions in funding costs can be substantial (in which circumstances, repo becomes attractive even for banks with access to cheap funds from other sources (e.g. AAA or AA-rated banks). Negative repo rates have occurred when there is extreme demand for a bond, e.g. where it is required for delivery into a futures contract;

- because repo involves a temporary exchange, it allows an investor access to cash without liquidating its bond positions at potentially unattractive market levels;

- because the collateral used in repo is issued by creditworthy names, it can provide financing for less creditworthy names; and

- as an alternative source of cash, repo offers diversification of financing.

**Lending cash**. For the supplier of cash:

- repo offers a secure, collateralised investment;

- as noted above, repo may enhance the yield which investors receive on cash and allow the investor to achieve better returns than are available on other money-market instruments (note that the collateral is generally highly rated and the return will reflect this); and

- central banks often use repo to add liquidity to the money markets through open market operations.

**Securities borrowed** can be used to cover failed trades, or short positions arising from:

- short selling of bonds in anticipation of a rise in bond yields, i.e. taking risk;

- short selling of bonds to hedge long positions in cash bonds or derivatives (e.g. interest rate swaps); and

- short selling of bonds for arbitrage against futures and options.

18

**Securities lent** can raise incremental income through the fee in securities lending or through raising cheap finance which might be reinvested at a higher rate.

## Economics

The purposes for which these types of transactions are entered into, as described above, explain the economics of the deals. As the exchanges of assets are intended and structured only to be temporary, the economic risks and rewards of the asset that each party is transferring to the other (whether cash or securities) are designed to be retained so far as possible by the original owner, despite the fact that the legal structure involves an outright transfer of ownership in each case.

This is reflected in:

- the treatment of coupons arising during the term of a repo; and
- the allocation of market risk and reward on the securities, (see the section on 'Other characteristics of repo' below).

The transaction decision of the counterparty taking securities as collateral through a classic repo or sell/buy-back is not influenced by the price of the securities, how the price is expected to fluctuate, or by the coupon on the securities (as long as the bonds are priced at market, including margins if applicable, and the collateral is saleable in the unlikely event of a default by the seller). Moreover, the return received by the counterparty who purchases securities as collateral does not depend (as in a normal purchase of securities) on the price, coupon or maturity of these securities. This is consistent with the fact that the market risk on these securities remains with the supplier of the collateral in spite of full title passing to the buyer.

As a result, from an economic viewpoint, classic repos and sell/buy-backs resemble secured (collateralised) short-term loans, where the cash 'lender' (buyer) receives collateral (purchased securities) as security against a default by the cash 'borrower' (the seller) in 'repaying' the cash (by buying back the securities on the maturity of the transaction). Indeed, a sell/buy-back or classic repo is often used in practice as an alternative to a deposit and, in this respect, it is usually classed as a money market instrument. However, counterparties frequently enter into sell/buy-back and classic repo transactions to borrow specific securities rather than to invest cash, which means that they should also be regarded as capital market instruments.

As the name implies, however, repo involves sales and repurchases rather than loans. The seller gives up full legal ownership of the securities to the buyer.

## *Other Characteristics of Repo*

## Legal structure

All forms of repo now involve an outright transfer of full legal title to the securities to the counterparty. In sell/buy-backs and classic repo, this is inherent in the structure. In both classic repo and securities lending it is provided for in the market standard governing documentation; the same is true for sell/buy-backs documented under the GMRA. The use of a sale and repurchase structure was originally developed in the US domestic market to allow participation by institutions which could not legally borrow or lend securities, but which could buy or sell them.

19

## Return

Return is a function of both supply and demand and of the purpose for which a transaction was entered into.

Any party providing **cash** will require payment from the other party for the use of that cash. In securities lending, this is only relevant where the securities borrower provides cash as collateral. In that case, it will charge an agreed rate of interest on the cash. In sell/buy-backs and classic repo, there is technically no interest but the same economic effect is achieved through the repurchase prices which take into account the relevant repo rate. The rate is implied in sell/buy-backs and quoted separately in classic repo (where it is sometimes called a 'pricing rate', which is the term used in the market standard governing documentation for classic repos).

On the **securities** side, whether a securities provider earns a return on the securities will again depend on supply and demand and the purpose for which the transaction is entered into. In securities lending, clearly the purpose is to borrow a specific issue or a generic group of issues, and consequently the securities lender will charge an agreed fee on those securities (see the earlier example). No fee is charged on securities provided as collateral, but if the collateral is in the form of cash, then the interest on the cash will effectively be reduced by the amount of any fee. In sell/buy-backs and classic repo, transactions are often cash driven and so no return will be paid on the securities. However, where a specific stock is being sought, there will be an implied return for the securities provider (the seller) through a reduced repo rate on the cash and thus a reduced repurchase price.

## Coupon

The right to receive any coupon on a security will generally rest with the legal owner of that security on the coupon payment date. But one of the consequences of the legal transfer of title to securities under all forms of repo is that the right to receive the coupon is technically given up for the period of the repo. However, because it is intended that the economic rewards of the assets temporarily transferred remain with the original owner, each form of repo provides in some way for the return of the coupon to the original owner.

In **securities lending** and **classic repo**, the borrower or purchaser of securities is required under the governing contract to pay to the lender or seller an amount equal to the amount of any coupon paid during the term of the transaction on the same day that the coupon is paid. In **sell/buy-backs**, any coupon accrued during the term of the repo is returned to the seller through the repurchase price calculation, but any actual coupon paid (which will include coupon accrued prior to the date of the transaction) is not legally recoverable because there is no contract documentation containing an obligation on the buyer to return it. Therefore, before the transaction is entered into the seller must ensure that proper account of the coupon is taken in the repurchase price; including, if appropriate, the payment of 'interest' by the buyer for the period for which it has had the benefit of the coupon (i.e. until it is repaid through the repurchase price).

## Collateral

Collateral is given by the party whose purpose is ancillary or secondary to the main purpose of the transaction; its effect is to ensure that this party performs its obligations. For example, in securities lending the main purpose of the transaction is the borrowing and lending of specific securities. The other leg of the exchange (cash or securities) will constitute the collateral. In sell/buy-backs and classic repo, the main purpose can be either to borrow or lend cash or to borrow or lend securities. Technically, in each case the collateral should be the other side of the exchange but in practice the securities are always considered to be, and called, the collateral. Despite the confusion this can cause, nothing turns on the terminology. The identification of which side of the exchange is collateral will affect the margining process and, in particular, overcollateralisation (see the section on 'Margin' below).

The collateral used in classic repo and sell/buy-backs is typically government securities, but eurobonds, corporate debt, equities, bills and in floating rate notes are also used, albeit rarely. In the US domestic repo market, Treasury securities are supplemented by Federal Agency debt. Mortgage-backed pass-through securities and money-market instruments (such as Certificates of Deposit, Bankers Acceptances and Commercial Paper) are also widely used in the US repo market. There is growing use of asset-backed securities, whole loans and corporate bonds.

Special collateral

- When a dealer seeks to borrow a specific security via a reverse repo or buy/sell-back, it is referred to as a special.

General collateral

- If a dealer is willing to accept any issues within a general category, this is called general collateral or, in the US, stock collateral.

## Market risk

It is apparent, from the examples given above, that all market risks and rewards on the securities are intended to be borne by the original owner and not by the buyer (in sell/buy-backs or classic repo) or borrower (in securities lending transactions). Whatever happens to the market value of the bonds during the term of the repo, whether they rise, fall or even default, the original seller/lender is obliged to reacquire them at the price originally agreed. In the case of sell/buy-backs and classic repo, the repurchase price is the original purchase price adjusted as necessary by the relevant repo rate and any coupon, and not the market value of the bonds at the time of repurchase. In securities lending there is no reacquisition price, but the securities lender is under an obligation to reacquire the bonds and return any collateral that it has received. Again, this ties in with the economics of the temporary exchange discussed earlier. Market risk does manifest itself, however, in the credit risk on the transaction, but this can be addressed through 'margining' (see the sections on 'Credit risk' and 'Margin' below). Market risk is examined in more detail in Chapter 6.

## Credit risk

Repo trades involve credit risk and, whilst the risk is clearly less than in unsecured transactions, there are risks that need to be identified and quantified. Essentially, the credit risk is two-fold: with the counterparty to the transaction and with the collateral supplied, although the latter is simply another element of counterparty risk. It is often mistakenly thought that the provider of cash has the greater credit risk but this is not necessarily so.

The first risk is that a repo counterparty defaults and on the termination date does not return the bonds or cash (depending on whether they reversed in or repoed out bonds). Under a repo transaction the buyer acquires full title to the bonds. The risk is therefore that the value of the bonds at the time of default is less than or greater than the original repo proceeds. That risk will be greater for longer term trades involving high duration bonds in volatile markets. Credit risk can be addressed through margining by agreeing a suitable haircut or initial margin (see the following section).

The second risk is that the issuer of the collateral might default during the period of a repo. However, in this case, we have seen that the provider of cash has recourse to its repo counterparty since the seller is still obliged to reacquire the collateral at the originally agreed repurchase price. In addition, in classic repo the margining positions will enable the cash supplier to call for further collateral. There is, however, the residual risk that the counterparty defaults before providing the top-up collateral or before the repurchase date. For this reason, in the case of general collateral (GC) repo trades, it is normal practice to agree a minimum credit quality of collateral supplied, e.g. AA rated bonds. Credit risk is examined in more detail in Chapter 6.

## Margin

'Margining' is a way of reducing credit risk, including any market risk inherent within that credit risk. Credit risk, as explained above, is essentially the risk that a counterparty will not perform its obligation to return cash or securities at the end of a transaction. The collateral side of the exchange is designed to eliminate or reduce that risk either through set-off (discussed in detail in Chapter 7 on 'The Legal Treatment and Documentation of Repo') or through retaining the collateral. In each case, the value of the collateral needs to be at least equal to the value of the obligation it collateralises (i.e. the cash in sell/buy-backs and classic repos, and the securities in securities lending). Since securities will rise and fall in value over any period of time, it is not unusual for the party receiving collateral to require a 'margin' above the value of the collateralised obligation. This is often called 'overcollateralisation' and involves two elements: first, an 'initial margin' or 'haircut' where the value of the collateral exceeds the value of the cash or securities given to the other party; and secondly, 'variation margin' or 'maintenance margin' where the original ratio between the value of collateral and value of cash/securities exchanged is maintained throughout the life of the repo. This is achieved by enabling either party to call for additional margin, or for the return of margin, if the value of the collateral has fallen below, or risen above, the original level.

Initial margin/haircut

In sell/buy-backs and classic repo, it will be the cash supplier (if anyone) that will require overcollateralisation, since 'cash is king' even if the purpose of the transaction was to enable one party to borrow a particular security issue. In securities lending, however, the loaned securities are considered to be the main purpose of the transaction and so the lender will require overcollateralisation. This is an inherent conflict between securities lenders and other repo dealers which will need to be worked out as the markets converge.

The amount of overcollateralisation or size of margin in a repo depends on:

- the credit standing of the counterparty supplying the collateral;
- the term of the repo: the longer the term, the greater the danger of a default;
- the maturity of the collateral: other things being equal, longer-term securities are more sensitive to interest rate changes than short-term securities;
- the likely volatility of the price of the collateral;
- the scarcity of collateral in general and of particular securities used as collateral;
- the current market price of the collateral; and
- the existence or absence of a legal agreement. Classic repos are inherently less risky than buy/sells and participants are likely to require greater initial margin in buy-sells, increasingly so as the effect of the Capital Adequacy Directive (see Chapter 10) is felt. Buy/sells documented under the GMRA, however, share a similar risk profile to classic repo and will be treated accordingly.

Variation margin

The two sets of market standard documentation used for classic repo and securities lending both give the parties the right to call for extra collateral (if its value has dropped in relation to the value of the other side of the exchange) or to call for the return of collateral (if its value has risen). There is no obligation to do so, but once credit lines become fully utilised, it is in the interests of both parties to make and meet margin calls. It is common practice, particularly between dealers, to attempt to minimise the frequency of margin calls by setting thresholds (e.g. USD 500,000) beyond which the value of the collateral must fall (or rise) before a margin call is triggered. This threshold will be agreed in the governing documentation. Sell/buy-backs documented under the GMRA have similar rights, structured as "repricing" rather than variation margin (see Chapter 7). However, undocumented sell/buy-backs have no such contractual rights and so remargining is not a legal obligation, although in practice participants may agree to 'reprice' transactions by closing out the original trade, sweeping up accrued interest and entering into a new trade at the then prevailing market rate, which achieves the same economic effect.

Coupon payments affect the value of collateral. In classic repo and securities lending, where the coupon is returned to the original owner of the securities upon receipt, this elimination of accrued interest will mean that the securities are worth less and extra margin should be called. In sell/buy-backs, the accrued interest is taken into account in the repurchase price but there are no rights to make margin calls (unless "repricing" is available for sell/buy-backs documented under the GMRA). In any event, if a coupon is paid, there is no obligation to return it to the original seller.

## Delivery

Where physical delivery of collateral takes place, it is made through the appropriate domestic or international clearing system, e.g. Euroclear and Cedelbank for international securities, Deutsche Börse Clearing for German securities, Sicovam for French securities, and so on. In the US, collateral is transferred over CPDwire or Fedwire. Physical delivery is usually against simultaneous or assured payment of cash, delivery-versus-payment (DVP), which is known in the international market as 'delivery-against-cash, receipt-against-payment', or simply 'DAC-RAP'. This is the safest form of delivery.

## Repo Variations

The following are examples of some of the different varieties of repo (true repo rather than securities lending) available in the market:

## Overnight repo

Overnight repo transactions are closed out (reversed) on the business day following their value date. This includes a repo agreed and executed on Friday for reversal after the weekend. In practice, overnight repo tends to be rolled over at maturity.

## Term repo

Term repos are reversed on a specified date more than one business day after the value date of the repo. Normally, classic repo trades can go out to one year, but they can extend beyond a year in special circumstances. It is possible for counterparties to allow term repo to be liquidated by mutual consent during the agreed term at agreed market rates.

## Open repo

Also known as demand repo. Open repo is classic repo for which the term is not fixed in advance. Instead, trades are automatically rolled over daily until one of the counterparties terminates the repo. The notice period for termination is predetermined and generally ties in with the usual settlement period for the collateral. At each rollover, the supplier of cash will change the repo rate and has the right to vary the amount of cash exchanged.

## Delivery repo

This is a repo which involves physical delivery of collateral to the supplier of cash where physical certificates exist, or a book-entry transfer. This is the most usual method of transfer in repo. While physical transfer provides good security for the supplier of cash, it suffers from the disadvantages of being slow, complex and expensive. Physical delivery also makes substitution difficult.

## Hold-in-custody repo (also called due-bill or letter repo in the US)

In this type of repo, collateral is not physically transferred but is simply segregated in the books of the supplier, or transferred from the supplier's clearing account to a special customer account. In the US, it is pledged in favour of the cash supplier. The supplier of collateral therefore retains physical possession and control of the collateral. Hold-in-custody repo, even involving pledges, may not therefore provide complete security for the supplier of cash. There are obvious risks, including the possibility that the same collateral is used several times and this type of repo is consequently becoming increasingly rare. Hold-in-custody repo is sometimes used by strong credits where the supplier of cash is of much lower credit standing. Hold-in-custody repo avoids the costs of transferring collateral across clearing systems, thereby allowing a higher rate of return to be paid to the lender of cash. This may also be useful where collateral is cumbersome or expensive to deliver, e.g. physical securities and odd lots. Moreover, some securities can only be used in hold-in-custody repo; e.g. it is not feasible to deliver unsecuritised mortgages (called 'whole loans' in the US). Hold-in-custody repo tends to be used for high-volume, low-value transactions.

## Triparty repo

Triparty repo avoids the expense and inconvenience of physical delivery on the one hand, and the credit risk of hold-in-custody repo on the other. Collateral is held by an independent third party, often the custodian of the securities to be used as collateral. The third party manages the exchange of collateral and cash internally. Custodians in triparty repo are usually the clearing organisation of whichever counterparty is the dealer (as opposed to the customer). This may be a bank (the principal clearing banks are the Bank of New York, Chase and Morgan Guaranty Trust) or a clearing system (like Euroclear or Cedelbank).

At the start of a repo, the clearer takes in money from the supplier of cash and credits the cash account of the supplier of collateral, simultaneously moving collateral from the securities clearing account of the latter to the custody account of the former.

On the termination date of the repo, the clearer will not return collateral to its original supplier until funds are returned. The clearer physically controls the collateral. It also ensures that collateral meets the credit requirements of the cash provider and handles all administration, including daily marking to market of collateral, margin calls, regular reporting to both counterparties and the supervision of any collateral substitutions.

Triparty repo should be cheaper than other forms of repo where collateral changes hands, because it does not involve delivery of collateral between institutions and so avoids clearing costs. A further advantage is that the customer is able to delegate the effort and expense of administering collateral. Triparty repo also allows a dealer to substitute collateral when wanting to change positions or if existing collateral goes special, without the extra cost of transfer. Under triparty repo schemes the dealer has a repurchase service agreement with the custodian and the dealer pays the custodian for its services. The customer and custodian also negotiate an agreement. In this, the customer will specify the types of collateral it will accept. The repo rate which it receives will reflect its flexibility on collateral. There is also the main master repurchase agreement between the dealer and the customer (see Chapter 7 for more details). Exhibit 1 to this chapter contains a paper by Cedelbank explaining the benefits of triparty repo in greater detail.

## Cross-currency repo

In the international markets, it is possible to trade repo where the cash and collateral exchanged are denominated in different currencies. In such transactions, the marking to market of collateral must take into account changes in the exchange rate between the two currencies. Securities are delivered against payment in a different currency from that in which the bond is denominated.

## Comparison of classic repo, sell/buy-backs and securities lending

It is apparent that the three alternative repo structures are closely related. In fact there are few differences of substance between them, legally or economically, and it is likely that, over time, the distinctions will become ever more blurred. Table 1 summarises the main differences between classic repo, sell/buy-backs and securities lending. The rest of this Handbook focuses on repo and sell/buy-backs.

### Table 1: Comparing classic repo and sell/buy-backs

| Transaction structure | Classic repo | Sell/buy-back | Securities lending |
|---|---|---|---|
| formal method of exchange | selling and buying with some lending/ borrowing characteristics | selling and buying | lending & borrowing (but with outright transfer of ownership) |
| form of exchange: | cash against collateral | cash against collateral | securities against collateral |
| collateral is: | bonds or equities | bonds | cash, bonds, letters of credit, guarantees |
| return is paid to the supplier of: | cash | cash | non-collateral securities |
| return is paid as: | difference between sale price and re-purchase price but quoted as separate repo rate | difference between sale price and purchase price | fee - for securities  interest - on cash collateral |
| initial margin | yes | possible | yes |
| variation margin | yes | no - but repricing available if documented under a GMRA | yes |
| overcollateralization (if any) | cash provider | cash provider | securities lender |
| coupon | returned to original seller | no obligation to return but may be factored into buy-back price | securities recalled over coupon date or coupon returned to original seller |
| events of default/ set-off | yes | No - if not documented under a GMRA Yes - if documented under a GMRA | yes |

# Exhibit 1 - TRIPARTY REPO

By Saheed Awan of Cedelbank

## Triparty Repo

Pick up the phone to a counterpart, negotiate a rate and term for your cash, pay it into your account at the custodian and ... that's it! You have just entered into a simple and secure money-market investment. For the counterpart - generally a broker-dealer borrowing the cash to fund the firm's securities positions - it is just as simple. By sharing a common custodian (the triparty agent), appropriate and sufficient securities are automatically selected from the broker dealer's portfolio at the agent and delivered into the triparty repo account against simultaneous transfer of the cash.

The first ever international triparty repo transaction was conducted on 22 September 1993. The trade was a USD.50 million transaction between the European Bank for Reconstruction & Development (EBRD) and Swiss Bank Corporation. The schematic below from the EBRD shows the easy-to-use nature of the product and the roles of the three parties.

Triparty repo has a number of significant advantages over other repo structures

### Triparty Repo - SECURE AND COST EFFECTIVE

The pre-settlement checks, settlement and all on going operational aspects of the repo are handled by an independent third party. There are no operations and system set-up costs for the Buyer, delivery costs are reduced, substitutions are easier and cheaper, margin movements are easily maintained and procedures in case of default of a counterpart are easily enforced.

Cost: LOW

Risk: LOW

Flexibility: GOOD

### Bilatateral (or Delivery) Repo - COSTLY

Securities are transferred from the Seller's custodian to the Buyer's. The systems and the operations staff required to settle, monitor and administer the repo make this an expensive structure. Substitutions are rarely allowed by the cash provider and therefore the repo rate is often lower than tri-party. Main benefit is that the transfer of securities ensures that in the event of the Seller's default, the Buyer can dispose of the securities with potentially less interference from the Seller (refer to section: Risks of Triparty Repo.)

Cost: HIGH

Risk: LOW

Flexibility: POOR

### Hold-in-Custody (or Trust Me) Repo - HIGH RISK

The securities are held in a safekeeping account with the Seller's custodian for the duration of the transaction. Although the set-up and administrative costs are limited, the risks of this arrangement are clear (remember the Wallace Smith Trust): The same securities could be used for a number of repo agreements simultaneously and, if the Seller were to become insolvent, the fact that the securities may not have been segregated could cause problems.

Cost: HIGH

Risk: HIGH

Flexibility: POOR

The simplicity and efficiency achieved with triparty repo does not undermine the benefits and security of a bi-lateral (or delivery) repo transaction:

- The investor still retains the credit quality of the counterpart and the additional credit of the purchased securities;

- The GMRA does not change;

- The daily valuation of the purchased securities is performed against the cash principal plus the accrued repo interest to date;

- The requirement for maintenance margin is maintained by the triparty agent's automatic margining facilities or chased up by the agent on behalf of the investor;

- Flexibility on the term and size of the transaction does not change. Triparty repo transactions can have a term ranging from overnight to 12 months. Sellers prefer longer term transactions under triparty as the repoed securities are easily accessible through substitutions.

**Transaction Maturities in Cedelbank**

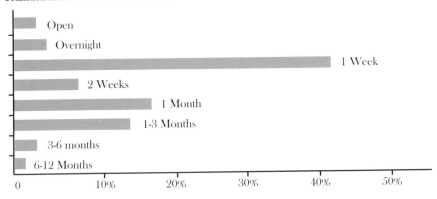

## Bottom line - how much does triparty repo cost me ... or save me?

Assume you have USD1 billion to invest and are looking at three options to place this cash - in triparty repo, delivery repo (or bi-lateral repo) or on time deposit.

The rule of thumb in calculating the cost of setting up a bi-lateral repo facility is that it will cost at least 2 basis points (0.02%) from the cash invested in operations staff costs and another 2 basis points in costs for building or buying a repo system, amortised over a year. These costs will naturally decline with economies of scale as your investment in repo builds up.

The second cost is the custody charge. In bi-lateral repo the custody fee charge is incurred by the purchaser of the securities, the cash provider. This fee can range from 0.9 basis points to 1.5 basis points (0.009% to 0.015%). With triparty repo, custody is included as part of the fee charged by the agent to the Seller. However, it is becoming more common for both parties - the cash provider and the taker - to share some of the costs. An all-inclusive fee of half a basis point (0.005%) may be paid by the cash provider.

The third element is the potential yield pick-up. In general giving the Seller the right of unlimited substitution is worth 3 basis points in extra yield.

The last and perhaps most important cost is the cost of capital associated with investment risk. It is not in the scope of this section of this book to provide a detailed study of the capital savings available through investing in collateralised instruments as opposed to investing unsecured. However in general a 100% secured reverse repo transaction will attract a zero capital cost, whereas a non-secured loan to an OECD commercial bank would attract a general risk factor of 8% of the 20% of risk capital the banking regulators would require for that class of counterparty. The opportunity lost is therefore the amount of capital held against the transaction multiplied by the firm's required return on capital.

Annual Costs & Revenues for supporting an investment of USD1 billion

| Item | Triparty Repo | Delivery Repo | Time Deposit (OECD Bank) |
|---|---|---|---|
| Operations Staff | $0.00 | -$200,000 | $0.00 |
| Systems | $0.00 | -$200,000 | $0.00 |
| Custody charges | $0.00 | -$140,000 | Not applicable |
| Substitution facility | +300,000 | - | Not applicable |
| Risk Capital Cost | - | - | -$1,600,000* |
| Bottom Line | Makes $300,000 extra | Loses $540,000 | Loses $1,600,000 |

- Assumes risk calculated according to the Solvency Ratio Directive and a required internal return on capital of 10%

## Who uses triparty repo?

International triparty was originally conceived to attract more cash investors into the nascent repo market of the early 1990s. By freeing up potential investors from the costs of setting up the systems and the back offices to process and administer multi-currency repo transactions, triparty would make "repo as simple as bank deposits." This, plus the opportunity to hedge credit risks that a documented repo transaction offers, has attracted a variety of cash lenders into international triparty:

- Central banks and supranational institutions who are required to invest in highly secure products like US or euro government bond repo through the convenience of the triparty structure.

- Medium and large European commercial banks that arbitrage the low cost cash obtained through their retail branch networks or through their commercial paper issuance programs.

- Financial institutions who experience irregular cash flows and require flexibility of tenure plus security in short term cash investments. This group includes building societies, insurance companies and the agency securities lending desks at custodians when they want to re-invest cash received as collateral against loans.

- Money market funds who are required to invest in products that ensure their AAA ratings and who need the flexibility and liquidity that over-night triparty repo offers.

However the one market segment that should have been strongly interested in using triparty repo - corporate treasurers - have proved to be an elusive group for the repo community and the triparty agents to attract. This, despite the ability of triparty repo to meet the most demanding needs of the corporate treasurer - security plus enhanced returns, flexible maturities and the low cost of entry. European corporate treasurers, unlike their American counterparts, generally seem to prefer unsecured bank deposits or commercial paper.

## Cash borrowers in triparty repo generally fall into three categories:

- Broker dealers use triparty repo to mainly finance their inventories and, to a lesser extent, to run a matched book. US broker dealers who lack access to cash deposits through a bank parent are the biggest users of triparty repo, followed by Japanese securities houses.

- Collateral-rich bank treasurers in Europe whose cost of funding through triparty repo is relatively cheaper than funds obtained internally or through the unsecured interbank markets. The pressure on such banks is also coming from their counterparts in the inter-bank deposits markets who are seeking a collateralised money market deposit.

- Commercial banks outside of the G7 block seeking to diversify their sources of finance and to lower the costs of such finance. The banks most likely to achieve this hold G7 government bonds and high quality Eurobonds. Triparty repo also serves as a back-stop facility for such banks when their normal lines of funding are cut by whenever military or political tension rises in their regions.

## Getting Started

The starting point to any transaction should be familiar:- credit analysis. Essentially, credit risk is a combination of three components: the creditworthiness of the counterparty, the volatility of the market in the securities of the repo trade and the identity of the issuer of the securities. Once suitability of the trading counterparty is concluded, the structure of a classic repo trade does accommodate and address the market value and issuer risk. It is in the Execution pages of the Triparty Repo Service Agreement that the rules to manage market and issuer risk are set by the cash provider. The volume of initial margin or haircut requested by the cash provider should cater for reasonable fluctuations in the market value of the securities. The margin maintenance obligations ensure that the cash provider's market exposure is not unacceptably increased (or decreased from the perspective of the Seller) during the life of the repo trade. As for the issuer risk, a responsible cash provider will minimise this exposure by defining comprehensible criteria of eligibility for securities. It is also recommended that to avoid duplication of exposure (and consequent increase of risk) eligibility criteria should exclude securities issued by the trading counterparty or any group entity.

Along with the completed Execution pages, the cash provider will need to send other supporting documentation to the triparty repo agent - a copy of the bi-laterally agreed Global

Master Repurchase Agreement, audited financial statements, articles of association, a list of authorised signatories and an agreement on the method to be used for collateralising the daylight overdraft exposure of the triparty agent. Upon receipt of the documentation, the triparty agent's credit unit will open an account in the name of the cash provider. Also, by this time, the triparty agent's staff will have come to train the new customers staff on procedures for sending trade details and the deadlines (most transactions are settled on a spot basis or on trade date +1). At this point the new customer may want to execute a test transaction to get familiar with the product without the weight of real money changing hands. After that, you are ready to deal.

# Chapter 3

# The Repo Markets

The largest and most important repo markets are the US, Japan and the Euro markets, namely Germany, France, Italy, Spain and Belgium and the U.K. Monetary union changed the face of Europe's repo markets, creating the potential for a single, large, liquid euro repo market. The distinctions between the individual markets are now blurring. Ultimately, the euro repo market may resemble its US equivalent. Some European repo desks have already been restructured to mirror US ones; instead of being responsible for individual countries, traders now look at the region as a whole, but focus on a specific part of the yield curve. At the time of going to press some 26% of the E3081bn of debt issued by six of the main european countries were on loan, via repo or securities lending, on any one day. This compares with the US market where USD 1, 854 bn of government debt is lent daily representing 55% of the US government debt outstanding.

In this chapter, the author explains the workings of the major European repo markets denominated in euro, namely the markets of debt issued by Germany, France, Italy, Spain, Belgium and the U.K., and the U.S. market. It concludes with an explanation of the market operations of the ECB.

### Exhibit 1
### European repo market estimated daily turnover in 1998

|  | Daily turnover (bn euros) | Outstandings USDbn |
|---|---|---|
| Germany | 60 | 121 |
| Italy | 50 | 101 |
| France | 40 | 176 - 257 |
| UK | 25 | 135 |
| Belgium | 25 | 73 |
| Spain | 20 | 46 |
| Other | 35 | 76 |
| **European repo market** | **255** | **809 (max)** |

Sources: national depositories, Cedel, Euroclear, Giovannini Group report 1999

nb: It is very difficult to obtain accurate data as to the turnover and outstandings in the European repo markets. This is largely due to the trade matching and settlement process. Most repo trades are matched and settled as two cash trades and are indistinguishable from outright purchases and sales. There are also inconsistencies in the authors' sources of data.

## Exhibit 2

### Table: Scale of activity in the government securities loan and repo markets (mns of US dollars)

| Country | Value of govt securities on loan (A) | Value of govt securities on repo (B) | Total value of govt securities on loan or repo (A+B) |
|---|---|---|---|
| Belgium | 1,338 | 72,749 | 74,087 |
| France | 2,797 | 256,866 | 259,663 |
| Germany | 41,193 | 120,833 | 162,026 |
| Italy | n.a. | 100,603 | 100,603 |
| Japan | 475,007 | 101,042 | 576,049 |
| Netherlands | 24,081 | 34,413 | 58,494 |
| Spain | n.a. | 46,488 | 46,488 |
| Sweden | 0 | 36,891 | 36,891 |
| Switzerland | 6,531 | 4,862 | 11,393 |
| U.K. | 45,045 | 134,593 | 179,638 |
| U.S.A. | 477,624 | 1,376,300 | 1,853,924 |

*Source: 'Securities Lending Transactions: Market Development and Implications' published by the Technical Committee of The International Organization of Securities Commissions (IOSCO) and the Committee on Payment and Settlement Systems (CPSS). July 1999*

### Germany

The German repo market is the largest in Europe in terms of daily turnover. For many years, it was an international one with trading dominated by London-based banks and investment banks. But in 1997, when the Bundesbank abolished minimum reserve charges on matched-book repo positions, volumes increased and a number of German banks in London moved their desks back to the domestic market. Despite this, the market in German repo is still centred in London. It makes up the largest proportion of the international multi-currency repo market.

German government bond repo received a boost in the form of the EU Capital Adequacy Directive (CAD) (see Chapter 10) implemented in 1999. The regulatory capital advantages which this provided made government repo more attractive than before, especially when compared to similar products such as deposits and placements.

The market has oustandings of USD 121bn equivalent market (estimate by IOSCO, CPSS) and average daily turnover of E60bn. In addition, there are on average Euro 1000 billion of repos matched monthly by ISMA's Trax trade confirmation matching system. This equates to E47 billion a day . The total nominal value of all German bonds outstanding as at September 1999 was E589 billion. Accordingly, daily turnover in the repo market is estimated at 10%, and outstandings at 20%, of debt outstanding in nominal terms.

The German government debt market is made up of the following securities. By definition, the vast majority of these constitute acceptable collateral in the repo markets.

## Exhibit 3 - The structure of the German bond and repo markets

| Type of issue | maturity | no. of issues | oustandings Euro bn | ISMA approved GC |
|---|---|---|---|---|
| Treasury bills | up to 1 year | 2 | 10 | |
| Bundesschatzanweisungen | up to 2 yrs | 9 | 45 | |
| Bundesrepublik -Bundes | up to 30 yrs | 42 | 327 | * |
| German Unity Fund | up to 3 yrs | 4 | 23 | * |
| ERP Sondervermoegen | up to 4 yrs | 2 | 6 | |
| Bundesobligation - Bobl Obl | up to 5 yrs | 22 | 121 | * |
| Treuhandanstalt | up to 30 yrs | 41 | 54 | * |
| Treuhand-Obligationen-Tobl | up to 5 yrs | 1 | 3 | * |
| Total | | | 589 | |

*Source: Bloomberg, ISMA*

nb1: ISMA'S list also includes World Bank global bond issues (2bn+)

nb2: All other bond types such as Bundesbahn or Bundespost are currently excluded as acceptable collateral on general collateral transactions unless otherwise agreed by the counterparties prior to the transaction.

One obstacle to growth is the unsecured nature of the interbank market in Germany. Unlike France where many loans are secured as repos, in Germany traditional inter-bank deposit and lending activity continues. Cross-border settlement problems from the Deutsche Börse Clearing (DBC) to Euroclear are a further obstacle. The majority of repos in German government securities settle in Euroclear and in many cases bonds are received too late and this results in additional funding costs. Accordingly many dealers are reluctant to deal with counterparties who do not deliver in the first settlement cycle, which impacts liquidity. However the introduction of CAD will lead to greater use of repo.

Securities lending in Germany takes the traditional fee-based form and is effected through lending programmes organised by DBC, the international central securities depositories and domestic banks. DBC has developed terms and conditions for collateralized loans between depository banks and their customers.

Repos are defined under the German Commercial Code; under German law, neither repo nor securities lending transactions depend on the use of a master agreement for their enforceability. Nevertheless, standard market documentation exists. The German Master Agreement (Deutscher Rahmenvertrag für echte Pensionsgeschäfte), is used for domestic repo transactions. In addition, many domestic trades in bonds and equities are structured as stock loans and use a securities lending agreement (Deutscher Rahmenvertrag für Finanztermingeschäfte.) In the event of a default, German law would support the enforceability of a repo both in the context of the buyer's ownership (no risk of recharacterization) and the availability of a statutory set-off mechanism providing for close-out netting even if no specific agreement to that effect has been entered into.

There is no trade confirmation matching system widely used for domestic transactions although Xetra is used by banks to access the ECB repo facility via the Bundesbank. The Bundesbank's repo operations have been growing quickly from 1985, when it started using this intervention tool more frequently. Repo continues to be the best method of maintaining orderly markets and ensuring that appropriate levels of liquidity are made available to the German money market. It is both a tool of liquidity supply and interest rate signalling, and since 1993 over 67% of total refinancing of the financial sector has been via repo.[1]

## France

The French repo market is one of the largest and most developed in the world. It enjoys several important advantages, including a relatively uncommon market-maker system and the support and encouragement of the Banque de France. Since 1994 the French Treasury (Tresor) has actively promoted repo as a way to promote liquidity in the French government debt market. It also benefits from an unusually watertight legal environment; repo legislation is enshrined in French law.

It is both a domestic and international market, with most securities settled domestically. OATs (59%) and BTANs (29%) make up the bulk of collateral. Daily turnover averages E40 billion and oustandings are estimated at E171 billion[2] to E250 billion[3].

## *Exhibit 4 - The structure of the French bond and repo markets*

| Type of issue | maturity | no. of issues | oustandings Euro bn | ISMA approved GC |
|---|---|---|---|---|
| Bons du Tresor a Taux Fixe et a Interet Precompte. BTFs | upto 1 year | 21 | 43 | * |
| Bons du Tresor a Taux Fixe et a Interet Annuel. BTNs | upto 5yrs | 14 | 158 | * Fixed coupon only |
| Bons du Tresor a Taux Fixe et a Interet Annuel Primaire. | upto 5 yrs | 64 | 2 | |
| Obligations Assimilables du Tresor OATs | upto 30 yrs | 56 | 381 | * Fixed coupon only |
| OATs principal strip | upto 30 yrs | 148 | 5 | |
| Total | | | 589 | |

*Source: Bloomberg, ISMA*

nb: ISMA also states that Index linked bonds are excluded unless specifically agreed by both counterparties.

The total nominal value of all French Government bonds outstanding as at September 1999 was E589 billion (coincidentally identical to the size of the German bond market). Daily

---

[1] *Source: BIS 03/99*   [2] *Source: Sicovam*   [3] *Source: IOSCO*

turnover is estimated at 7% of debt outstanding in nominal terms, and outstandings at between 29% and 42%, depending on which source of data is used. In addition, there are, on average, E200 billion of repos matched monthly by ISMA's Trax trade confirmation matching system. This equates to E10 billion a day[4]. France was the first to enjoy a centrally cleared repo market when SBF introduced its Clearnet product for French government bond repo in November 1998.

This exceptional liquidity reflects the fact that the principal interbank trades are secured and the domestic banks, which are the main repo dealers, use repo to take risk positions. Since the introduction of the euro, however, the demand for French bonds by international and even French houses has decreased as the futures market moves to the Bund contract on Eurex from the OAT contract on Matif. This has led to a quieter French repo market.

The market in French government repo is expensive to the euro general collateral curve and for the period January-March 1998, repo traded below uncollateralized money by 4bp for overnight trades, 5bp for 1 week, and 8 bp for 1 and 3 month trades[5].

The French government debt market is made up of the following securities. By definition the vast majority of these constitute acceptable collateral in the repo markets.

### Exhibit 5 - Composition of the repo market in French Government Securities[6]

| Repo trades | 1998 | Q1- 99 | Q2- 99 |
|---|---|---|---|
| Number | 242,341 | 52,042 | 51,654 |
| Daily | 966 | 826 | 795 |
| Repo trades (in bn euros) | | | |
| Value | 10,281,328 | 2,046,385 | 1,893,590 |
| Daily | 40,961 | 32,482 | 29,132 |
| Average size of repo trades | | | |
| (in million euros) | 42 | 39 | 37 |
| Underlying securities | | | |
| OAT | 43% | 54.5% | 59% |
| BTF | 14% | 13% | 9.5% |
| BTAN | 41% | 30.5% | 29% |
| **French Government debt** | **98%** | **98%** | **97.5%** |
| Other securities | 2% | 2% | 2.5% |
| Interest rate | | | |
| Fixed | 53.38% | 41.36% | 39.89% |
| Floating | 46.57% | 58.45% | 59.94% |
| Zero | 0.05% | 0.19% | 0.17% |
| - Outstanding value - end | | | |
| of period (in bn euros) | 170,846 | 184,063 | 171,169 |

Source: Sicovam

[4] Since this source is unlikely to include trades executed between two continental European counterparties, or those of counterparties dealing via their Paris-based entity, it understates the market size.
[5] Source: BIS Implications of repo markets for central banks. March 1999
[6] Contribution: Virginie Bourcier (ClearnetSBF SA)

A unique feature of the French market is the predominance of floating-rate repo. Previously known as TMP[7] (Taux Moyen Pondéré, the rate at which major banks borrowed from, and lent to, each other unsecured overnight) this has been superceded by Eonia. It is very difficult for individual repo dealers to control the rate, since it is determined by a wide range of participants, many of whom are outside the repo market.

On average, 60% of French government debt repo takes place on a floating-rate basis. The repo rate is the arithmetic mean of the overnight rate over the period of the trade, plus the spread over or under this index at which the repo was dealt.

In 1994, 12 primary dealers in French government securities (SVT's) were named as primary dealers (Spécialistes de la Pension sur Valeurs du Trésor or SPVTs) in French government debt repo. In February 1996 the SPVT's designation was dropped when the SPVT group was merged with the SVT group. The Tresor requires the SVT's active in the repo market (currently 12 out of the 19 SVT's) to make markets in fixed income repos. They must quote on screen in real time prices for all repo transactions in BTFs, BTANs and OATs, with the following maturities and amounts:

- next day: EUR 100 million;
- one week: EUR 100 million;
- one month: EUR 50 million;
- three months: EUR 20 million.

A number of screen prints are shown below and following:

## *Exhibit 6 - REUTERS BSGY*

```
1355        SOCIETE GENERALE - REPO DESK - 0142136190        BSGY
       PENSION  LIVREE  ON  FRENCH  GOVERNMENT  SECURITIES


MATURITY    -    ASK    -    BID    -    SIZE
TN               2.47   -    2.57   -    100 X 100
1S               2.51   -    2.61   -    100 X 100
1M               2.46   -    2.56   -    50 X 50
2M               2.51   -    2.61   -    20 X 20
3M               2.58   -    2.68   -    20 X 20
6M               2.73   -    2.83   -    20 X 20
9M               2.90   -    3.00   -    20 X 20
12M              3.04   -    3.14   -    20 X 20


OPEN
```

[7] taux moyen pondere

## Exhibit 7 - BLOOMBERG CCFC9

```
CCFC9                                          DG8 2a Corp   CCFC

16:38 CREDIT COMMERCIAL DE FRANCE              PAGE  1  /  1
```

| FRENCH REPO RATES | BID | ASK | TIME |
|---|---|---|---|
| 1) T/N | 2.4700 | 2.5600 | 9/02 |
| 2) 1 Week | 2.4600 | 2.5800 | 9/02 |
| 3) 1 Month | 2.4700 | 2.5700 | 9/03 |
| 4) 2 Month | 2.5100 | 2.6100 | 9/03 |
| 5) 3 Month | 2.5500 | 2.6500 | 9/03 |
| 6) 6 Month | 2.7200 | 2.8200 | 9/03 |
| 7) 1 Year | 2.9800 | 3.0800 | 9/03 |

```
                     Contact: Jean-Michel Meyer
                     Tel: 01 53 67 05 11
```

## Exhibit 8 - BLOOMBERG CLMM1

```
CLMM1                                          DG8 2a Corp   CLMM
CREDIT LYONNAIS
                                          Page 1 of 1    11:02 GMT
                     REPO / PENSION LIVREE                08-Sep-99
                     OAT - BTAN - BTF
TEL: 01.49.24.76.38
```

| MATURITY | ASK | BID | SIZE | COMMENT |
|---|---|---|---|---|
| T/N | 2.450 | 2.600 | 100×100 | |
| 1W | 2.450 | 2.600 | 100×100 | |
| 1M | 2.450 | 2.600 | 50×50 | |
| 3M | 2.550 | 2.700 | 50×50 | |
| 6M | 2.780 | 2.930 | 25×25 | |
| 9M | 2.950 | 3.100 | 25×25 | |
| 1Y | 3.020 | 3.170 | 25×25 | |
| 1M | 2.850 | 3.000 | 50×50 | |

```
STATUS: ADJUST
```

## Exhibit 9 - BLOOMBERG SOCB14

```
                                                           Page 1 of 1
15:39:30              SOCIETE  GENERALE

           PENSION LIVREE  ON  GOVERNMENT  SECURITIES

  MATURITY   -   ASK    -   BID    -    SIZE
    TN           2.47   -   2.57   -   100 X 100
    1S           2.44   -   2.54   -   100 X 100
    1M           2.46   -   2.56   -    50 X 50
    2M           2.47   -   2.57   -    20 X 20
    3M           2.52   -   2.62   -    20 X 20
    6M           2.71   -   2.81   -    20 X 20
    9M           2.89   -   2.99   -    20 X 20
   12M           3.01   -   3.11   -    20 X 20

          CLOSED        VALUE TOM DOMESTIC CLEARING
```

## Settlement Systems

OATs, BTANs and BTFs are cleared through the Sicovam system. Delivery in each case is versus payment. Repo transactions are booked as such with deals automatically reversed at termination. Repo is usually dealt 'tom-next' (tomorrow to the next day) although it is possible to deal cash (same day).

## Background

Traditionally used as a money-market instrument, the technique of structuring temporary transfers of securities as sales and repurchases became increasingly popular in the late 1980s, as an alternative to the riskier réméré. The repo structure, formerly known as 'pension livrée', is now simply called 'pension'.

During 1993 and 1994 a secure legal framework for pension transactions was implemented. This law:

- confirms the legal nature of the transactions as outright sales and repurchases, so that there is no risk of recharacterisation as secured loans;

- permits any legal entity (except individuals) to enter into repos (subject to any internal corporate restrictions);

- expressly contemplates (but does not require) margining, which again involves the outright transfer of any margin;

40

- permits the buyer to retain the purchased securities in the event of a default by the seller;
- requires delivery of the securities if the transaction is to be enforceable against third parties; and
- permits the termination of repos and the exercise of set-off between repos in the event of the insolvency of a French counterparty.

However, this last 'privilege' is only conferred on repos carried out under a master repo agreement approved by the Banque de France which used to be exclusively the 'Convention - cadre relative aux operations de pension livrée' (known as the 'Pension Livrée Agreement') but now also includes the GMRA.

## Participants

While financing has always been a low priority for universal banks, which have access to cheap in-house funding, it is a major concern at securities houses[8], which do not have access to retail deposits. A key factor in the development of the French repo market has been an underlying supply of cash in the form of money-market mutual funds or Sicavs monétaires[9], which aim to provide retail investors with a return close to wholesale market rates while preserving capital. The Sicavs monétaires are excluded (as non-banks) from the interbank deposit market and have to choose from CDs, repo or BTFs.

BTFs were the traditional Sicav investment. Repo represents a compromise between higher-yielding CDs and lower-yielding BTFs, with the added bonus of being secured against government paper. Furthermore, repo offers the benefit of being indexed against the same money-market index - Eonia - that provides the accepted benchmark for measuring the performance of Sicavs monétaires. It is worth noting that BTFs remain very popular with Sicavs monétaires, but the popularity of Eonia means that there is a large market in money-market swaps into Eonia.

## Balance Sheet Treatment

As with classic repo, the securities sold under a 'pension' remain on the balance sheet of the seller and the repo monies are treated as a liability. The bonds sold are then recorded as 'securities given under pension'. Similarly, the money lent by the buyer is registered as an asset and securities bought are recorded as a liability under 'securities received under pension.

Pension transactions are fiscally neutral because the start and end prices are the same. Interest received by the cash lender is taxed as ordinary income. These transactions are exempt from VAT and stamp duties.

---

[8] *maison(s) de titres*
[9] *SICAV is an abbreviation of 'société d'investissement à capital variable' (in UK terminology, a unit trust)*

# Italy

The Italian repo market is one of the oldest in the world. In 1979, the central bank began to transact repos, or rather buy-sells, with banks and securities houses as a means of supplying and absorbing liquidity.

Like many European repo markets, the flow of business tends to be one way - bonds from London and cash from Milan - and that flow has been driven by foreign demand for high-yielding bonds. On the other side of the market is a huge retail repo sector reflecting Italy's unusually high household savings ratio. Italian banks essentially intermediate between the foreign and domestic sectors.

The Italian government bond market is the largest in Europe with outstandings of E997 billion as at September 1999. Daily repo turnover averages E50 billion and oustandings are estimated at E98 billion. Accordingly, daily turnover is estimated at 5% and outstandings at 10% debt outstanding in nominal terms.

In addition, there are on average E1300 billion of repos matched monthly by ISMA's Trax trade confirmation matching system. This equates to E63 billion a day. (Since this source is unlikely to include trades executed between two continental European counterparties, or those transacted by counterparties dealing via their Milan entity, it understates the market size and is inconsistent with the market estimate above.)

## Exhibit 10 - The structure of the Italian bond and repo markets

Repo is mainly of BTPs and CCTs.

| Type of issue | maturity | no. of issues | oustandings Euro bn | ISMA approved GC |
|---|---|---|---|---|
| Buoni Ordinari del Tesoro - BOTs | upto 1 year | 31 | 131 | * |
| Buoni Poliennali del Tesoro - BTPs | upto 30 yrs | 66 | 534 | * |
| Certificati di Credito del Tereso - CCTs | upto 10 yrs | 41 | 240 | * |
| Certificati di Credito del Tereso - ICTZ | upto 2 years | 15 | 87 | * |
| Credito Tesoro - CTES | upto 2 years | 6 | 5 | |
| Total | | | 997 | |

Source: Bloomberg, ISMA

The retail origin of the Italian market differentiates it from most other repo markets, which originated for bond borrowing purposes, although the introduction of the BTP[10] contract on LIFFE in 1991 increased the demand for specials.

---

[10] Buoni Tesoro Poliennali (Treasury Bonds)

Until 1992, the retail market was driven by tax anomalies such as exemptions on supranational and Italian government Eurobonds which could be swapped into synthetic lira debt. There are also fundamental economic factors driving retail investors into repo. These include the lack of collective investments such as pension funds as well as the market size in, and yields on, government debt.

Settlement of Italian repo is generally effected via a domestic custodian bank especially for BTPs, CCTs[11] and BOTs[12] and via Euroclear/Cedel Bank for CTEs[13]. Failure to deliver is regarded as extremely serious in Italy, despite there being no official securities lending facility. Italian banks remain reluctant to lend securities, both because they are naturally on the other side of the market and also because of a lack of familiarity with the idea of securities lending. Most securities lending is effected only to cover failed trades and must be arranged personally by contact between dealers, usually for no fee. Spreads, when quoted, are several points wide.

## Taxation

The Italian repo market is almost entirely sell/buy-back and there has been little or no movement towards classic repo. The use of the sell/buy-back structure is entrenched for two reasons: the retail nature of the market and the possibility that classic repo may be regarded as two deals and attract double stamp duty. The most popular tenor is one week and overnight repo is limited to cross-border or large wholesale deals. This also reflects the fact that stamp duty is imposed at a flat rate on domestic deals, which encourages longer, larger and cross-border repo. The retail repo sector is intermediated by another 200 banks without international access.

## Spain

The development of the repo market in Spain can be traced back to a decision by the Bank of Spain to issue government debt in the form of Treasury bills (Letras) in 1987.

There are three main types of paper traded under repo in Spain:

- Letras (Treasury Bills), with maturities of between six and 12 months;
- Bonos with initial maturities of between three and five years; and
- Obligaciones (Treasury Bonds), with initial maturities of between 10 and 15 years.

NB. Certain regional government and government agency issues are also acceptable for repo. The Spanish repo market has an average daily turnover of E20 billion and outstandings of E45 billion.

The total nominal value of all Spanish Government bonds outstanding as at September 1999 was E251 billion. Accordingly daily turnover is estimated at 8% and outstandings at 18% of debt outstanding in nominal terms. In addition, there are on average E141 billion of repos matched monthly by ISMA's Trax trade confirmation matching system. This equates to E7 billion a day[14].

[11] *Certificati di Credito Tesoro (Floating rate Treasury certificates - credit notes)*
[12] *Buoni Ordinari del Tesoro (Treasury bills)*
[13] *Certificati del Tesoro in ECU (Treasury notes)*
[14] *Since this source is unlikely to include trades executed between two continental European counterparties, or those executed by counterparties who deal via their Madrid based entity, it understates the market size.*

## Exhibit 11 - The structure of the Spanish bond and repo markets

| Type of issue | maturity | no. of issues | oustandings Euro bn | ISMA approved GC |
|---|---|---|---|---|
| Letras del Tesoro | upto 1 year | 49 | 51 | * |
| BONOS | upto 30 yrs | 31 | 200 | * |
| Total | | | 251 | |

*Source: Bloomberg, ISMA*

Market participants range from large domestic and non-domestic banking institutions and fund managers to local Cajas[15] that - in a development almost unique to Spain - offer repo as a savings product to account holders through their branch networks.

Useful information on Spanish money markets is included below:

## Exhibit 12 - BLOOMBERG CIMD

```
4                                          DG8 2a Corp   CIMD
C.I.M.D.  - Madrid


                                                      Page 1 of 1
      * C.I.M.D.MADRID TREASURY BILLS AND REPOS TF.4326425 * CIMF
    SIMULT.  LET-REPO LETRAS 12 MES  LETRAS 18 MES  -DECENALES-
DD 2.45-48   2.45-49  GR-1A          GR-18          4.75
1W 2.48-50   2.48-52  11-02 2.75-82  29-09 3.09-16  5.15 2.45-50
DC 2.49-53   2.48-53  03-03 2.79-85  13-10 3.10-16  6/30 2.45-50
2W 2.49-51   2.48-53  31-03 2.80-86  27-10 3.10-18  4.50 2.35-45
1M 2.50-53   2.50-53  28-04 2.85-91  10-11 3.15-25  7.90 2.45-50
2M 2.53-58   2.54-60  12-05 2.88-00  24-11 3.17-27  4.25 2.45-50
3M 2.59-61   2.58-63  09-06 2.92-00  07-12 3.20-30  6.00 2.45-50
6M 2.79-81   2.77-82  21-07 3.00-09  19-01 3.23-35  5.25 2.35-45
9M 2.90-00   2.90-00  18-08 3.11-16  02-02 3.28-37  5.00 2.45-50
12 3.00-10   3.00-10  01-09 3.08-16  02-03 3.34-37  6.15 2.45-50
PAGINA INDICE <CIMDA>   PAGINA RESUMEN <CIMD>




Copyright 1999 BLOOMBERG L.P.  Frankfurt:69-920410  Hong Kong:2-2977-6000  London:171-330-7500  New York:212-318-2000
Princeton:609-279-3000    Singapore:226-3000    Sydney:2-9777-8686    Tokyo:3-3201-8900    Sao Paulo:11-3048-4500
                                                                        I665-262-0 08-Sep-99 16:37:27
```

---

[15] Cajas are equivalent to UK Building Societies

## Exhibit 13 - REUTERS EURIBOR01

```
09:07 13SEP99          EURIBOR RATES          UK31108        EURIBOR01

  RATES AT 11H00 BRUSSELS TIME 13/09/1999    VALUE DATE 15/09/99
  EURIBOR RATES   ACT/ 360
  ================================================================
    1WK   2.547   <EURIBORSWD=>  EURIBOR  (Euro Interbank Offered Rate)
    1MO   2.584   <EURIBOR1MD=>  is the rate at which Euro interbank
    2MO   2.644   <EURIBOR2MD=>  term deposits within the Euro zone are
    3MO   2.693   <EURIBOR3MD=>  offered by one Prime Bank to another
                                 Prime Bank. It is computed as an average
    4MO   3.081   <EURIBOR4MD=>  of daily quotes provided for thirteen
    5MO   3.096   <EURIBOR5MD=>  maturities by a panel of 57 of the most
    6MO   3.114   <EURIBOR6MD=>  active Banks in the Euro zone.
                                 It is quoted on an act/360 day count
    7MO   3.139   <EURIBOR7MD=>  convention, and is fixed at 11:00am(CET)
    8MO   3.167   <EURIBOR8MD=>  displayed to three decimal places.
    9MO   3.202   <EURIBOR9MD=>  ================================================
                                 See <EURIBOR> for details of Panel Bank
   10MO   3.237   <EURIBOR10MD=> contributions and historical recap
   11MO   3.277   <EURIBOR11MD=> displays
   12MO   3.314   <EURIBOR1YD=>  ================================================
For EONIA please refer  to page  <EONIA>, LIBOR master index see <BBALIBORS>
Composite displays: (a/360) see <EURIBOR=>, (a/365) see <EURIBOR365=>
```

## Exhibit 14 - REUTERS CIMF

```
1049 CIMD MADRID TREASURY BILLS & REPOS    TLF.+341 4326425   CIMF
   SIMULT.  LET-REPO LETRAS 12 MES   LETRAS 18 MES    -DECENALES-
DD 2.45-49  2.45-49  GR-1A           GR-18            4.75
1W 2.48-52  2.48-52  11-02 2.75-85   29-09 3.10-19    5.15 2.45-50
DC 2.50-53  2.48-53  03-03 2.78-83   13-10 3.10-20    6/30 2.45-50
2W 2.50-53  2.48-53  31-03 2.80-86   27-10 3.10-20    4.50 2.35-45
1M 2.50-52  2.50-53  28-04 2.85-91   10-11 3.15-25    7.90 2.45-50
2M 2.55-59  2.54-57  12-05 2.88-00   24-11 3.17-27    4.25 2.45-50
3M 2.59-64  2.60-64  09-06 2.93-02   07-12 3.20-30    6.00 2.45-50
6M 2.80-85  2.80-86  21-07 3.00-09   19-01 3.26-40    5.25 2.35-45
9M 2.95-02  2.95-02  18-08 3.10-15   02-02 3.30-43    5.00 2.45-50
12 3.05-15  3.05-15  01-09 3.10-19   02-03 3.37-45    6.15 2.45-50
PAGINA INDICE <CIMDA>    PAGINA RESUMEN <CIMD>
```

In line with other money-market instruments, Spanish repo is quoted on a 360-day basis. The bid/offer spread, for terms of up to three months, is usually up to five basis points (0.05%); however, spreads may widen as the period of the proposed trade lengthens. Repo historically trades below Eonia, although the spread can be as narrow as five to 10 basis points.

The number of bond issues which trade as 'specials' are relatively few. Demand is normally seen in the 'cheapest-to-deliver' (CTD) bonds deliverable against the 10-year futures contract. In normal market conditions, one would expect to pay between five and 10 basis points through general collateral (GC) levels when bidding for a specific bond but on occasion a particular issue will become scarce. Trades are transacted either as repo or as buy/sells, but the latter is more prevalent, since buy/sell is recognized by the Bank of Spain as transferring ownership. A move towards repo documentation, in the light of margin concerns, is a possibility.

As the volume of securities repoed in the market has increased, the Bank of Spain has developed a smooth and efficient book-entry accounting system allowing same-day settlement for resident counterparties and next-day settlement for non-resident counterparties. This flexibility, together with the loss of one day value, has accounted for a contraction in the number of trades settled via Euroclear and Cedel.

The tax treatment of coupon paper is net of 25% withholding tax for residents. This, however, does not apply to Letras or repo with non-residents, which receive an almost instant return of withholding tax.

## *Belgium*

The Belgian repo market is one of the most developed in Europe with daily turnover of E25bn and outstandings of USD 73bn equivalent (estimate by IOSCO, CPSS). The total nominal value of bonds and bills outstanding as at September 1999 was E236bn. Accordingly daily turnover in the repo market is estimated at 11%, and outstandings at 30%.

Like the French market it enjoys several advantages. In 1991 the Belgian parliament passed an act which recognised repurchase agreements and afforded protection to users. A legal agreement known as the Convention de Place was developed in the same year . Dealers only need to sign this once and a copy is held by the National Bank of Belgium (NBB). In 1997 the GMRA was recognised in Belgian law and may be used for repos domestically. NBB also maintains a register of the signatories of the GMRA .

Belgian government bonds are dematerialised and settle domestically on a delivery versus payment basis through the NBB. Indeed all Belgian banks are obliged to hold their OLO's in the NBB and an automatic bond lending system operates to ensure orderly settlement. It is also possible to settle via Euroclear and Cedel.

The debt market is vast in proportion to GDP. It reached a peak in 1993 of 135% of GDP and has since stabilised. However this deep and liquid pool of bonds has been mobilised by repo participants and despite the proportion of debt to GDP, 30% of bonds are out on repo at any one time.

The Belgian government debt market is made up of the following securities . By definition, the vast majority of these constitute acceptable collateral in the repo markets.

## Exhibit 15 - The structure of the Belgian bond and repo markets

| Type of issue | maturity | no. of issues | oustandings Euro bn | ISMA approved GC |
|---|---|---|---|---|
| Treasury bills | up to 1 year | 28 | 40 | |
| Belgian Government bonds - OLO's | up to 20 yrs | 62 | 193 | * |
| Belgian Governement bonds - OLO's strips | up to 30 yrs | 7 | 3 | * |
| Total | | | 236 | |

*Source: Bloomberg, ISMA*

OLO's, which are government book-entry securities and which are fungible with other issues, are the securities offered as collateral in most repo trades. There are exchange auctions of maturing OLO's for longer dated instruments. Less frequently, repo is undertaken in Treasury bills and dematerialised Phillippe bonds which are bonds generally held by retail investors.

Fixed term repos are the only form of repo recognised by Belgian law. One noticeable difference between Belgian Government bond repo and other markets is that the seller of the bond in a repo receives the coupon if it is paid during the term of the repo. Tri-party repo is popular with Belgian banks who act as cash providers against government and corporate bonds.

The Ministry of Finance, through a series of parliamentary acts since 1991, has encouraged the development of an efficient and liquid market in Treasury bills and OLO's.

The National Bank had used repo as its main instrument in open market operations to supply and absorb funds since 1991 and, by 1997, 73% of all refinancing of the financial sector was made via reverse repo. On average 15 banks accessed this facility in order to raise short term funds. From the advent of EMU these banks have been able to access Euro via the NBB by pledging OLO's as collateral. Accordingly the major participants in the Belgian market are familiar with the workings of the repo markets both as a primary supplier of liquidity by the central bank and in the domestic and international markets.

Since the introduction of the euro, however, demand for Belgian bonds by international and domestic houses has increased. The availability of such a large and mobile pool of collateral has meant that OLO's have become not only an acceptable form of collateral in Euro general collateral trades but also the bonds of choice in term GC trades.

The repo market in OLO's is 'cheap' to the euro general collateral curve compared with other collateral such as French and Spanish government bonds.

A useful screen for information on the Belgian repo market is BBLB13:

## Exhibit 16 - BLOOMBERG BBLB13

```
BBLB13                                        DG8 2a Corp   BBLB
16:40 BANQUE  BRUSSELS  LAMBERT                PAGE  1  /  1
TERM     EUR DEPOSIT RATE       EUR REPO RATE         TREASURY CERTIF
         BID    ASK   TIME      BID    ASK   TIME     BID    ASK   TIME
1M   1)  2.51   2.63  9/03  12) 2.55   2.60  8/31  18) 2.46   2.51  8/23
2M   2)  2.57   2.69  9:49  13) 2.58   2.63 14:10  19) 2.49   2.54  8/23
3M   3)  2.61   2.73  9:49  14) 2.62   2.67  8/30  20) 2.54   2.59  8/30
6M   4)  3.01   3.17  9:49  15) 2.89   2.94 14:10  21) 2.77   2.82 14:07
9M   5)  3.10   3.26  9:49  16) 3.02   3.07 14:10  22) 2.96   3.01 14:07
1Y   6)  3.18   3.34  9:49  17) 3.19   3.24 14:10  23) 3.10   3.15 14:07

              FRA EUR
3/6  7)  3.27   3.32  8/31
3/9  8)  3.33   3.38  8/31
6/12 9)  3.46   3.51  8/31

              IRS EUR
1Y/3M 10)  3.30   3.35 14:09
1Y/6M 11)  3.36   3.41 14:09
     J.Goffaux      M.DeBrucker   C.Mortier  A.Jardon  J.Van Mierenhoucht
    Tel: 32 2 547 3512    2716      3972       2255        2268
    Fax: 32 2 547 2795

Copyright 1999 BLOOMBERG L.P.  Frankfurt:69-920410  Hong Kong:2-2977-6000  London:171-330-7500  New York:212-318-2000
Princeton:609-279-3000        Singapore:226-3000    Sydney:2-9777-8686   Tokyo:3-3201-8900   Sao Paulo:11-3048-4500
                                                                      I665-262-0 08-Sep-99 16:39:27
```

NBB acts as lender of last resort in the bond market and the Ministry of Finance can create additional bonds to fill short positions. Accordingly there are few specials in the market.

Repos in Belgium are free of withholding tax if the securities are held by eligible institutions e.g. pension funds, Belgian corporations and non-residents in X accounts.

It is possible to engage in securities lending but, as Exhibit 17 below suggests, the vast majority of trades are undertaken as repos.

## Exhibit 17 - Scale of activity in the Belgian government securities loan and repo market (millions of US dollars)

| Country | Value of govt securities on loan (A) | Value of govt securities on repo (B) | Total value of govt securities on loan or repo (A+B) |
|---|---|---|---|
| Belgium | 1,338 | 72,749 | 74,086 |

*Source: IOSCO/CPSS Report, July 1999 - see Exhibit 2.*

48

# United Kingdom

## Open gilt repo market

An open repo market in UK government debt was established in January 1996, supported by reformed tax structures to facilitate the efficient functioning of the market. Prior to this, gilts were only lent via authorized intermediaries, known as Stock Exchange Money Brokers (SEMBs). These firms were specialist businesses whose principal function was to serve Gilt-Edge Market Makers (GEMMs) and investors who lent securities. The SEMBSs on-lent the gilts to the GEMMs and to discount houses.

The liberalization of the market meant that for the first time ever, anyone could borrow or lend gilts, via repo, reverse repo or stock lending/borrowing, directly or via an intermediary. Following a quick start, the gilt repo market is now established as an important component of the sterling money markets. Outstandings grew from £94 billion at the end of November 1998 to £105 billion at end of February 1999. This is a return to the previous peak achieved in oustandings in Aug 1998[16].

The gilt repo market has an average daily turnover of £25 billion according to market estimates. The total nominal value of gilts outstanding as at September 1999 was £261 billion. Accordingly, daily turnover is estimated at 6%, and outstandings at 40%, of debt outstanding in nominal terms (based on BOE statistics).

## Exhibit 18 - The structure of the U.K. bond and repo markets

| Type of issue | maturity | no. of issues | oustandings GBP bn | ISMA approved GC |
|---|---|---|---|---|
| Gilts | upto 30 yrs | 75 | 261 | * |

Source: Bloomberg, ISMA

## Exhibit 19 - Scale of activity in the government securities loan and repo markets (millions of US dollars)

| Country | Value of govt securities on loan (A) | Value of govt securities on repo (B) | Total value of govt securities on loan or repo (A+B) |
|---|---|---|---|
| United Kingdom | 45,045 | 134,593 | 179,638 |

Source: Bloomberg, ISMA

Following the liberalization, the Bank of England extended its use of repo, which is now the main platform of liquidity management. By June 1998, repo accounted for 70% of the refinancing provided to the financial sector.[17]

---

[16] Source: BOE Quarterly bulletin May 1999)
[17] Source: BIS

49

## Characteristics of the Bank of England repo

Frequency : up to four times per day

Maturity: overnight or 14 days

Acceptable collateral: gilts, bills

Counterparties: banks, securities houses, discount houses

Number of active counterparties: 20

Margining practices: daily mark to market, margin calls and haircut

The Bank of England has reserved the right to lend gilts on repo to facilitate orderly market trading. If, for example, a gilt issue comes under pressure in the repo markets because it is the cheapest to deliver into a futures contract, the Bank of England can step in and offer to lend the bond at a rate of zero per cent to GEMMs or their clients who would have been subject to failed deliveries.

A useful screen concerning the Bank of England repo and the Gilt repo market in general is shown below:

## Exhibit 20 - Reuters BOE/MONEYOPS1

```
08:45 10SEP99        BANK OF ENGLAND           UK00181     BOE/MONEYOPS1
The weekly sterling Treasury bill tenders takes place today; bids for the
Stg 900 mn 28 day bills and Stg 200 mn 91 day bills on offer must be received by
12.30 pm. The results of the tenders will be published shortly after 1pm on the
fifth page in this series.

9.45 am Initial liquidity forecast Stg 100 mn shortage
Principal factors in the forecast
Treasury bills & maturing outright purchases +247
Bank/Exchequer transactions +995
Rise in note circulation -1325
Bankers balances above target +5
```

## Settlement

Settlement is via the Central Gilts Office (CGO), a department of the Bank of England. This is an electronic book-entry settlement system with payment for transactions 'assured' by settlement banks. It is also possible to settle via the two big International Central Securities Depositories (ICSDs), Euroclear and Cedelbank.

In the late 1980s, the CGO introduced a new collateral management facility. Delivery-by-Value (DBV) enables members to deliver and receive packages of securities, to a specified value, against the creation of an assured payment obligation, on the basis that equivalent stock is returned automatically the following business day. Each day, participants seeking to borrow securities call likely counterparts with their borrowing needs, and pledge gilts DBV as security.

A selection algorithm notionally allocates the seller's securities to the buyer until the value sought plus the margin for each DBV has been satisfied. This is run by the CGO according to the timetable overleaf.

DBV co-exists with repo and reverse repo transactions on a member-to-member delivery basis. DBV is also available in CREST, the central securities depository for equities. While the CREST system facilitates members' ability to give and receive packages of securities as collateral, there is, however, no connection within CREST between stock loans by one member to another and DBVs given as collateral.

The CGO operational timetable is as follows:

Current

| | |
|---|---|
| 07:00 | Start of day - system available for enquiry |
| 08:00 | Start of day - system available for input |
| 08:30 | Start of gilts settlement |
| 09:30 | Circles run |
| 09:30 | DBVs returned |
| 13.30 | Circles run |
| 14:30 | Circles run |
| 14:50 | End of DVP settlement |
| 14:55 | Start of DBV settlement |
| 16:05 | End of DBV settlement |
| 16:19 | Final payments |
| 16:20 - 18:30 | Input enabled |
| 17:15 | Reference prices updated |
| 19.00 | System closes |

The CGO does not have a matching function and all gilt trades are traditionally 'called over' (the seller's settlement office telephones the buyer with details of the trade on value date). Margin may be delivered in cash or gilts. The method of repricing will be the same as for any other repo market.

## Legal Agreement and Code of Best Practice

The legal agreement used is the GMRA, a document already well established in the London repo market, and issues of application to gilts are covered in an annex to this document (see Chapter 7) and a Gilt Repo Code of Best Practice for market participants published by the Bank of England.

The Code of Best Practice was formulated after a period of consultation and debate with market participants and focuses on setting general standards. It covers action required prior to trading, explains the standards expected of market professionals, their agents and brokers, suggests minimum requirements to be covered in a legal agreement and recommends standards for margin, custody treatment of collateral, and default and close-out procedures.

## Taxation

From the start of 1996, all gilt holders, other than individuals, have received interest payments gross of tax. This made gilt repo available to all professional participants without penalties from withholding tax, provided that they held Gilts in a special CGO account. Tax, where it is due, is accounted for quarterly, and the previous distinction between bonds which were tax-free to overseas holders (FOTRA stocks) and taxed if held domestically disappeared. All gilt interest is paid gross unless otherwise specified.

# United States

Although it dates back to 1918, it wasn't until the 1980s that the US repo market really took off, spurred by greater sophistication in investment strategies and the growth of proprietary trading, particularly arbitrage. A further boost came in the shape of increasing numbers of corporates investing cash through primary dealers. Repo was seen as a secure investment for a specific period with no risk.

Securities dealers, smaller provincial banks, municipalities and state funds soon joined the market. Mutual funds are now a key source of cash since they have large daily cashflows. Repo is seen as a convenient same-day tool for enhancing yield and avoiding inconvenient capital gains/losses (for which mutual funds have to account), and it is treated as a normal money-market instrument by a wide range of cash investors. Securities lenders are users of repo as a method of investing collateral and there is no shortage of securities in supply.

## Exhibit 21 - Scale of activity in the government securities loan and repo markets (millions of US dollars)

| | A<br>Value of govt<br>securities on<br>loan | B<br>Value of govt<br>securities on<br>repo | C<br>Total value of<br>govt securities<br>on loan or repo<br>(A+B) | D<br>Total value of<br>govt securities<br>issued | E<br>% on loan<br>or repo<br>(C/D*100) |
|---|---|---|---|---|---|
| United States | 477,624 | 1,376,300 | 1,853,924 | 3,355,500 | 55.3 |

Interbank repo, mainly in government securities, is brokered by many firms, of which the majority are blind brokers; that is, they provide anonymity to both sides of the trade and pass instructions to the GSCC which novates and nets these down.

The US domestic market is screen-based and those screens are usually limited to broker-dealers, although there are some telephone brokers. The next tier of repo trading is the market in mortgage-backed pass-through securities. Securities come to the marketplace (via broker-dealers, from their proprietary or matched books positions ), from smaller lenders and thrifts as a result of the attractive higher yields and broader investor base.

The US government bond market is the largest in the world with the total value of government securities outstanding of USD 3356 billion. Correspondingly, it is the largest repo market with outstandings of USD 1376 billion. The total of bonds that are lent via the repo and securities lending markets is USD 1854 billion which represents 55% of the debt market.

A useful screen is Reuters: REPO Exhibit 22 (overleaf).

There is a developing market in corporate and high-yield bonds and asset-backed securities and a developed one in emerging-market debt (e.g. Brady bonds). In this sense, therefore, the growth of repo is part of the wider processes of securitization and disintermediation, whereby traditional credit transactions through banks have been replaced by securities-based transactions. This is due to the choice of security, availability of triple-A collateral, mark-to-market of collateral or over-collateralization, and the availability of DVP.

## Exhibit 22 - REUTERS REPO

```
1500............REUTERS REPURCHASE AGREEMENT RATES           REPO
REPO U.S. TREAS  *    MORTGAGE   *     OPEN SPECIALS   * GOV'T
8:08             * 5.31 - 5.26 * 02Y          -        *TERM O/N
O/N  5.10 - 5.08 * 5.20 - 5.18 * 2YR          -        *  REPO
1WK  5.13 - 5.09 * 5.24 - 5.19 * 03Y          -        *  5.09
2WK  5.21 - 5.11 * 5.31 - 5.21 * 3YR          -        *-------
3WK  5.26 - 5.16 * 5.36 - 5.26 * 05Y          -        *FEDRAL
1MO  5.26 - 5.16 * 5.36 - 5.26 * 5YR          -        *FUNDS
2MO  5.31 - 5.26 * 5.41 - 5.36 * 01O  2.60  - 2.40     *B 5 1/4
3MO  5.31 - 5.26   5.41 -5.36  * 10Y  4.20  - 3.80     *A 5 5/16
       -       -             * 03O          -          *L 5 1/4
       -       -             * 30Y          -  4.80     *
```

Triparty repo emerged in 1981 and is well established. The two main providers are the clearing banks for broker-dealers: Bank of New York and Chase Manhattan. Over the last five years, the proportion of repo traded triparty has grown considerably and is estimated at 50% of the total market in repo. It also facilitates smaller repo transactions, and offers better rates when compared to delivery repo because of lower collateral requirements. Triparty can also be used for portfolio swaps: a portfolio of government securities is swapped for lower-grade (eg mortgage-backed) securities in return for a guaranteed fee. This is popular among municipalities, state funds and insurance companies.

Repo is a key tool of the Federal Reserve's open market operations. When there is a shortage, it adds cash by undertaking repo, and when it wishes to drain reserves from the banking system it undertakes matched sale/purchases, or MSPs (these equate to reverses from the dealers' viewpoint). This occurs daily at 11.30 a.m. New York time. The rate at which the Fed undertakes system repos or MSPs is a closely-watched indicator of official interest-rate policy. The Fed also undertakes 'System MSPs' on behalf of clients - generally major foreign central banks - and normally announces the size of that transaction in advance.

Participation in the repo market is broadly-based, with activities grouped as follows:
- firm financing for securities dealers, hedge funds, arbitrageurs, etc;
- bond lending by investors and central banks;
- matched and mis-matched book trading by primary dealers; and
- cash investment by banks, municipalities and state funds.

### Documentation

The Bond Markets Association (BMA) (formerly the Public Securities Association (PSA)) Master Repurchase Agreement was originally issued in 1986 after a number of scandals relating to repo and a long internal consultation process. The PSA agreement is based on New York law and is the model for the GMRA.

### Securities lending

Securities lending has been in existence in the US for 25 years. It usually takes place through agents; typically commercial banks with extensive custodial operations. Some larger pension funds lend directly. The agent, who typically splits the fee with the lender, provides five key services:

- custody of the lendable securities;
- negotiation of the terms and conditions of the loan;
- collecting and marking-to-market the securities pledged as collateral;
- collecting fees from the borrower; and
- sourcing potential borrowers and monitoring their creditworthiness.

A typical loan of treasuries is initiated by a government securities dealer seeking a specific issue. The dealer will telephone several banks which have agreements, with their custody or trust customers, to lend treasuries. Loan fees and the form of collateral are negotiated between agent bank and dealer.

## The European System of Central Banks

### Introduction

Prior to the introduction of the euro, the 11 individual central banks of the member states that adopted the euro used repos extensively to add and withdraw liquidity and to signal policy stance and changes in it. Since the introduction of EMU in January 1999, monetary policy has been undertaken on a more uniform basis, through the European Central Bank. The national central banks are still involved, but only as the conduits through which the ECB carries out its open market operations.

Essentially it is a de-centralized system relying on the national central banks to produce a single monetary policy. Accordingly the different processes and procedures previously carried out by the Bunbesbank, Banque de France and other central banks ceased from the end of 1998.

### Monetary policy framework

The European System of Central Banks is made up of the European Central Bank and the national central banks (NCB's) of the European Union member states e.g. Bank of Italy, Bank of Spain, and so on. The NCBs of the countries that have adopted the single currency carry out the operations of monetary policy on a uniform basis.

### Monetary policy instruments

### 1. Open Market Operations

Open market operations are used to steer interest rates, manage liquidity and signal policy stance and changes in it. The ESCB has five instruments at its disposal:

1. reverse transactions
2. outright transactions
3. issuance of debt certificates
4. foreign exchange swaps
5. collection of fixed-term deposits

Reverse transactions:

- Regular liquidity providing reverse repo transactions usually weekly for a period of two weeks. The majority of refinancing comes about through this route.

- Longer term refinancing operations are provided via reverse repos each month for a period of three months. The longer term financing is not intended to signal policy stance.

- Fine tuning operations are conducted as and when required to counter unexpected liquidity changes. These may take the form of reverse repos, outright purchase or sales, foreign exchange swaps or by taking term deposits. These, by their nature, have to be executed quickly and may take the form of bilateral transactions or by tender. Active participants in the foreign exchange market are used for FX swaps.

Structural operations are also carried out by the ESCB using issuance of debt certificates, outright transactions and reverse repos as and when structural imbalances occur such as surplus liquidity or too large a deficit.

## 2. Standing Facilities

Two standing facilities are available, the marginal lending facility and the deposit facility. The marginal lending facility is open to eligible counterparties who may borrow cash overnight secured against eligible assets. Generally there is no limit to how much may be borrowed. The deposit facility allows eligible banks and investment banks to place overnight deposits with the NCB.

These facilities are in place so as to limit the volatility of short-term rates and rates are targeted; the interest rate on the marginal lending facility is the ceiling, and the rate on the deposit facility is the floor. The ECB conducts open market operations within this band.

## 3. Minimum Reserves

A minimum reserves system is used to stabilize interest rates and manage liquidity in the system. The reserve requirement is calculated according to the composition of the balance sheet of each credit institution in the euro area and is based on an average daily reserve holding over a one month maintenance period. These are interest bearing at the ESCB reverse repo rate.

### Eligible assets

Two categories of assets are eligible as collateral for all ESCBs credit operations. Tier one consists of marketable debt and tier two consists of other assets marketable and non-marketable, both debt and equity, which are important for and meet the eligibility criteria of some national central banks but are subject to ECB approval. No distinction in pricing is made between the two tiers.

Tier one assets must be:

- highly rated;
- located in the euro area;

- transferable in book entry form;
- deposited with a national central bank or an approved securities depository; and
- listed or quoted on a regulated market or traded on certain non-regulated markets.

Tier two assets must be:

- debt instruments (marketable or non-marketable) or equities traded on a regulated market;
- securities issued by a financially sound entity;
- easily accessible to the NCB;
- located in euro area;
- denominated in euro; and
- issued by or guaranteed by entities established in the euro area.

Securities which were issued by or guaranteed by the counterparty or by an entity which has close links to the counterparty are invalid. Bonds maturing or paying a coupon or equities with a payment of any kind during the monetary policy operation may be excluded.

These securities may be used on a cross border-basis e.g. to borrow from the central bank of the member state where they are established by making use of assets located in another state. It is possible, for example, to borrow euros from the Banque de France using Bunds held in Germany.

## Eligible counterparties

### Eligibility criteria

- institutions are subject to the ESCB's minimum reserve system
- they must be financially sound and EU-supervised (although non-European financially sound firms which are subject to comparable supervision may be eligible).
- they must fulfill required operational criteria.

An eligible institution accesses the standing facilities and open market operations via the national central bank of the country where it is established. If, however, it has branches in other countries within the euro zone it may access the national central bank where these are located.

## The reverse repo tender process

### Step 1: Tender Announced

The ECB announces via the usual public information wire services (and to individual counterparties if it is necessary) its intention to inject cash to euro-area banks under 14-day refinancing loans, generally at a fixed rate, e.g. 2.5%. This is usually on a Tuesday for the main refinancing operations and on the first Wednesday of each minimum reserve maintenance period for longer term refinancing operations.

The key details announced are:

- The reference number of the tender
- The date of the tender operation (announcement date + 2 days, e.g. Aug 4th)
- The type of operation (e.g. 14-day refinancing loans)
- The maturity date (usually announcement date + 14, e.g. August 18th)
- The type of auction (e.g. fixed-rate tender)
- Allotment method
- Maximum bid limit (if any)
- Minimum allotment (if any)
- Time schedule for submission of bids (e.g. August 3rd at 9:30am)
- Minimum amount of bids (e.g. 1.00 million euros, multiples of euro 100,000 thereafter)

## Step 2: Counterparties prepare and submit bids

Each individual NCB has its own set of procedures. In fixed-rate tenders the bank bids the amount of money that it is willing to borrow from the NCB. In variable-rate tenders, banks may submit multiple bids at up to ten different rates at a minimum of 1bp difference, stating against each bid how much they are willing to borrow.

The ECB may impose a maximum bid limit; this will be included in the tender announcement. A bank bidding for cash should have sufficient collateral available to meet its bids and may be fined if it does not. The NCBs have the right to check that sufficient collateral is readily available.

## Step 3: ESCB compiles bids

In fixed-rate tenders, the bids are added together and if the result exceeds the amount of liquidity alloted the bids will be scaled down on a pro-rata basis. However, the ECB has the right to allot a minimum amount to each bidder.

In variable-rate tenders, liquidity is allocated to the highest bidder and successive lower bids are filled until the tender is exhausted. If, by the lowest accepted rate - the marginal rate - the total amount of bids exceeds the offer of liquidity, the firms who bid at this rate have their bids filled on a pro-rata basis at the marginal rate of interest. Again, the ECB has the right to allot a minimum amount to each bidder.

## Step 4: Tender allotment results announced

The tender results are announced publicly via the wire services. The public tender result contains the following information:

- Reference number of the tender operation
- Date of the tender operation (e.g. July 29th)

- Type of operation (e.g. variable rate tender, 91 day refinancing loans)
- Maturity of the operation (e.g. October 28)
- Total amount bid (e.g. 64.973 billion euros)
- Number of bidders (e.g. 281)
- Total amount allotted (e.g.15 billion euros)
- Percentage allotted at marginal rate: (e.g. 69.17%)
- Marginal rate : (e.g. 2.65%)
- Minimum rate bid (e.g. 2.40%)
- Maximum rate bid (e.g. 2.71%)
- Allotment method (e.g. multiple)

## Step 5: Individual allotment results certified

Many banks and eligible securities houses can and do access these facilities depending on the liquidity position of the market, the rate at which the cash is offered and the general availability of eligible collateral. Often, over 800 banks apply.

An example of the outcome of a reverse tender is shown in ECB17 below.

## Exhibit 23 - ECB17

```
09:17 31AUG99    EUROPEAN CENTRAL BANK, FRANKFURT a.M. GE66608              ECB17
Main Refinancing Operation-Allotment
Reference Number: 19990048              Min Allotment:
Transaction Type: Reverse Transactions  Fixed Rate: 2.50 %
Operation Type: Liquidity Providing     Max Bid Limit:
Procedure: Standard Tender
Tender Date: 31/08/1999                  % of Allot.: 4.43
Start Date: 01/09/1999                   Tot Amount Allotted: 66000.00 mn
Maturity Date: 15/09/1999
Duration (days): 14                      Tot Bid Amount: 1490634.50 mn
                                         Tot Number of Bidders: 808
Auction Type: Fixed Rate Tender
Allotment Method: Single Rate
```

## Settlement

The cash side of these transactions is settled in the counterparty's account with the national central bank or on the accounts of settlement banks participating in Target, a real-time gross settlement system in use in the EU.

The cash is settled only after or precisely when the collateral is transferred. Accordingly, the collateral needs to be in place at the NCB or be settled intra-day on a DVP basis. The collateral is delivered from the custody account with the NCB or via approved securities settlement systems. The ECB aims to settle these transactions at the same time across all NCB's.

## Initial margins, valuation haircuts and variation margins

Initial margin is 1% for intraday and overnight transactions, and 2% for transactions of one day or more. No margins are applied in liquidity absorbing transactions.

## *Valuation haircuts:*

Fixed-rate instruments

    0 %    for securities maturing within one year

    1.5%   for securities maturing after one and before three years

    2 %    for securities maturing after three but before seven years

    3 %    for coupon bonds maturing in 7+ years

    5 %    for zero coupon bonds and strips with a residual maturity of 7+ years


Floating-rate instruments

    0%    for instruments where the coupon has been fixed for the next period

# Conventions and Methodologies

This Chapter summarises some of the more important conventions in the repo market and concludes with a brief checklist of issues and methodologies for those contemplating setting up a repo business.

## Repo Market Conventions

### Point of trade

Agree:

- collateral; term including value and termination dates; rate; amount (nominal of bond or quantity of cash); start price ('all-in' or 'dirty' for repo or 'clean' for buy-sells);

- settlement depository or agent (usually this is agreed and known prior to trading and is held in the static data file of both parties);

- right(s) of substitution (if any);

- treatment of coupon (if paid during the term of the trade):

  (i) if repo, manufactured coupon is paid to 'seller' on coupon payment date;

  (ii) if buy-sell, treatment of coupon is open for discussion - either re-invested (at original rate or a different repo rate) until maturity of the buy-sell OR the manufactured coupon is paid to seller on coupon payment date;

- Initial margin(s) (haircut) - to be factored into the start price.

(NB. It may not be possible to assign collateral at the point of trade. Accordingly, the trade ticket is written only when the collateral is known.)

### Collateral

The ISMA CRD Repo Sub-Committee has agreed a list of acceptable general collateral for issuers in the major markets, a copy of which is included as Appendix 1.

### Pricing basis

Collateral is priced with reference to a market standard source, eg ABN-AMRO, Frankfurt Stock Exchange fixings or CGO reference prices. Collateral is priced at the prevailing mid-market level (with an adjustment for haircut, if applicable). These prices are provided via electronic quote vendors such as Bloomberg or Reuters.

The repo rate is determined by a number of factors including: demand for/supply of the particular issue; prevailing money market rates; and other term repo rates. Whilst an index such as EONIA / LIBOR is often a good benchmark, trades are not executed with reference to it (eg EONIA / LIBOR less 1/8 %) but rather as a specific rate, ie 2.5%. The 'all-in' price of a repo is usually taken to two decimal places. The clean price of a buy-sell is usually taken to two decimal places and the termination price is taken to six decimal places.

For details of the relevant day count conventions for the cash and securities, see Appendix 2.

## Margin choices

In classic repo, the market standard documentation (see the section on 'The GMRA' in Chapter 7) permits the party receiving a margin call to choose to provide margin in the form of either securities or cash. The choice of security must be reasonably acceptable to the party making the call (except in the case of a margin excess, where, according to the GMRA, securities of the same issue as the collateral for the outstanding repo trade(s) must be returned) and the securities will be delivered free of payment. (NB. As margin calls are made on a portfolio basis, ie netting all repos and reverses between the parties, the choice of deliverable collateral may be wide, since it is unlikely that a party can reasonably refuse to accept collateral of the same type as that already accepted in the underlying trades except in extenuating circumstances).

If cash is chosen, it is delivered in the currency agreed in the governing legal agreement. Under the GMRA, interest is paid on cash margin at a rate agreed between the parties.

It is simplest to deliver securities booked as a free delivery repo with a termination date matching that of the repo with the nearest maturity.

The delivery date for margin is agreed in Annex I of the GMRA but generally ties in with the settlement cycle of the bonds/cash market in the delivery currency. The currency of the margin is agreed prior to trading, also in Annex I of the GMRA.

## Repo broking

In the gilt repo market, the Bank of England's Code of Best Practice requires that so called name-passing brokers should:

- not act as principal to a deal;
- only quote firm prices substantiated by another market participant;
- only receive payment for successfully bringing counterparties together in the form of brokerage, which is freely negotiated; and
- pass counterparty names immediately when a bid is 'hit' or an offer 'lifted' and not before, and then only to the parties involved (ie client confidentiality must be maintained).

Nothing is stated concerning the 'posting' of trades. Repo brokers are required to broadcast to the market generic trade details of repos that have been executed.

## What to do in an event of default

Once the decision to declare a default has been made, and it is a major decision, it is vital that the non-defaulting party realises the collateral (ie sells bonds in the market), or uses cash to buy bonds, to minimise any potential for loss. However, the Code of Conduct recommended that:

'Once a decision to declare a default has been taken, it is important, in the interest of the participant, the defaulting party and the market, that the process be carried out carefully. In particular:

(a) the non-defaulting party should do everything within its power to ensure that the default market values used in the close-out calculations are, and can be shown to be, fair;

(b) if the non-defaulting party decides to buy or sell securities consequent to the close-out, it should make every effort to do so without unnecessarily disrupting the market.'

## Checklist of Issues and Methodologies

### Compliance

As a preliminary step, participants contemplating the commencement of a repo business should ascertain whether there are any legal reasons preventing them undertaking repo transactions and, if applicable, they should obtain any necessary permission from their regulators.

### Credit

We have seen in Chapters 2 and 6 that there is credit risk in repo and that this can be addressed through margining. Consequently, once the creditworthiness of the counterparty and the collateral has been assessed, a suitable haircut or initial margin should be agreed. Collateral should be marked to market daily and margin calls made when net exposure breaches agreed thresholds. However, in spite of the credit and capital advantages of taking an initial margin, in practice many firms do not. The volatility of the underlying instruments, the fragmented nature of the market and the different degrees of counterparty creditworthiness would suggest that haircuts should become standard. However, many participants consider this to be an internal credit issue and assign haircuts case-by-case. Additionally, the ability to mark-to-market and call for top-up collateral as and when required, under the terms of the GMRA, provides additional comfort. It is not standard market practice for inter-dealer repo trades via a broker to be margined, whatever the term.

An additional way to limit credit risk is to develop a notional risk system reflecting potential market movements based on the term of the repo, the underlying security and the term of that security. A list of authorised counterparties, with their notional and/or gross limits, should then be maintained and any drawings marked against it. Most institutions will have a credit policy regarding the maximum percentage of an issue that may be held, whether outright or under repo, and it is important that any system can assess that risk. It is also normal practice to ensure that all large exposure reporting rules are complied with.

### Creation of false or distorted markets in repo

In the Code of Conduct it states that 'participants in the gilt repo market must not in any circumstances enter into transactions designed to limit the availability of specific gilt-edged stocks with the intention of creating a false or distorted market in repo, the underlying securities or derivatives.'

## Controls

Repo transactions should be properly authorised before bonds or cash are released, especially in the case of margin calls where free deliveries may occur. Clearly defined trading limits need to be set and monitored effectively.

## Systems

Basic requirements of a repo trading system are:

**Position management**

- the ability to identify outright positions from trading books;
- the ability to identify matched-book trading positions.

**Profit and loss management**

- the ability to calculate profit and loss on either an accruals or mark-to-market basis;
- the ability to calculate profit and loss in the firm's base currency.

**Credit risk management**

- the ability to mark-to-market collateral against a notional or nominal credit line;
- the ability to mark excesses to a general credit line;
- the ability to signal margin calls as a percentage or nominal amount threshold basis.

**Cash management**

- the ability to provide cash balance information for trading books.

**Risk management**

- the ability to provide interest rate risk information such as cash ladders, and identify market exposure.

## Legal

For classic repos, legal documentation should ideally be signed up before trading. This should take the form of a master repurchase agreement with the following facets:

- the full passing of legal title, including any securities transferred via margining;
- daily marking-to-market of collateral;
- margining provisions, including agreed absolute or percentage thresholds for margin calls;
- 'events of default' allowing bonds to be sold/cash retained and claims for differences to be made;
- netting rights (across transactions and currencies); and
- the rights of each party with respect to the treatment of coupon and substitution.

The GMRA satisfies all of these requirements and, as the market standard agreement for international repo, should be the preferred choice of agreement for participants.

Legal advice should also be sought, case-by-case, as to whether a proposed counterparty has the legal ability to undertake repo transactions and has authorised the trading, and whether the documentation will be effective in its country of domicile even in the event of the counterparty's insolvency. There are more details on the legal aspects of repo in Chapter 7.

## Accounting

Companies should be aware of the accounting treatment of repo and the resulting profits or losses. Generally, the bonds remain as an asset on the balance sheet of the seller, despite the outright transfer of title, and the corresponding liability is the repo cash. Accordingly, coupon continues to accrue to the seller and the return on the repo monies is treated as the payment of interest and is taken as a charge on an accruals basis. The collateral is usually marked to market. A detailed examination of repo accounting can be found in Chapter 8.

## Taxation

The tax treatment of repo is a major issue in itself and differs in each jurisdiction. In the UK, the return on the cash leg of a repo is treated as interest and is taxed as income, not as a capital gain or loss. Management should satisfy itself that the tax status of the securities traded as repo collateral is known and understood. Whilst most government bonds are gross paying securities, some are not. The treatment of withholding tax on these bonds is complex. A fuller explanation of tax issues can be found in Chapter 9.

### Settlement

Settlement of repo should be undertaken in much the same way as in the underlying bond market, ie through a secure payment system such as Cedel Bank, Euroclear or CGO, utilising delivery-versus-payment or assured payments.

## Partialling and shaping

Unless otherwise agreed a partial delivery of a security to effect a larger delivery may be declined by the recipient in most markets. However, in the Code of Conduct participants 'are encouraged to act in such a way as to facilitate the settlement of trades and, in particular should shape their trades according to their settlement capability.' Indeed it is now ISMA CRD Repo sub-committee policy to encourage shaping of settlement of trades to Euro 50mn nominal.

## Fails

In the event that a seller fails to deliver a bond on the first leg of a repo transaction the buyer does not deliver its cash and the repo rate starts to accrue as if the delivery had occurred and the buyer earns extra interest by reinvesting the cash same day. This is known as a positive fail. If the buyer fails to redeliver bonds on the closing leg of the repo, the repo rate ceases to accrue as the seller was willing to repurchase the bonds on the due date.

## Custody

Collateral should be held separately from the repo counterparty wherever possible (e.g. in a segregated account) to prevent fraud or the pledging of the same collateral to more than one counterparty (often known as 'double-dipping'). In the case of 'hold in custody' repo, adequate systems for segregating and monitoring collateral are required.

## Gilt repo

Before dealing in gilt repo with a client for the first time, market professionals need to ensure that the client is aware of the Bank of England's Gilt Repo Code of Best Practice and its key contents, or draw them to the client's attention.

Market professionals will need to explain that the Code recommends that:

- transactions should be effected under the gilt repo legal agreement or equivalent;
- transactions should be marked-to-market and recollateralised; and
- collateral should be held independently from the repo counterparty.

They should also inform the client that there may be tax consequences arising from entering into gilt repo transactions, and that professional advice may need to be sought.

## Methodology for calling for margin

The following trade is a working example of the margining process:

1) **No haircut**

   The terms of the trade are:

   | | |
   |---|---|
   | Nominal | £10,000,000 |
   | Issue | Bond 6%, 10th August '09 |
   | Repo rate | 5.28125 % |
   | Clean price | 95.00 |
   | Accrued interest | 0.887671 |
   | Dirty price | 95.887671 |
   | On side date | April 5th |
   | Off side date | May 5th |
   | On side amount | £9,588,767.12 |
   | Return on cash | £9,588,767.10 x 5.28125% x 30/365 = £41,622.47 |
   | Off side amount | £9,630,389.59 |

2) **Haircut of 2.5%**

   If a haircut of 2.5% was taken, the trade details would be as follows:

   | | |
   |---|---|
   | Nominal | £10,000,000 |
   | Issue | Bond 10th August '09 |
   | Repo rate | 5.28125 % |
   | Clean price | (93.490479 - 0.887671 =) 92.602808 |
   | Accrued interest | 0.887671 |
   | All in price | (95.887671 x 0.975 =) 93.490479 |
   | On side date | April 5th |
   | Off side date | May 5th |
   | On side amount | £9,349,047.94 |
   | Return on cash | £9,349,047.94 x 5.28125% x 30/365 = £40,581.91 |
   | Off side amount | £9,389,629.85 |

Assume we are one day into this trade. If the market price has not moved, the repurchase price would be calculated as follows:

| | |
|---|---|
| Clean price: | 92.602807 |
| Return on cash: £9,349,047.92 x 5.28125% x 1/365 | = £1352.73 |
| Accrued: £10,000,000 x 6% x 1/365 | = £1643.84 |
| Total: (return on cash minus accrued) | = £(291.11) |
| New clean price: | 92.599896 |

Action: None. Since a 2.5% margin was taken, and the cash investor bought at an effective price of 92.60280, the cash investor is covered.

As the yield curve is upward sloping, the investor has positive cost of carry. This is reflected in a repurchase price that is lower than the original sale price. Using the first example of a trade with no haircut, the dirty current yield is 6.257322 (against a funding rate of 5.28125) which equates to 97.6072 basis points on £9,588,767, ie £256.42 per day. (NB. Repo and gilt markets both price on an Actual/365 day count convention.)

Returning to the example of a 2.5% haircut, if, on the following day, the market price of the gilt has fallen from 95.00 to 92.00, the securities are now worth:

| | |
|---|---|
| Principal: | £9,200,000.00 |
| Accrued: | £90,410.96 |
| Total: | £9,290,410.96 |

The cash investor, however, has lent £9,349,047.92 against this security and is deficient by £58,636.96 and now has the right to call margin from the counterparty in the form of eligible securities or cash. To return the trade to the original haircut of 2.5%, the cash investor should call for the following amount:

$$(0.929041096 \times 1.025 \times £10,000,000) - \text{original monies}$$

$$= £9,522,671.23 - £9,349,047.92$$

$$= £173,623.31$$

Having made the margin call, the cash investor's counterparty has the right to offer margin either in cash or similar quality securities to those in the original trade. Taking each of these choices in turn:

## 1. A cash movement is agreed and a reprice of the original trade is agreed for value April 6.

### Option A

The original trade is closed out for value April 6, and a new trade agreed from April 6 - May 5. The offside of the original transaction has accrued return on cash of £1352.73, i.e. one day. The offside of the old trade of £9,347,695.21 (original repo monies minus one day's return on cash) pairs off against the new onside of £9,058,000. Bonds do not move and the cash of £289,695 is paid to the cash investor.

67

The terms of the trade are now:

| | |
|---|---|
| Nominal | £10,000,000 |
| Issue | Bond 6%, 10th August '09 |
| Repo rate | 5.28125 % |
| All in price | 90.58 (92.9041096 x 97.5% rounded) |
| On side date | April 6 |
| Off side date | May 5 |
| Onside cash | £9,058,000 |
| Return on cash | £9,058,000 x 5.28125% x 29/365 = £38,007.93 |
| Offside cash | £9,096,007.93 |

## Option B

The repo return on cash of £1,352.73 may be rolled until the end of the trade. Accordingly, the offside of the new trade will be £9,096,007.93 + £1352.73 = £9,097,360.66

This method is asymmetrical - had the bond rallied in price, the buyer (cash investor) would have invested more cash at the original repo rate. The major drawback with this method is the change in the amount of the cash investment. If the bond market had risen dramatically, the cash investor, had he elected to pledge cash as margin, would effectively have increased the amount of the cash investment. As margin calls may occur at any point during a trade, prevailing rates may offer more attractive alternative investment opportunities but the cash investor is obliged to supply more cash at the original repo rate.

## 2. A delivery of bonds is made to satisfy the margin call.

## Option A

The original trade is closed down, for value April 6, and a new trade is booked for the period April 6 - May 5. The nominal amount of bonds is increased. The offside of the old transaction, of £9,349,047.94 versus £10,000,000 nominal, pairs off with the new transaction of an increased nominal of £321,000.

The new trade looks as follows:

| | |
|---|---|
| Nominal | £10,321,000 |
| Issue | Bond 6% 10th August '09 |
| Repo rate | 5.28125 % |
| All in price | 90.58 |
| Onside date | April 6th |
| Offside date | May 5th |
| Onside cash | £9,349,047.94 |
| Return on cash | £39,229 18+ £1,352.73 = £40,581.91 |
| Offside cash | £9,389,629.85 |

In this example, the bonds are delivered free of payment and the cash amount invested remains the same throughout the trade.

## *Option B*

A free delivery of the same amount of bonds could be made leaving the original repo trade intact. This delivery, essentially a repo at an all-in price of zero and a repo rate of nil, should have an offside date the same as the first trade.

Most dealers claim to reprice repo using one of the four methods above, and some claim to reprice undocumented buy-sells under a gentlemen's agreement. Repricing is generally based on a combination of price and net exposure and most dealers choose to take collateral rather than reprice.

If cash is provided as margin most dealers pay interest but the choice between a prevailing market rate, original repo rate(s) or nothing differs from firm to firm. The vast majority of dealers claim to reprice on coupon payment dates and, generally, they clean up the accrued return on the cash even though they are not obliged to do so until the trade terminates.

# Chapter 5

# Netting & Clearing

In the United States, the establishment by the Government Securities Clearance Corporation in 1995 of a repo netting service fundamentally changed the repo market.

The volumes traded increased, the maturity of repos and reverses lengthened and the range and sophistication of products offered expanded. In Europe two clearing houses currently offer similar services namely London Clearing House's (LCH's) RepoClear and the Paris Market's Clearnet. A third, European Securities Clearance Corporation (ESCC), a joint venture between Euroclear and Government Securities Clearance Corporation (GSCC ), is considering offering a service.

## Definitions and Overview

The term "netting" is used to describe the process of offsetting mutual obligations e.g. to offset an obligation owed by Bank A to Bank B with an obligation Bank B has to Bank A.

There are three principal techniques for netting:

- netting by novation: the process of replacing a set of obligations involving gross payments/deliveries with another set of obligations providing for net payment/delivery;

- close-out netting: the right to close out transactions on the default of a counterparty and reduce the parties' obligations to a single net payment obligation; and

- settlement netting: the process of settling all deals between two counterparties on a net basis.

Netting can either be "bilateral" when it is between two counterparties, or "multilateral" when it involves three or more parties.

The use of netting techniques can bring significant benefits for balance sheet purposes, capital usage, credit risk and operational efficiencies, provided that the netting is legally enforceable in all relevant jurisdictions in all situations, including the default or insolvency of the parties.

This chapter is principally concerned with repo netting services offered by clearing houses, which utilise these techniques on a multilateral basis. It provides examples of the different types of repo netting utilised by clearing houses, examines the benefits of netting, and goes on to consider the related services offered by clearing houses.

In essence, where repo/reverse repo trades are settled through a clearing system such that the clearing entity acts as the counterparty to all repo/reverse repo contracts then there may be scope for significant netting across an entire repo book. The opportunities afforded to a bank of bilateral netting are effectively extended to multilateral netting.

## Examples of netting services within a clearing system

### Netting by novation

We have seen that novation is a legal term that refers to the replacement of one group of obligations with another. In the context of repo netting by a clearing house, novation netting is used as the central platform. All repos and reverse repos between counterparties using the clearing house service are novated to the clearing house (referred to in this context as the central clearing counterparty (CCC)) which becomes counterparty to and responsible for the corresponding trade obligations arising from the original bilateral trades. Essentially, it interposes itself between the two parties to the original transactions and becomes the buyer to the seller and the seller to the buyer as shown in Example 1. The terms novation and registration are used interchangeably in this context, so the affected repos are said to have been "registered" with the CCC.

### Example 1 - Novation of bilateral trades to the CCC

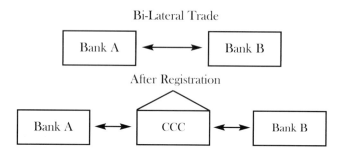

In this example it can be seen that the original bilateral trade between Bank A and Bank B has been replaced by two bilateral trades with the CCC. When this process is repeated across a range of counterparties, a qualifying member of the clearing service is able to replace its existing bank-to-bank bilateral repo relationships with a single multilateral relationship with the CCC representing its net position, as demonstrated in Example 2.

### Example 2 - Multilateral netting

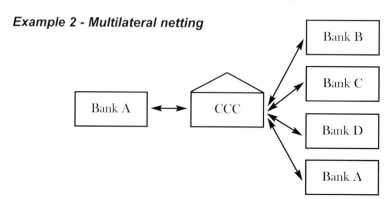

Here we can see that Bank A's series of bilateral trades have been novated to the CCC with the result that Bank A (and each of its counterparties) has a single relationship with the CCC in place of its bilateral trades, representing only the net positions of the original trades with all of its counterparties. The result is that instead of having a series of obligations to pay, deliver or receive cash and securities to Banks B, C, D and E, Bank A has a single series of trades with the CCC to pay, deliver and receive only the net balance of the original trades.

The original bilateral repo trades will typically have been subject to a master repurchase agreement such as the GMRA but at the point of registration or novation the transaction becomes subject to the CCC's own standard legal documentation.

## Settlement netting

When settlement is due, a netting process is run by the CCC which results in a single net long or short position per member, per issue, per settlement date, per depository. Both bonds and cash amounts are netted down, on both the opening and closing legs of the repo. The net position is the difference between all the long and short positions resulting from repos or reverses. The netting is run according to the cut-off times dictated by the relevant settlement depository.

This net position is settled in the member's designated settlement depository. In the US this is across the Fed Wire, in RepoClear it is via the chosen national or international settlement depository, in Clearnet it is Sicovam for French government securities and in ESCC it will be Euroclear in the initial stages.

## Example 3 - Settlement netting

The main principles of settlement netting are explained in a detailed example in Appendix 1 to this chapter.

## Reasons for and the benefits of repo netting

### Current environment

The greatest current threat to the repo business is its on-balance sheet treatment. While capital treatment by the major regulators is favourable for documented repos in firms with adequate credit and risk policies, repo is a balance sheet 'hog' and the return on competing, albeit longer dated products, is by definition often greater. Whilst return on assets long ago lost much of its importance as a measure of financial performance for banks it remains a focus of analysts, especially the ratings agencies.

In recent years government bond repo has become very competitive and now bears many of the characteristics of a commoditised market. Dealing spreads have been reduced and a 'bid-offer' spread such as exists in the unsecured deposit and placement market no longer apply to government repo.

There are low barriers to entry to new firms and margins have been squeezed by new entrants. The market is visible, brokers who are integral to the inter-professional market are not restricted as to whom they transmit prices to. Historically the barriers to entry to new brokers have been low - very little capital was required and technology demands were limited.

The cost of settlement and brokerage charges has led many firms to reduce their matched book activities. Brokerage costs often act as a disincentive to trading. Currently both sides to a deal pay up to 0.01% per annum of the nominal value of the trade with discounts for major dealers. Clearly the larger the trade and the longer the period, the greater the brokerage. The major houses have negotiated bilateral brokerage reductions and brokerage rates in general are under pressure from competition.

## Balance sheet reduction

A party repoing a bond - the seller - will retain the securities on its balance sheet as an asset and include the obligation to repay the cash advanced by the buyer as a liability. The party reversing in the bond - the buyer - will include the cash advanced to the seller as an asset. Accordingly repo including matched book repo is on-balance sheet.

When a bank or investment bank enters into several repo and reverse repo contracts with the same counterparty there will therefore be a series of assets (collateralised loans - from reverse repos) and liabilities (borrowings - from repos) on its balance sheet. Balance sheet netting is the ability to offset these assets and liabilities in the balance sheet.

Repo netting reduces balance sheet usage by offsetting the cash assets and liabilities relating to the same counterparty, provided certain conditions are met. The extent of the netting is determined by the accounting treatment applied. Bilateral repo netting has been undertaken for many years and with the advent of central clearing counterparties in the US and Europe, it has become possible to net on a multi-lateral basis across an entire repo book.

Refer to Chapter 8 for a full explanation of the UK accounting treatment of repo and the requirements for balance sheet netting.

## Settlement efficiencies

Repos involve two movements of cash and bonds namely the opening and closing legs. With settlement netting, parties to repo trades 'pair off' - that is, buys are netted versus sells and the cash difference is exchanged, or partially 'pair off' deliveries. with the net. The introduction of a central counterparty extends this process.

When settlement is due a netting process is run which results in a single net long or short position per member, per issue, per settlement date, per depository used. The net position is the difference between all the long and short positions resulting from repos or reverses due for settlement on the opening or closing leg.

In practice the number of trades that actually settle, the 'net', are a fraction of the original undertaken and both same-depository and cross-border deliveries are reduced. In the US up to 90% of deliveries are netted down. This affords the banks and investment banks significant operational savings and reduces the settlement chain leading to fewer delivery fails. In addition the central counterparty is often permitted by its members to instruct their net deliveries on their behalf under a Power Of Attorney which, in theory, reduces the likelihood of instructions being input incorrectly or not input at all.

In order to reduce the risk of dealers failing to make full delivery of their net obligations, securities are settled in a maximum nominal size known as 'shaping' e.g. such as $50mn, Euro 50mn. The contra cash value that moves in the opposite direction is divided in value and pro-rated against the nominal of the security.

A prerequisite to registration is that all details to a repo transaction are matched or compared beforehand. Those that do not meet the central counterparty's requirements are either rejected or held as pending awaiting correction. In most markets where bilateral repo trading is the norm, matching systems are either not present or they are used inefficiently which means that not all details to the trade are matched and 'out-trades' may occur e.g. if the term is not matched problems may arise in the future if the two dealers had misunderstood the terms of trade. Real-time matching of both legs reduces 'out-trades' and fails, and assists straight-through-processing of repos.

In those markets where settlement of outright bond trades and repos is netted further operational efficiencies are achieved.

## Reduction of credit risk

It will be evident from the novation process that the amount of bilateral credit lines required in a cleared environment are substantially less than would otherwise be the case as any participant will have a single counterparty, the CCC, in place of its other counterparties. However, dealers do need to maintain some counterparty limits for the period between trading and matching or, in the case of the GSCC, trades for the period until the on-leg has settled (usually within the same day). Also, should the trade not meet the CCC requirements or be too late to enter netting, it will have to revert to a bilateral trade.

## Margin offsets

Margin offsets with other products, such as futures or swaps, cleared by the same or related central counterparties are possible. This frees up collateral which may be used for other purposes, or cash which will then be available to finance other positions. While no central clearing counterparty currently offers such offsets they are expected to be introduced in the near future.

## Trade anonymity

Currently the information of a dealer's outright positions may be inferred through the activity of the repo desk who are charged with financing the firm's long and short positions. Also, details of trades executed through IDBs are 'posted' (i.e. advised to the market as a matter of course). There have been occasions when proprietary information (such as the identity of the two parties) has been leaked by brokers or dealers. In an era of Automated Trading Systems, trade anonymity is secure. (This is a contentious issue. Many dealers and brokers are keen to know the positions of their competitors which can be deduced in the current environment. Indeed liquidity may be hindered by trade anonymity.)

## Potential brokerage savings

Automated trading of repos should become cheaper than 'voice broked' repo as it relies less on broker input. This should lead to lower brokers' fees per trade. However, in the US the volume of repos traded doubled as repos were intermediated by blind brokers and cleared by GSCC.

## Services of a Clearing system

Trade confirmation matching system / Trade comparison service

Registration / Novation

Multi-lateral netting

Risk monitoring & Margining

Collateral substitution

Settlement netting, including cross border netting

Coupon passback

Fails management

Reporting

## Trade confirmation matching system

Eligible repo transactions may be delivered to the CCC by a number of routes:

1. Direct dealer to dealer. In this case, instructions are passed by an eligible trade confirmation matching system.

2. IDB 'name give-up' broker. Matching instructions are received just from the dealers in the same way as above.

3. IDB 'hybrid' system. Prices are posted to a screen and trades are executed by dealer calling the broker on a direct telephone line who then executes the trade via a keypad. This is essentially a combination of dealer and broker input, and matching instructions are received in the same way as above.

4. IDB 'Blind Broker'. Dealers trade on an anonymous or 'blind' basis with approved inter-dealer brokers. They settle the first leg directly with the broker

and all parties to the transaction submit trade details to the central counterparty for comparison, netting and settlement. This is common in the USA, but not yet available in Europe.

5. Automated Trading Systems. Trades are matched and reported to the CCC via a secure network or secure messaging system e.g. S.W.I.F.T.

Generally the CCC is independent of the trading system.

## Trade confirmation matching system / Trade comparison service

In the US, GSCC uses a real time trade comparison service which automatically matches repo and reverse repos using a standardised reporting format. This eliminates the need for paper confirmations and reduces the likelihood of 'out-trades' and fails.

In RepoClear, TRAX is used to match trades. Upon receipt of matched details of both legs of a transaction from both parties, TRAX sends details to LCH which registers the transaction. In the future, LCH will accept other sources of trade confirmation matching but at the time of going to press only TRAX was suitable.

ESCC intends to use EuroClear's pre-settlement matching system EUCLID or S.W.I.F.T. messaging to match and thereby novate repos.

With the imminent arrival of automated trading systems in the European markets the matching service will be provided by the ATS which will electronically supply matched trade details to the CCC.

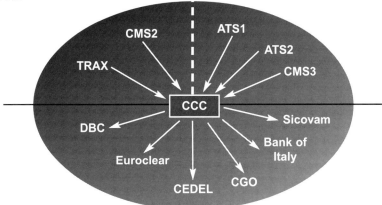

At the point the terms of trade are matched, the CCC registers the trade and becomes the counterparty.

## Settlement

Net settlement takes place in the normal depository(s) for the market e.g. Bunds in DB Clearing, Euroclear or Cedel, BTPS in Bank of Italy (Monte Titoli), Gilts in the Central Gilts Office (CGO), Oats in Sicovam, Euroclear or Cedel, and so on.

# Risk management

In order to protect itself from market, credit and settlement risk the CCC calculates its exposure and calls for margin. Margining is made up of three basic components:

- Variation margin,
- Initial margin
- Delivery margin.

## 1) Variation margin

Variation margin is calculated daily overnight on all outstanding repo contracts for each repo leg. It represents the change in the net present value (NPV) of a repo over a one day period (yesterday minus today).

The CCC marks-to-market repo trades using daily close of business dirty bond prices and daily end of day repo rates obtained from the most reliable market sources. Repo rates are applied bond by bond according to whether it is specific or general collateral. It charges or pays variation margin (VM) daily, in cash, throughout the life of the trade on the basis of this mark-to-market calculation and an intra-day margin call is issued should the movement be considered significant.

The VM called by the CCC from one member is passed onto the relevant counterparty. These monies are returned on an assumed settlement basis.

## 2) Initial margin

This is an amount of cover that the CCC will require a member to deposit with it to cover potential losses that it might incur from the time that the member defaults (or, to be precise, the time the member last pays margin) to the time the CCC can close out its positions.

It will have two components:

(a) an amount assessed on a portfolio basis to cover the member's exposure to general market movements over the close-out period; and

(b) a top-up to cover losses which could arise from price movements in the 'specials' over the close-out period.

It ensures that the CCC has sufficient liquidity to guarantee orderly settlement and to provide the collateralisation required to cover each member's overall exposure.
Both parties to a transaction pay initial margin which may be paid in cash (which is generally interest bearing), eligible securities which attract a haircut or letters of credit/bank guarantees. It is recalculated daily and intra-day margin calls are made if necessary.

## 3) Delivery margin

This is an amount, in the days immediately before a bond settles, to cover the CCC for the risk of settlement failures. Delivery margin is treated like initial margin and can usually be covered in cash, bank guarantees or approved securities.

## In summary:

- Current exposure is captured by a daily mark to market known as variation margin

- Future exposure is estimated at one day's variation margin and is captured by initial margin

- Settlement exposure is captured by delivery margin

## GSCC (Government Securities Clearing Corporation)

GSCC provides automated trade comparison or matching, netting and settlement services for US Government securities. It was established in 1986, started cash bond netting in 1989, initiated repo netting in 1995 and in 1998 it processed $213trillion in transactions of which repos accounted for $130 trillion.

It is principally owned by its member firms who are the major dealers and brokers in US securities repos and many of these are represented on its Board. It operates on a 'not-for-profit' basis. It is a SEC Registered Security Clearing agency and is an affiliate of National Securities Clearing Corporation (NSCC).

| GSCC | Now | Future |
|---|---|---|
| Products | Treasury Bills, notes, bonds, Zero Coupon securities Book-entry non-mortgage-backed agency securities Cash bonds and repos Repos to maturity Settlement T+0 | |
| Members | 75 netting 29 comparison-only i.e. trade matching 2 clearing agent bank members | |
| Membership Types / Membership requirements | Membership requirements depend on whether a member is classified as a bank/trust co, a dealer, a FCM, an IDB, an insurance company or a foreign entity | |
| | Bank / Trust Company $100mn equity<br>Category 1 Dealer $50mn net worth, $10mn excess net/ liquid capital<br>Category 2 Dealer $25mn net worth, $10mn excess net/ liquid capital<br>Category 1 FCM $50mn net worth $10mn adj. excess net capital<br>Category 2 FCM $25mn net worth $10mn adj. excess net capital<br>Category 1 IDB $10mn excess net liquid / excess net capital<br>Category 2 IDB $25mn net worth, $10mn excess net/liquid capital<br>Insurance companies $500mn statutory capital (plus ratings requirements) | |
| Trade Capture | GSCC proprietary system | |
| Clearing System | Developed by SPC Software Services, subsidiary of Security Pacific | |
| Services | Trade comparison (matching) Multilateral netting Calculation of initial and variation margins on net positions Collateral management On line collateral substitution Treasury Auction Takedown Service Risk monitoring Fails management | Cash/ derivatives cross margining |
| Depositories | Fed Wire | |

## RepoClear

RepoClear is the London Clearing House's (LCH) centralised clearing service for the European repo market. LCH was established in 1888 and acts as central counterparty for trades executed by its members on the London International Financial Futures Exchange (LIFFE), the London Metal Exchange (LME) and the International Petroleum Exchange (IPE).

RepoClear was launched in August 1999. It provides multilateral netting and settlement services for European Government repos. It is 75% owned by its 110 member firms who are the major dealers and brokers in the European financial markets (a number of which are represented on its Board) and 25% by LIFFE, LME and IPE. It operates on a 'not-for-profit' basis. It is registered under the U.K Clearing House. Act and is regulated by the Financial Services Authority (FSA).

Its primary protection in the event of failure by a member is the initial margin collateral collected from that firm.

Its financial backing is as follows:

- Defaulters initial and variation margin
- Defaulters Default Fund Contribution
- LCH profits year to date (up to a maximum of £10mn)
- Default fund which acts as a common backing pool contributed by members according to their volume of business which is set quarterly and represents roughly 10% of interest margin
- insurance backing £100mn after £150mn of loss
- LCH capital (circa £50mn)

|  | Now | Future |
|---|---|---|
| Products | German Government bond repo Settlement T+1 | Belgium, Italian, U.K., French Government bond repos |
|  |  | Extension to all Eurozone Government bonds and repos |
|  |  | Settlement T+0 |
| Members | 8 members | Extension to other major repo and bond market participants |
| Membership requirements | RepoClear Dealer (RD): Participant in wholesale market for European repos |  |

81

| Membership requirements continued/... | Investment grade (S&P BBB) or be a subsidiary of an RCM that is of at least investment grade | |
|---|---|---|
| | RepoClear Clearing Members (RCM): | |
| | RD or £250mn in capital Own LCH share Contribute to default fund | |
| Confirmation matching system | ISMA's TRAX | Automated Trading Systems other trade or settlement matching systems |
| Clearing System | London SPAN adapted for Repos | SPAN / LCH PAIRS |
| Services | Registration Multilateral netting Start leg settlements Closing leg settlements Collateral management Calculation of margins Risk monitoring Collateral substitution Cross border netting Reporting Fails management | Cross margining between LCH cleared positions Cross margining between cash bonds and repos Cross margining with other central counterparties Enhanced collateral substitutions Enhanced functionality: Open repos, floating rate repos, reverse to maturity, Delivery by Value ( DBV) Adoption of 'Blind Broking' |
| Depositories | Member choice: DBC, Euroclear, Cedel | Member choice: extension to other national depositories |

## European Securities Clearing Corporation (ESCC)

ESCC is a joint venture between Euroclear the international settlement depository and GSCC. It is a separately capitalised legal entity with banking status in Belgium. It is an independent 'not-for-profit' organisation. It will begin netting European government bonds and repo in 2000.

| | Now | Future |
|---|---|---|
| Products | None | German, French, Belgian Italian and Austrian Government bonds and repos |

| | | |
|---|---|---|
| Members continued/... | None | European based banks and broker dealers U.S. based banks and broker dealers, IDBs, ATSs Exchanges |
| Trade Capture | None | EUCLID server or PC( the Euroclear-proprietary communications channel) via single S.W.I.F.T. message type MT 515. ATSs Exchanges |
| Clearing system | None | Adapted version of GSCC system |
| Services | None | Trade Capture, Centralised Comparison (matching) Registration / Netting by novation Risk management Collateral management Reporting Adoption of Blind Broking |
| Depositories | None | Euroclear, possible extension to other depositories |

## Clearnet

Clearnet is the Paris Bourse's centralised clearing service for the Euro-denominated government bond, repo and other over the counter fixed income markets. BCC (Banque Centrale de Compensation), a wholly owned subsidiary of SBF with banking status, acts as the central clearing counterparty.

Clearnet was launched in November 1998. It provides multilateral netting and settlement services for European Government repos. It was created by the SBF Group, Sicovam and Prominnofi, a French inter-dealer broker.

Paris Bourse is the operating entity for the Societe de Bourse Francaise which is the French stock market. It has capital of Euro 310mn and insurance backing of a further Euro 150mn.

## Clearnet

| | Now | Future |
|---|---|---|
| Products | French and German government security markets (cash and repos) Settlement T+1 | Extension to other Euro zone government security (Belgium, Dutch, Italian etc) and repo markets; Corporate bonds; OTC derivatives. |
| Members | 28 members | Extension to other major bond, repo and OTC derivatives market participants. Main European banks |
| Membership Requirements | ownership of ISP Euro passport; minimum capital adequacy of Eur 150 million; minimum credit rating of A ; possible membership with a capital of Eur 30 million and a A credit rating or capital of Eur 150 million and a B credit rating, provided increased margin requirements (+20%) | |
| Trade capture | Via an IDB Prominnofi | Partnership with other IDBs and brokers Trade capture via other matching systems eg RGV terminals |
| Clearing system | Adapted derivatives clearing system | Clearing 21®, a single software for cash & derivatives (2000) |
| Services | Novation Multilateral netting Collateral management Calculation of margins Risk monitoring Fails management Reporting | Cash / derivatives cross-margining |
| Depositories | Sicovam, Cedel and Euroclear | Extension to other national depositories |

## Appendix 1 to Chapter 5

### *Example of the main principles of settlement netting*

This example is designed to illustrate the main principles behind the allocation of deliveries, specifically where cross border settlement is involved. In this example, eight members have booked a series of trades that have been registered by the CCC. For simplicity cash amounts are ignored.

The trades are as follows:-

| Seller | Seller Depository | Buyer | Buyer Depository | Nominal (m) |
|--------|-------------------|-------|------------------|-------------|
| B | EOC | A | EOC | 10 |
| B | EOC | C | EOC | 40 |
| B | EOC | G | DBC | 10 |
| C | EOC | D | EOC | 10 |
| D | EOC | H | DBC | 10 |
| E | DBC | A | EOC | 20 |
| E | DBC | B | EOC | 20 |
| F | DBC | B | EOC | 10 |
| F | DBC | G | DBC | 60 |
| G | DBC | C | EOC | 40 |
| G | DBC | H | DBC | 20 |

or represented pictorially

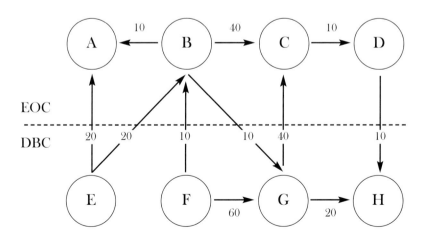

The CCC's main principle of netting is to ensure that the smallest possible number of movements occurs. The netting routine will first address the cross-border deliveries then net the remaining deliveries as follows:

1. Select cross-border trades i.e. all those involving two depositories such as EOC/Cedel, EOC/DBC or Cedel/DBC.

The trades are as follows:-

| Seller | Buyer | Seller Depository | Buyer Depository | Nominal (m) |
|--------|-------|-------------------|------------------|-------------|
| B | G | EOC | DBC | 10 |
| D | H | EOC | DBC | 10 |
| E | A | DBC | EOC | 20 |
| E | B | DBC | EOC | 20 |
| F | B | DBC | EOC | 10 |
| G | C | DBC | EOC | 40 |

2. From the cross-border trades, determine the net amount of bonds (and cash) that need to move across the bridge, i.e. the cumulative net position of all trades incorporating two depositories.

| Seller | Buyer | Seller Depository | Buyer Depository | Nominal (m) |
|--------|-------|-------------------|------------------|-------------|
| B | G | DBC | EOC | 10 |
| D | H | DBC | EOC | 10 |
| | total | DBC | EOC | 20 |
| E | A | EOC | DBC | 20 |
| E | B | EOC | DBC | 20 |
| F | B | EOC | DBC | 10 |
| G | C | EOC | DBC | 40 |
| | total | EOC | DBC | 90 |
| Net | | EOC | DBC | 70 |

This shows that cumulatively there are 20m of bonds to be delivered from EOC into DBC, and 90m of bonds due to be delivered in the opposite direction from DBC into EOC. The CCC will net these two figures and produce settlement tickets that move only the required 70m bonds from DBC into EOC. This will be the Net Cross-Border Delivery amount.

3. Ascertain all parties who may be required, because of their original trading, to make or take cross-border deliveries. The CCC therefore nets together bonds movements, for each member for each cross-border depository combination:

| Member | Member Depository | Counterpart Depository | Nominal (m) |
|--------|-------------------|------------------------|-------------|
| A | EOC | DBC | +20 |
| B | EOC | DBC | +20 |
| C | EOC | DBC | +40 |
| D | EOC | DBC | -10 |
| E | DBC | EOC | -40 |
| F | DBC | EOC | -10 |
| G | DBC | EOC | -30 |
| H | DBC | EOC | +10 |

For example, member B who originally had 3 cross-border trades, buying 20, buying 10 and selling 10, nets to one entry of buying 20. These netted amounts are the Members' potential Cross-Border Deliveries.

4. The CCC will then allocate the Net Cross-Border Delivery amount (determined in 2 above) to one or more members according to their potential Cross-Border Delivery amounts (determined in 3 above).

So in this case the 70m delivery from DBC to EOC will have to be apportioned to members E, F and G who all have net deliveries from DBC to EOC. In apportioning that amount the CCC will seek to minimise the number of cross-border deliveries. (Members A, B, C, D and H who are not due to make net deliveries from DBC to EOC will not be allocated any cross-border deliveries.)

In this example the cross-border deliveries are allocated to members E and G. These members will then be asked to deliver the relevant amounts to the CCCs account cross-border as follows:

| Member | Member Depository | Counterpart Depository | Nominal (m) |
|--------|-------------------|------------------------|-------------|
| E | DBC | EOC | -40 |
| G | DBC | EOC | -30 |

5. After the cross border deliveries have been determined in 4, all remaining deliveries for each member will be netted into a single delivery between the member and the CCC's account in the member's local depository. The following are then the complete netted settlements, with the cross border movements determined in 3 shown highlighted.

| Member | Member Depository | Counterpart Depository | Nominal (m) |
|---|---|---|---|
| A | EOC | EOC | +30 |
| B | EOC | EOC | -30 |
| C | EOC | EOC | +70 |
| D | EOC | EOC | 0 |
| E | DBC | EOC | -40 |
| F | DBC | DBC | - 70 |
| G | DBC | DBC | +40 |
| G | DBC | EOC | -30 |
| H | DBC | DBC | +30 |

Member D's bond movements net out, and the net cash amount for the trades will be moved within EOC.

Pictorially the netted amounts are as follows:

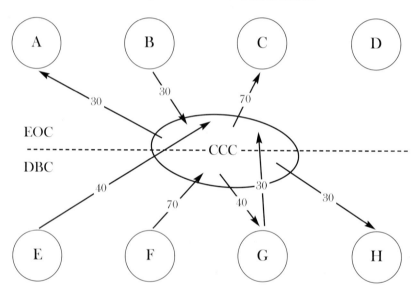

## The main principles worth noting are:

a) as with any other 'like for like' depository settlements, individual member's cross-border long and short positions will be netted off;

b) where members have net cross-border movements they will not know until the results of netting are published whether they will actually be required to participate in a cross-border delivery or not; and

c) members will only ever be required to make cross-border bond deliveries to the CCC, not cross-border cash deliveries. Members should ensure that cross-border deliveries occur in the overnight run not the daylight runs.

# Chapter 6

# Risks in Repo Transactions

Repos and reverse repos are effectively secured transactions backed by legal documentation and consequently they should be one of the safest forms of investment in the money market, assuming that two elements - counterparty and collateral - are of the highest quality.

In the major repo markets both counterparties and collateral are of the highest quality. Default by either is considered unlikely and market risk in the form of collateral price volatility remains with the original seller. The returns, however, often reflect the limited risk and in recent years repo markets have developed in lower-rated collateral securities with weaker counterparties. Accordingly the probability of issuer or counterparty default is not insignificant and in this chapter we therefore consider the residual market risk (add-on risk or potential exposure) together with counterparty exposure.

While active risk management of repos may not be standard market practice yet, it appears to be an appropriate approach for international repo markets where higher yields are often combined with greater default probabilities and market risks.

This chapter will explain to the reader a number of the risks involved in repo trading. The overview section considers the risks associated with the two key elements of a repo transaction mentioned earlier: counterparty and collateral. The later sections of this chapter consider a more detailed risk classification along traditional risk matrix lines, separating the risk on repo transactions into credit, market, liquidity, systems/operational and legal risks.

## Overview of Credit Risk

In the classic repo transaction there are two areas of protection  - counterparty and collateral. These areas of protection are also areas of risk exposure: the following figure shows risks associated with each area and those that are not immediately related. This latter set of risks - those unrelated to counterparty and collateral - will be covered later in the chapter.

## Counterparty risk

If the counterparty in a repo transaction defaults, the cash investor has a legal right to sell the collateral in the market at the then prevailing market price and the non-defaulting party is covered (i.e. has no loss attributable to the default) if proceeds from the sale of the collateral at least cover the cash value of funding including accrued repo interest.

Counterparty risk comprises two elements: replacement cost  (or current exposure) and potential exposure. Replacement cost is  the difference between the value of assets (both cash and securities) held by one party  and the value of assets (both securities and cash) held by the other.  It measures the cost of replacing the current position held at current market rates in the event of a default.

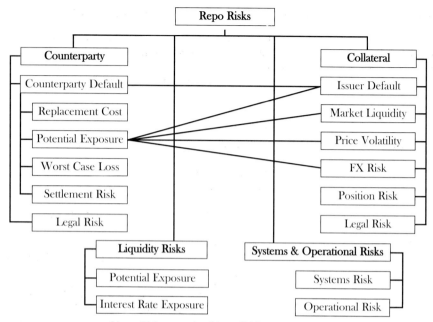

*Note: Risks connected by solid lines are related*

Add-on risk or potential exposure is an additional loss that may be incurred over a period between the counterparty's default on its repo obligations and the subsequent liquidation of the position. A detailed explanation of counterparty risk measurement will be given in the Counterparty Risk section below.

## *Collateral issuer risk*

The most obvious risk associated with the collateral on a repo transaction is issuer default which could theoretically leave the collateral holder with a bond worth zero and a resultant loss. However, if the collateral issuer defaults the collateral holder does not automatically make a loss. In most cases the collateral supplier will replace the defaulted collateral by an equivalent performing security according to parameters (equivalent yield, credit rating, maturity, price volatility, market liquidity, market demand, etc.) agreed in the legal agreement prior to trading.

Another form of issuer risk involves dealing with a counterparty in securities issued by itself or related entities. Common sense suggests that these type of trades be avoided with a requirement set that the credit risk of the collateral be independent from the credit risk of the counterparty, unless the counterparty is a Zone A Central Bank.

The joint issuer and counterparty default probabilities derived from their credit ratings should help determine a list of approved collateral securities for each counterparty.

Other risk factors associated with collateral include price volatility and market liquidity which define the size of initial haircut or margin ("overcollateralisation") required by the cash supplier to protect itself against potential exposure in the event of a counterparty default.

When the security is first bought and then repoed, or when it is sold and then reversed, a long or short position is taken in the collateral security, which creates a position risk. The risk is similar to the risk of forward trades and is not repo-product-specific. It is better measured and controlled at the aggregate level of the entire security trading portfolio rather than at the repo desk level.

### Repo Risk Classification

Using a more traditional matrix, repo risks can be classified into the following groups:

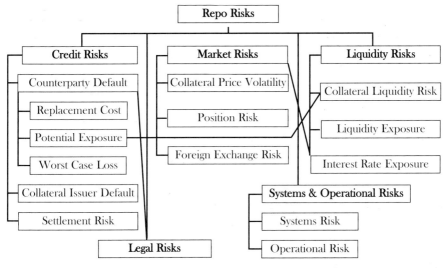

Note: Risks connected by solid lines are related

## 1. Repo Risk - Credit Risk

Credit risk comprises both counterparty (default) risk and collateral issuer default risk ("issuer risk") and because of the importance of these two risks in repo transactions, most of the rest of this chapter concentrates on these areas.

### 1.1 Counterparty Risk

Counterparty default risk is the loss that may be incurred by a firm in the event of a counterparty default if the proceeds of liquidation of the firm's position do not cover the value of the assets, including accrued interest, held by the counterparty.

Counterparty default risk is measured by net counterparty exposure composed of current exposure (replacement cost) and potential exposure (add-on risk).

## 1.1.1. Current exposure measurement

Current exposure or replacement cost, is any positive excess of the value of assets given to the counterparty, including any interest accrued, over the value of assets currently held by the firm, including any interest accrued, that will be lost in case of the counterparty's immediate default.

For the cash investor in a reverse repo deal, current exposure is the excess (if any) of the cash value of the loan, including accrued repo interest, given to the counterparty over the current mark-to-market value of collateral held by the firm:

> Current Exposure = MAX (0, Cash Value of Loan - MtM Collateral Value);
>
> Note: Cash Value of Loan = Initial Value of Funding + Accrued Repo Interest

Most often, though, the cash investor will have a negative net value in the above equation due to overcollateralisation (i.e. an initial margin, or haircut), which can be interpreted as a current cushion for the cash investor.

For the cash borrower in a repo deal, current exposure is the excess (if any) of the mark to market value of collateral given to the counterparty over the cash value of the loan held by the firm, (and most often it will have an exposure due to overcollateralisation):

> Current Exposure = MAX (0, MtM Collateral Value - Cash Value of Loan)

In a securities lending transaction with no cash involved, the cash value of the loan in the above equations will be substituted by a mark to market value of securities lent or borrowed[1].

Where there is a legally enforceable netting agreement (such as the GMRA - see Chapter 7 for further details), the total current counterparty exposure is calculated on a portfolio basis as the total of all securities and cash, including accrued interest, lent or given as collateral to the counterparty less the total of all securities and cash, including accrued interest, received from the counterparty.

> Current Counterparty Exposure = Σ (MtM Securities Lent + MtM Collateral Given
> + Cash Lent + Interest Accrued) - Σ (MtM Securities Received +
> MtM Collateral Received + Cash Received + Interest Accrued)

Netting will effectively reduce the total exposure figure offsetting current exposures against current cushions in different deals with the same counterparty.

---

[1] For the security lender, current exposure will be the excess (if any) of the mark to market value of securities lent to the counterparty over the mark to market value of the collateral taken:

Current Exposure = MAX(0, MtM Securities Value - MtM Collateral Value)

For the securities borrower, current exposure will be the excess (if any) of the mark to market value of the collateral supplied to the counterparty over the mark to market value of securities borrowed:

Current Exposure = (MAX, MtM Collateral Value - MtM Securities Value)

## Current exposure measurement - introduction of margin maintenance

The margin is set at the start of the repo and should be maintained at the same level throughout the life of the repo transaction by marking the collateral to market at least daily and calling variation margin as and when required. Whether a margin call is made depends on whether there is a haircut and a margin call threshold (trigger).

When there is no haircut and no margin call threshold, the margin call amount is equal to the current counterparty exposure:

> Cash Investor Margin Call = Current Counterparty Exposure =
>
> Old Cash Offside - Current MtM Collateral Value > 0
>
> Cash Borrower Margin Call = Current Counterparty Exposure =
>
> Current MtM Collateral Value - Old Cash Offside > 0

If no margin call threshold has been agreed either in the documentation or at the point of trade, the margin may be called by either party each time the collateral price changes regardless of the magnitude of this change. This may occur every day or every other day and can be quite costly operationally. Accordingly parties often agree on a certain margin call threshold or trigger amount to limit excessive operational costs. This margin call threshold may be expressed as a fixed cash amount or as a percentage of the original collateral value. When there is a margin call threshold in the form of a fixed cash amount, margin will be called when the current counterparty exposure exceeds this threshold amount:

> Cash Investor Margin Call = Current Counterparty Exposure =
>
> Old Cash Offside - Current MtM Collateral Value > Margin Call Threshold Amount
>
> Cash Borrower Margin Call = Current Counterparty Exposure =
>
> Current MtM Collateral Value - Old Cash Offside > Margin Call Threshold Amount

If the margin call threshold is expressed as a percentage of the original collateral value, margin will be called when the change in value of the collateral exceeds the threshold:

> Original Collateral Value - Current MtM Collateral Value > Margin Call Threshold =>
>
> Cash Investor Margin Call = Current Counterparty Exposure =
>
> Old Cash Offside - Current MtM
>
> Current MtM Collateral Value - Original Collateral Value > Margin Call Threshold =>
>
> Cash Borrower Margin Call = Current Counterparty Exposure =
>
> Current MtM Collateral Value - Old Cash Offside

When there is a haircut, there is an agreed ratio of the original repo monies to the original collateral value which has to be maintained at the same level throughout the life of the repo.

This ratio can be defined as follows (overleaf):

> Margin Ratio (MR) = Original Repo Monies/ Original Collateral Value =
>
> New Cash Onside / MtM Collateral Value = 1 - Haircut

As the collateral is marked to market daily, a new cash onside will be calculated according to the prevailing market price and when the difference between the new cash onside and the old cash offside exceeds an agreed threshold amount (or the change in collateral value exceeds an agreed threshold), margin will be called by the affected party for this difference between the new cash onside and old cash offside.

When the collateral price declines, the old cash onside will be greater than the old cash offside, which will affect the cash investor who will call for margin to restore the margin ratio. Conversely, if the collateral appreciates, the cash borrower will be affected and will call for margin equal to a positive difference between the new cash onside and old cash offside.

> New Cash Onside = MtM Collateral Value x MR =
>
> MtM Collateral Value x (1- Haircut) = (New All-in-price) x Nominal
>
> Old Cash Offside = Original Repo Monies + Return on Cash
>
> Cash Investor Margin Call = Old Cash Offside -
> New Cash Onside > 0 (Margin Call Threshold Amount)
>
> Cash Borrower Margin Call = New Cash Onside -
> Old Cash Offside > 0 (Margin Call Threshold Amount)

Once made, the margin call may be satisfied in either cash or securities reasonably acceptable to the party making the call. The cash amount is calculated following the example above. Security margin can then be calculated from the cash margin call amount:

> Security Margin Call* (Nominal) = (Cash Margin Call / MR) / New Dirty Price  = (Cash Margin Call/(1-Haircut))/ New Dirty Price (rounded to '000)

*Note: *The sign (direction) of the security margin call will be determined by the cash margin call sign (direction).*

Margin will be called when the collateral mark to market exceeds the threshold level.

> Original Collateral Value - Current MtM Collateral Value > Margin Call Threshold =>
> Cash Investor Margin Call = Old Cash Offside - New Cash Onside
>
> Current MtM Collateral Value - Original Collateral Value > Margin Call Threshold =>
> Cash Borrower Margin Call = New Cash Onside - Old Cash Offside

Where repo transactions are carried out under a legal agreement which provides for netting and which is legally enforceable, variation margin will be calculated and called on a portfolio basis.

As the trades may have different haircuts the portfolio is often calculated on a trade by trade basis and then netted down.

Cash Investor Margin Call = Σ Old Cash Offside - Σ New Cash Onside

Cash Borrower Margin Call = Σ New Cash Onside - Σ Old Cash Offside

Netting will effectively reduce the total amount of margin callable due to the portfolio diversification effect which will reduce current exposure both from deals and from related margin calls.

## Current exposure measurement - margin calls in practice

If the margin call is not met by the counterparty by the end of the customary settlement period for spot deliveries of the relevant cash or securities (or any other period agreed between the parties), the firm which called for margin has a legal right to send a default notice to the counterparty and to liquidate the collateral. This creates a few days' time lag between the margin call and collateral liquidation in the event of a counterparty default.

When there is a margin call threshold, a cash investor may not have a current exposure at the time of margin call and therefore may not be concerned. However, over the period between the margin call and the sale of collateral following a default there is a potential risk that the mark to market value of the collateral declines below the cash offside amount in which case the cash investor may incur a loss. This potential loss, or potential market exposure, depends on the collateral price volatility and may be significant in volatile markets.

Conversely, a security seller may also incur an additional loss on top of the current counterparty exposure in the event of a counterparty default, but this time it will potentially be caused by an increase in the collateral price.

## 1.1.2. Potential exposure measurement

Potential exposure is the additional loss - on top of current exposure - that may be incurred by a firm due to collateral price volatility following a counterparty default over the period between a margin call notice and the liquidation of the defaulter's collateral.

Potential exposure can be measured by Value at Risk (VaR), a widely accepted market risk measure. Value at Risk (VaR) is a probability weighted estimate of a potential loss over a given future period of time at a given confidence level (from 95% to 99%). A 5% three-day VaR at a 99% confidence level means that the biggest three day potential loss will not exceed 5% in 99 out of 100 business days based on historical price volatility. VaR measurement techniques will be discussed in the Market Risk section below.

The future time period for the VaR estimate (VaR horizon) is chosen based on the predicted number of days between a margin call date and the liquidation of the defaulter's collateral and will depend on the agreed margin call deadline and market liquidity of the collateral. Often, the margin call is to be met no later than the end of the next business day following the confirmed receipt of the margin call. In most cases collateral can be sold in one day without materially moving the market. In total, this will amount to a 3-4 business day VaR horizon depending on the margin call provisions.

When there is no margin call threshold, potential exposure will be equal to VaR multiplied by the original collateral value:

$$\text{Potential Exposure} = \text{VaR} = \text{VaR \% x Original Collateral Value}$$

When there is a margin call threshold, margin will be called only when this threshold is exceeded and therefore potential exposure will be equal to VaR plus the margin call threshold expressed as a percentage of the original collateral value multiplied by the original collateral value:

$$\text{Potential Exposure} = (\text{VaR \% + Margin Call Threshold \%}) \text{ x Original Collateral Value}$$

Potential exposure is calculated identically for cash investor and cash borrower.

Potential exposure will be calculated up to the default notice sent to the counterparty and the subsequent sale of collateral in the market. Once the counterparty is technically in default and a decision is made to liquidate the position, potential exposure will no longer be important; instead, the firm will need to monitor closely the break-even price of the collateral to be able to sell the collateral without a loss.

### 1.1.3. Net counterparty exposure

Net counterparty exposure will be equal to the sum of current exposure (current margin) and potential exposure.

$$\text{Net Counterparty Exposure} = \text{Current Exposure (Current Margin) + Potential Exposure}$$

$$\text{Cash Investor Net Counterparty Exposure} = \max (0, \text{Old Offside Cash -}$$
$$\text{MtM Collateral Value + Potential Exposure})$$

$$\text{Cash Borrower Net Counterparty Exposure} = \max (0, \text{MtM Collateral Value - Old Cash}$$
$$\text{Offside + Potential Exposure})$$

When there is a legally enforceable netting agreement, the net counterparty exposure on a portfolio of deals will be calculated as follows:

$$\text{Cash Investor Net Counterparty Exposure} = \max (0, \Sigma(\text{Old Offside Cash -}$$
$$\text{MtM Collateral Value + Potential Exposure}))$$

$$\text{Cash Borrower Net Counterparty Exposure} = \max (0, \Sigma(\text{MtM Collateral Value -}$$
$$\text{Old Cash Offside + Potential Exposure}))$$

### 1.1.4 Haircut calculation

Potential exposure is closely related to the calculation of the haircut, since the haircut is designed to protect the cash investor against potential exposure. Accordingly, in order to fully protect the cash investor against potential loss due to collateral price volatility in the event of a counterparty default the haircut should be greater than the estimated potential exposure for the security:

The haircut may be obtained from the potential exposure estimate by rounding up the potential exposure figure to full or half percent points depending on existing market convention.

## Haircut calculation - examples

### Example 1

| Security | 95% Confidence Level VaR (over 4 business days) | Margin Call Threshold | Potential Exposure (VaR + Margin Call Threshold) | Initial Haircut (rounded Potential Exposure) |
|---|---|---|---|---|
| Emerging Markets Brady Bonds | | | | |
| Brazilian Capitalization Bonds | 5.45% | 5.00% | 10.45% | 11.00% |
| Bulgaria Interest Arrears Bonds | 6.86% | 5.00% | 11.86% | 12.00% |
| Korea Global Bonds | 2.46% | 5.00% | 7.46% | 8.00% |
| Macedonia Capitalization Bonds | 5.89% | 5.00% | 10.89% | 11.00% |

However, actual haircuts may be lower than the potential exposure and zero haircuts are not uncommon. The reason for this is that haircut size depends first and foremost on the counterparty credit standing and then on collateral price volatility.

Conversely, for lower credit counterparties with whom the firm is not prepared to take any unsecured credit risk (which do not have an available credit line), initial haircut size may be increased from VaR (+ Margin Call Threshold) to VaR multiplied by some cushion factor (+ Margin Call Threshold) or to the worst historical loss (+ Margin Call Threshold) depending on the credit rating.

### Example 2

Using an emerging markets example for counterparties with credit ratings of Ba or B
Initial haircut = VaR x Safety Cushion Factor (1.5 or 2)

| Security | 95% CL VaR | MC Threshold | VaR x Cushion Factor of 1.5 + MC Threshold | Initial Haircut (rounded) | VaR x Cushion Factor of 2 + MC Threshold | Initial Haircut (rounded) |
|---|---|---|---|---|---|---|
| Brady Bonds | | | | | | |
| Brazilian Capitalization Bonds | 5.45% | 5.00% | 13.18% | 14.00% | 15.90% | 16.00% |
| Bulgaria Interest Arrears Bonds | 6.86% | 5.00% | 15.29% | 16.00% | 18.72% | 19.00% |
| Korea Global Bonds | 2.46% | 5.00% | 8.68% | 9.00% | 9.91% | 10.00% |
| Macedonian Capitalization Bonds | 5.89% | 5.00% | 13.84% | 14.00% | 16.79% | 17.00% |

## Example 3

For counterparties with credit ratings of B and below:

Initial Haircut = Worst Historical Loss + Margin Call Threshold

| Security | 95% CL VaR | Margin Call Threshold | Worst Historical Loss (over 4 business days) | Worst Historical Loss + Margin Call Threshold | Initial Haircut (rounded) |
|---|---|---|---|---|---|
| **Brady Bonds** | | | | | |
| Brazil Capitalization Bonds | 5.45% | 5.00% | 19.80% | 24.80% | 25.00% |
| Bulgaria Interest Arrears Bonds | 6.86% | 5.00% | 22.20% | 27.20% | 28.00% |
| Korea Global Bonds | 2.46% | 5.00% | 12.38% | 17.38% | 18.00% |
| Macedonia Capitalization Bonds | 5.89% | 5.00% | 14.87% | 19.87% | 20.00% |

## Example 4

For counterparties with available credit lines initial haircut size can be reduced within the available limit:

Line Usage = Potential Exposure - Initial Haircut < Available Credit Line

| Security | 95% Confidence Level VaR (over 4 business days) | Margin Call Threshold | Potential Exposure (VaR + Margin Call Threshold) | Initial Haircut | Line Usage (Potential Exposure - Initial Haircut) * |
|---|---|---|---|---|---|
| **Brady Bonds** | | | | | |
| Brazilian Capitalization Bonds | 5.45% | 5.00% | 10.45% | 10.00% | 0.45% |
| Bulgaria Interest Arrears Bonds | 6.86% | 5.00% | 11.86% | 10.00% | 1.86% |
| Korea Global Bonds | 2.46% | 5.00% | 7.46% | 10.00% | -2.54% |
| Macedonia Capitalization Bonds | 5.89% | 5.00% | 10.89% | 10.00% | 0.89% |

Note: * As a percentage of the original security value

Generally speaking, the initial haircut size should always reflect the counterparty credit rating, collateral price volatility and market liquidity. An available credit line does not mean that lower credit counterparties can be assigned zero haircuts within the available limit as this may lead to losses in the event of a default by the counterparty.

Since counterparty credit ratings, collateral price volatility and the market liquidity of securities may change significantly over time, initial haircut tables should be regularly updated and reviewed to reflect the latest changes.

## 1.1.5 Expected, Unexpected and Worst Case Loss

While the counterparty net exposure figure shows a potential loss in the event of a counterparty default (default probability = 1), there is an alternative approach to estimating credit loss in the event of default which takes into account both the probability of default and the recovery value net of costs associated with recovery, such as litigation costs. The formula is as follows:

Credit Loss = Exposure Value x Default Probability % x (1 - Recovery Rate %)* = Exposure Value x Credit Loss Rate = Loss Given Default - Recovery Value**

*Note:* * *(1 - Recovery Rate) is sometimes referred to as severity of loss;*

** *Recovery value should be estimated net of litigation costs if any*

With this approach three types of estimates can be obtained:

- Expected Loss uses expected values (arithmetic mean or weighted average of historical data) for each component in the above equation: default probability, recovery rate and litigation costs.

Expected Loss = Exposure Value x Average Default Probability % x (1 - Average Recovery Rate %) = Exposure Value x Average Credit Loss Rate

- Unexpected Loss estimates a range of possible deviations from the mean or central tendency represented by the expected loss figure. It covers all possible historical deviations from the mean to the biggest historical loss at a given confidence level. This range estimate is not very useful for risk management purposes as it is difficult to make any decisions based on a wide range of possible outcomes.

Expected Loss < Unexpected Loss <= Worst Case Loss

- Worst Case Loss estimates the largest loss based on the historical data at a given confidence level, which is unlikely to be exceeded in future except on a very low number of occasions referred to as tolerance level (i.e. once in 100 cases for a 99% confidence level which corresponds to a 1% tolerance level). The 'Worst Case' loss estimate is based on the Value at Risk conceptual framework.

This is a relevant credit loss measure for risk management purposes, provided sufficient historical data is available which is relevant to the particular counterparty. Worst case loss is estimated based on a selected sample of historical credit loss rates applied to the net counterparty exposure figure for a given counterparty credit class.

The easiest way to estimate worst case loss, or VaR, is by using a percentile function which simply takes the n-th worst loss for each 100 data for a n% tolerance level (or 1-n% confidence level). Alternatively, worst case loss, or VaR, can be estimated by multiplying a historical credit

99

loss volatility by a multiple a which is a point estimate of the confidence band limit, beyond which only exceptional losses may occur with an extremely low probability (see Figure 1 below).

While a values are tabulated and commonly available for known probability distributions, such as a standard normal distribution which has a bell shape (a = 1.65 for a 95% confidence level; a = 2.34 for a 99% confidence level), estimating a for a credit loss distribution which is highly skewed to the right is not a trivial task. Using the percentile function which makes no assumption regarding the shape of probability distribution will help avoid this complication.

### Figure 1 The shape of credit loss distribution

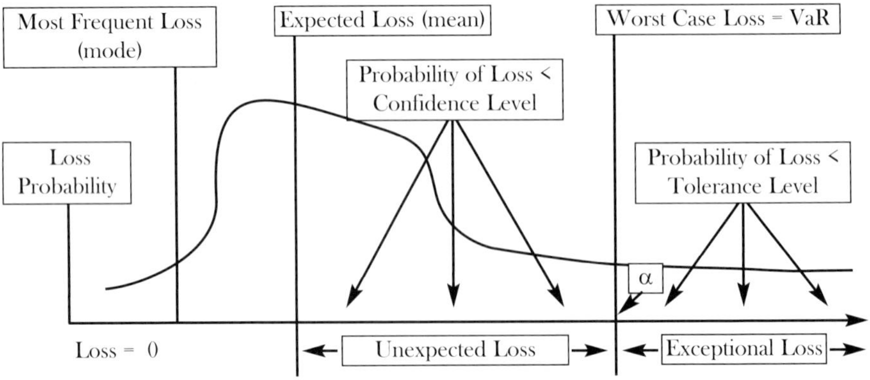

Techniques for estimating default, recovery rates and credit loss rates are beyond the scope of this chapter. For rated counterparties these statistics can be obtained from international credit rating agencies, such as Moody's, or Standard & Poor's. However, care should be taken when applying default and recovery rates observed in one market to a different market for which data is not available for some reason, as the overall number of defaults observed within one credit class may vary significantly from country to country and from year to year, because the default frequency is highly dependent on the strength of the economy and economic cycles.

Also, while international credit ratings have been accurate indicators of relative counterparty credit standing or counterparty specific credit risk in a particular market, they have often failed to predict the absolute amount of credit risk, including systemic risk of the market which may account for a lion share of defaults in cases of economic downturn or systemic crisis.

One Year, Weighted Average Default Rates by Rating

| Rating | Average Default Rate |
|--------|---------------------|
| Aaa | 0.00% |
| Aa | 0.03% |
| A | 0.01% |
| Baa | 0.12% |
| Ba | 1.34% |
| B | 6.78% |

*Source: Moody's Historical Default Rates of Corporate Issuers report, 1970-1997*

Average One-Year Loss Rates

| Rating | Average Default Rate |
|--------|---------------------|
| Aaa | 0.00% |
| Aa | 0.02% |
| A | 0.00% |
| Baa | 0.06% |
| Ba | 0.70% |
| B | 3.57% |

*Source: Moody's Historical Default Rates of Corporate Issuers report, 1970-1997*

Default and recovery rates are not stable over time. They may vary significantly within one credit class or rating from year to year. Volatility increases as credit quality deteriorates from the top of the investment grade scale, where both default probability and its volatility are close to zero, down the speculative grade scale where both default probability and its volatility can run into double digit figures.

Also, credit quality tends to change over time with credit ratings migrating across different credit classes. Over the near term, investment grade credits tend to improve their credit quality while speculative grade credits tend to deteriorate.

Over the longer term, the probability of investment grade credits shifting down the scale increases while speculative grade credits either default or survive and improve their credit quality. All these observed tendencies need to be taken into account when estimating default and recovery rates based on the international credit ratings.

Alternatively, for newly established institutions or those without international credit ratings assigned, default probability can be inferred from the current asset price volatility, assuming that the counterparty is most likely to default when the current market value of assets declines below the current market value of liabilities and estimating the probability of this event, which is assumed to be a proxy for the counterparty default probability.

Default probability can also be inferred from the credit spread of debt securities issued by the counterparty provided they are actively traded in the market.

It should be noted that the loss incurred on a documented repo transaction in the event of a counterparty default might be recovered provided the standard repo agreement is fully enforceable in the local jurisdiction. A loss incurred on an undocumented repo transaction e.g. a 'buy-sell' has a much lower chance of recovery.

## 1.2 Collateral and Issuer Default Risk

Issuer risk is the loss that may be incurred by the cash investor (collateral holder) in the event of the issuer defaulting on the collateral prior to the maturity of the repo and, simultaneously, of the counterparty defaulting on the repo transaction. This loss is conditional on the counterparty default, since standalone issuer default does not necessarily lead to a loss as long as the counterparty does not default on the repo transaction. (See Figure 2 below)

## Figure 2  Issuer and Counterparty Default Loss Outcomes

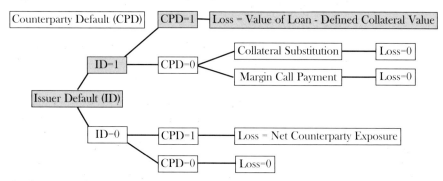

In the event of issuer default, the affected party will either demand suitable collateral replacement, provided this is stipulated in the repo agreement or has been agreed between the parties at the point of trade, or will make a margin call.

Clearly, collateral replacement provides better protection from counterparty default risk for the affected party (cash investor), since market liquidity in the defaulting issuer's securities may be temporarily or even permanently suspended leaving the cash investor fully exposed to the counterparty.

Often, however, the defaulting issuer's securities will retain some residual market value and liquidity, and any loss incurred in the case of simultaneous counterparty and issuer default will therefore be equal to a difference between the loan value and residual market value of defaulting issuer's securities:

| Counterparty and Issuer Loss = Value of Loan - Defaulted Collateral Value |
| --- |

This loss may be greater than a worst case loss predicted in the event of a standalone counterparty default (when the issuer does not default), since the likely decline in the value of the defaulted security will be greater.

The probability of such an exceptional loss will be equal to the joint probability of both counterparty and issuer defaulting at the same time, which will be much lower than the single default probabilities provided they are not linked to each other.

When the counterparty default is independent from the issuer default, their joint default probability will be equal to the product of the single default probabilities:

| Joint Default Probability = Counterparty Default Probability x Issuer Default Probability |
| --- |

If the counterparty and the issuer have a 5% and 10% default probability respectively and their defaults are not linked to each other, the joint default probability becomes 5% x 10% = 0.5%. However, the counterparty and issuer defaults can be partially and totally linked when they are parent and subsidiary or when both counterparty and issuer are the same entity. In case of the parent - subsidiary relationship, the parent default will likely trigger the subsidiary default and while the reverse is not true, the default of the parent company may become more likely if the subsidiary defaults.

In this case the joint default probability will be close to the parent company default probability. The parent and subsidiary default probabilities can be totally linked if the subsidiary cannot default unless the parent defaults and vice versa.

In such case the default probability is the same for the parent and subsidiary and the joint probability is equal to that common value. When both the counterparty and the issuer are the same entity the joint default probability becomes effectively a single one.

Clearly, such situations should be avoided unless the counterparty is a top rated institution, government agency or central bank in Zone A with a default probability equal to or very close to zero. This can be achieved by demanding that the issuer is independent of the counterparty. A simultaneous default of formerly unrelated counterparty and issuer may occur in case of a systemic crisis in an emerging market when one large default may trigger a series of defaults due to the high volume of mutual obligations between the financial institutions.

However, a financial institution operating in such a volatile market can assess potential risks in the event of a systemic crisis by running a stress test (sensitivity) report on its repo positions at default level prices and assuming simultaneous issuer and counterparty defaults at relevant price levels to evaluate the impact of potential losses on its P&L. This may help make informed decisions on the size of the book, quality and quantity of collateral taken and credit quality of existing counterparties.

In a recent attempt to address issuer risk enhancement, the International Swaps and Derivatives Association (ISDA) published a set of credit derivative definitions for documenting privately negotiated credit default swaps and options. In a credit default swap or option transaction, one party mitigates against the risk of a default on a loan or a bond by transferring that risk to another party willing to accept the risk of such an event. This latest ISDA publication provides definitions of restructuring and default events, and outlines what to do if a procedure is not written into the master agreement. The need for such a standardized framework was highlighted by Russia's debt default last year, as well as the Asian economic crisis. If the market in credit derivatives develops, it will help diversify issuer default risk and reduce the potential loss in cases of simultaneous issuer and counterparty default.

## 2. Repo Risk - Market Risks

Market risk is a potential loss that may be incurred due to an adverse movement in market rates during the minimum period required to liquidate securities or close positions in the market. There are several types of market risks inherent in repo transactions:

· Collateral price volatility

· Position risk

· Foreign exchange risk

## 2.1 Collateral Price Volatility

Collateral price volatility, or potential exposure, introduced and discussed earlier in this chapter, is the potential loss that may be incurred after a counterparty default due to an adverse move in collateral price (decline for the cash investor and increase for the security supplier).

Collateral price volatility can be measured by a standard measure of market risk (such as VaR). There are a number of approaches to measuring VaR. The two most common VaR measures are:

- Parametric VaR assumes some known historical probability distribution of price returns (most often standard normal distribution) and uses parameters of this known distribution to calculate a VaR figure. Unlike credit loss distribution, which is visibly skewed to the right, security price returns often have a symmetrical bell shaped distribution close to a normal standard distribution, as price moves in either direction often have roughly the same frequency and magnitude.

Parametric VaR = $\alpha$ * $\sigma$ * MtM Security Value, where

$\alpha$ - point estimate for the confidence band limits. For a standard normal distribution, $\alpha$ = 1.65 for a 95% confidence level and $\alpha$ = 2.34 for a 99% confidence level
$\sigma$ = standard deviation of N day price returns usually taken on a sample of the last 100 business days, where N is the number of days from the margin call date to the collateral liquidation in case of the counterparty default.

## Figure 3 Market Risk Loss Distribution

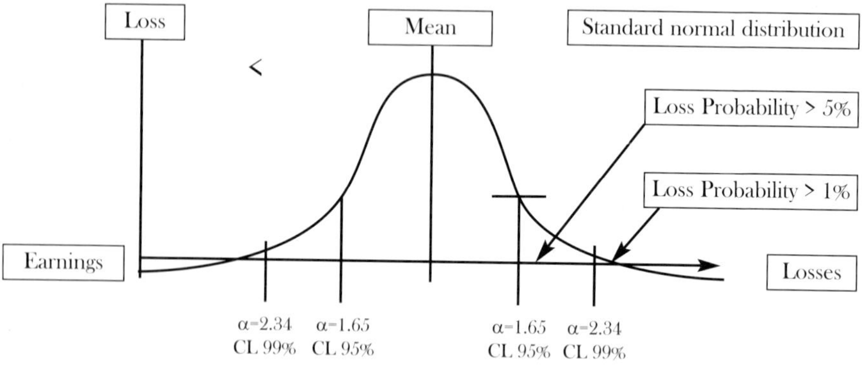

Note: Actual market loss distribution needs to be tested for normality (test for kurtosis or "flat tails" and skewness) before parametric VaR can be effectively applied:

- Historical VaR makes no assumption regarding the shape of historical distribution and derives a VaR value from the percentile function which simply takes the second (at a 99% confidence level) or fifth (at a 95% confidence level) worst historical loss every 100 past business days and assumes that any future potential loss should not exceed this value with a 99% or 95% probability.

Note: Though bond VaR is usually measured in terms of modified duration as a measure of price sensitivity with respect to yield (interest rate) changes, the first two VaR measures seem more relevant for measuring the volatility of security price returns.

Aggregating potential exposures for a portfolio of trades by means of a simple sum of potential exposures for individual securities would assume that there is no portfolio effect, and therefore overestimate the total potential exposure figure (i.e. this would be overly conservative).

Provided there is a legally enforceable netting agreement, this can be rectified by estimating potential exposure using either historical simulation or a variance-covariance matrix to calculate portfolio VaR for each counterparty, although this will considerably increase the amount of calculations and require a more sophisticated system.

## 2.2 Position Risk

Position risk is a potential loss which may be incurred due to an adverse market rate movement when repo trading has resulted in a long or short position taken in the underlying security. If a security is purchased and repoed (buy + repo, or buy + sell-buyback), a long position has been taken. If a security is reversed in and then sold (reverse repo + sell, or buy-sellback + sell), a short position has been created. If a security is purchased in a reverse repo and then repoed out as in a matched repo deal, no position in that security results.

Position risk on long and short positions taken in the security is similar to the forward purchase and sale risk when the purchase or sale price is locked in at the origination of the trade until the repo maturity. An adverse deviation from this locked in price adjusted for repo interest will result in a loss; a favorable deviation will result in a profit.

This risk can be measured using sensitivity measures such as a modified duration and convexity for bonds, or by running stress testing reports evaluating the impact of significant market rate moves on the security position values and P&L figures. Position risk resulting from repo trading should be considered, monitored and managed in the broader context of the entire security-trading portfolio as it is not repo-product-specific.

## 2.3 Foreign Exchange Risk

Foreign exchange risk arises when either the security or cash collateral is denominated in a foreign currency. The FX risk is a potential loss that may be incurred due to a possible fall in the value of the foreign currency versus the base currency of the contract and the subsequent devaluation of the collateral which may lead to a loss in the event of a counterparty default.

Foreign exchange risk on less volatile currencies can be estimated from historical exchange rate volatility. For weaker and more volatile currencies, the probability of a devaluation of the currency and its potential size can be estimated from the currency's relative valuation and interest rate parity.

The currency risk can be hedged by indexing all contract payments and security valuation to the base currency of the contract and - where the foreign currency has a greater historical volatility than the base currency - requiring an initial haircut for the cash collateral denominated in the foreign currency.

## 2.4 Liquidity Risks

The market liquidity of the security in a repo transaction should be sufficient for a prompt liquidation in the event of a counterparty default where this liquidation should be accomplished without materially moving the market. Collateral with low liquidity may fail to provide the required cushion in the event of a counterparty default, and this may result in a significant loss. Also, in times of market volatility volumes traded are often reduced and the size of counterparty trading limits are reduced; this may make a liquidation without materially moving the market more difficult to achieve.

Illiquid collateral is also hard to mark to market on a daily basis for margin call purposes since - by definition - few reliable price sources exists. Illiquid securities may be considered as acceptable collateral only when dealing with top rated counterparties with zero or near zero probability of default. In all other cases the market liquidity of the security involved should be a key approval requirement for any proposed repo transaction.

The market liquidity of the security is reflected in the size of the haircut applied on the repo. This haircut is estimated based on the potential price decline over the number of days between the margin call date and liquidation of the security in the event of a counterparty default. This predicted number of days would reflect the security's liquidity (including the relative size of the transaction).

If the collateral can be easily liquidated in one day, the period to liquidation is estimated at 4 business days (3 + 1) with the first three business days given to the counterparty to meet the margin call.

If two days are needed to liquidate a given amount of the collateral without triggering market price decline, the number of days to liquidation will be increased by one business day to 4 or 5 business days respectively and potential exposure will be estimated over the 4 or 5 day horizon.

# 3. Repo Risk - Settlement Risk

Settlement or delivery risk is a loss that may be incurred if counterparty fails to honor its commitment at settlement of a leg of a repo trade. Default in this case is defined not only as a permanent failure to deliver the asset (most obviously cash) but also as any significant delay in such delivery without any acceptable reason provided. Acceptable reasons may include operational problems which may be rectified within one or two business days.

Settlement risk arises when the firm delivers the asset before the counterparty delivers cash (or vice versa). Clearly in a DVP world this will not happen but in a safe settlement environment, often seen in emerging markets repo, it could. Settlement exposure is equal to the total transaction amount delivered by the firm which may be lost if the counterparty fails to deliver the asset.

The probability of a fully-fledged counterparty default and subsequent loss of the total transaction amount on a properly documented repo trade done with a professional well-rated counterparty is low. However, settlement delays are not uncommon even with good credits and professional dealers. Given the large size of repo books with significant numbers of individual transactions maturing on different dates, complex delivery chains and schedules exist and any such delay may therefore force the firm either to delay delivery on other trades, potentially resulting in a cost in the form of funding and - in some markets - fines[2] , or to borrow the asset (cash or security) in the market at a cost to the firm.

Settlement risk is increased significantly in undocumented trades and when dealing with lower rated counterparties. In such cases repo trades should only be done on safe settlement terms; these exclude settlement exposure by requiring prior delivery of the asset by the counterparty. However, safe settlement terms are likely to be accepted only by counterparties with comparably much lower credit standing.

To further mitigate against settlement risk, internal control procedures need to be enforced that limit or prohibit trading on an undocumented basis or require trading with lower rated counterparties to be done only on safe settlement terms or on Delivery Versus Payment (DVP) terms.

## 4. Repo Risk - Systems and Operational Risks

Systems risk is a loss that may be incurred by the firm due to design and implementation deficiencies in their systems which support repo trading. Like the next set of risks - legal risks - systems risks are not repo-product-specific but may nevertheless lead to significant losses and hinder product development if not addressed properly.

Despite the apparent simplicity of repo it requires relatively sophisticated system and operational support. This is due to a variety of functions that the repo system is expected to perform from online data capture, position keeping and settlement to P&L calculation, daily collateral mark to market and margin maintenance, and a large number of reports that it is expected to generate, such as cash and security position reports, margin call reports, counterparty exposure reports, P&L reports and sensitivity (stress testing) reports.

These operational complexities call for integrated system solutions which would enable centralized data capture, position keeping, settlement, margin maintenance, risk management and reporting to ensure data consistency and integrity at all levels and for all users and departments. In reality, however, different functions are often performed by different systems which creates room for data discrepancies and calls for regular data reconciliations between front, middle and back offices and with counterparties.

Online trading systems offer centralized data capture, position keeping, settlement and reporting, which improves data quality and consistency. However, these online trading systems may lack flexibility when it comes to customization, improvement or enhancement, or any kind of change in their design, as they are protected from outside modification by the customer. This limits their potential of becoming a fully integrated repo system for a firm.

---

[2] *Such fines are not often included in the repo agreements such as the GMRA but may be in other jurisdictions and are used to penalize the counterparty for any potential delay in asset delivery.*

# 5. Repo Risk - Legal Risks

Legal risk may stem from inadequate legal documentation supporting repo trades, which may prevent the firm from being able to sue to recover its losses incurred in the event of a counterparty or collateral default; or the documentation used (if any) may simply not provide for the important protections of margin maintenance and close-out netting.

This issue can be addressed by requiring appropriate legal and compliance procedures that would prohibit repo trades from being concluded with a counterparty prior to the signing of the standard repo agreement, the GMRA, or another appropriate agreement.

In addition to signing repo agreements, legal opinions may need to be sought from overseas jurisdictions in which the counterparty is based to establish the enforceability in those jurisdictions of the agreement and, in particular, the close-out netting provisions. If this is not done, there is a risk that, if the counterparty defaults or becomes insolvent, the non-defaulting party will not be able to rely on the agreement to establish a net exposure and may be at risk for the full amount of the cash or collateral provided to the counterparty under the repo.
Refer to Chapter 7 for a full explanation of close-out netting and the risk of unenforceability.

# The Legal Treatment and Documentation of Repo

## Introduction

The first part of this chapter sets out the legal framework for repo and considers the principal legal issues which arise. The second part examines the attempt by repo practitioners to develop documentation for classic repos (and, more recently, sell/buy-backs) designed to ensure that, despite the difficulties of classifying repo in legal terms (discussed under 'Legal Framework' below), participants can construct a valid and enforceable set of rights and obligations for their trading. This aim has been achieved through the development of the PSA-ISMA Global Master Repurchase Agreement, referred to in this Handbook as the "GMRA" (see the section entitled 'Documentation' below). The discussion of legal issues is confined for the most part to those of English law and is not exhaustive. By their nature, cross-border trades will involve the laws of at least one other jurisdiction. Although many of the issues discussed below are equally applicable in other jurisdictions, the full extent of a participant's rights and obligations in respect of transactions involving a non-UK counterparty will be determined not just by English law but also by the law and regulation of the counterparty's jurisdiction. This applies particularly to the efficacy of close-out and netting provisions, which needs to be considered by reference to the law governing the insolvency of the counterparty (generally that of its jurisdiction of incorporation) as well as the proper law of the contract. To some extent, the laws of the place where the securities are held will also be relevant, but these issues will be no different from those arising in an ordinary sale and purchase of securities, and therefore will not be considered here.

## Legal Issues

### Legal Framework

England has no legislation specifically dealing with repo, unlike some other countries such as France, and there are no reported court cases on the subject. This leaves the legal issues to be considered according to general legal principles. Chapter 2 explained the special nature of repo and its differences from buying/selling and borrowing/lending. Inevitably, the hybrid nature of repo gives rise to some difficulties of classification within the traditional legal concepts and principles built on conventional buying/selling and borrowing/lending transactions. Despite this, the legal issues in repo are, on the whole, well established. Sell/buy-backs are fairly simple transactions and as such do not pose any particular problems of classification. Whilst classic repos are much more of a hybrid, the use of the GMRA to document them is of great assistance in providing a clear legal framework for trading.

### Contract

Both classic repos and sell/buy-backs constitute an immediate sale of securities and a simultaneous agreement to purchase equivalent securities at a later date. The relationship between the parties is thus one of contract: a contract of sale and purchase. Accordingly, to understand the relationship between the parties and the rights and obligations which it entails, general principles of contract law need to be considered. It is not proposed to set out here the detailed rules relating to contracts, which occupy whole text books in themselves, but rather the basic elements which must be satisfied in order to create a binding contract.

There are five basic requirements for a valid contract:

· offer and acceptance of the subject matter of the contract;

· certainty and completeness of the terms of the contract;

· an intention by the parties to create legally binding relations;

· consideration for the contract (i.e. a 'price'); and

· valid execution of the contract by the parties, if the contract is in writing.

Generally, it will be apparent that these elements are present in the vast majority of classic repos and sell/buy-backs involving professional market participants, but particular care should always be taken to ensure that the requirements of certainty and completeness of terms are met.

The general English legal principle of freedom of contract means that parties are free to include any commercial terms they wish in their contract, provided that they do not act illegally. Commercially, parties will be restricted to some extent by market practice and the trend towards standardisation of classic repo documentation (see the section on 'Documentation' below) and also by the willingness of competitors to offer more favourable terms, but there is no legal requirement to adopt one form of contract or one set of terms over another. This may be particularly important in structured transactions where the repo element may be just one part of a larger deal and where flexibility of terms is required.

There is no legal requirement that a classic repo or sell/buy-back contract be in writing, and it is therefore perfectly possible to conclude the contract orally (although in some jurisdictions it may not be enforceable without written evidence, in order to prevent fraud). Since classic repo and sell/buy-back transactions are typically executed over the telephone, it is at this stage that a contract will be concluded and both parties become bound. It is for this reason that most financial institutions record telephone conversations between dealers and this practice is generally encouraged by the industry's regulators. Care should clearly be taken to ensure that the dealers state all the relevant terms when dealing.

The confirmation by fax or telex which follows the deal merely serves as evidence of the transaction and provides a useful opportunity for either side to query any discrepancies if they do not believe that the essential terms have been correctly stated. For this reason, confirmations should pass before delivery of cash or securities. The London Code of Conduct (see Chapter 10 on 'UK Regulation of Repo'), provides that parties should have the capability to despatch confirmations so that they are received and can be checked within a few hours of when the deal is struck.

Under the GMRA, confirmations are stated to constitute prima facie evidence of the agreed terms. This means that they are rebuttable by other proof, but the burden of proving otherwise lies with the party which disputes the confirmation. The tape recordings of the actual deal would be the best means of rebutting such evidence (most jurisdictions require the prior consent of the other party to such recording for it to be used as evidence), although deal tickets, other correspondence, evidence of market custom or a usual course of dealing between the parties will also be admissible.

## Sales v. secured cash loans: recharacterization risk

A question which has traditionally occupied participants in the classic repo and sell/buy-back markets and their advisers is that of "recharacterization" - the fear that repo or sell/buy-back transactions will be treated by the courts as borrowings of cash secured by a charge or pledge of securities, rather than as an outright sale of the securities.

Such a recharacterization could have a number of adverse consequences. Probably the most serious is that the transaction, as recharacterized, would contravene applicable legislation (for example legislation relating to money lending) or fail to comply with formalities required for the valid creation of security interests. This could have the result that the buyer of securities would be required, on the insolvency of the seller, to surrender the securities to the liquidator (since he would not have acquired a valid title) and prove as an unsecured creditor for the amount owed to him. Clearly, this would often have a disastrous result. Other possible consequences of recharacterization include problems of capacity or authority of the counterparty; breach of "negative pledges" (contractual restrictions on borrowing and the creation of security) or other contractual restrictions; differences in tax or accounting treatment and possible challenges to the validity of linked transactions (on the ground that the repo buyer, having only a limited interest, had no authority to sell).

The risk of recharacterization is a particular concern in relation to repos and sell/buy-back transactions because of their hybrid nature and the economic blurring of the distinction between buying/selling and borrowing/lending (see Chapter 2). This makes them more vulnerable than most kinds of transaction to the argument that they should be analysed legally by reference to their underlying substance rather than to the description which the parties have applied to them.

English courts are, in principle, able to recharacterize transactions, but the circumstances in which they are prepared to do so have in practice been narrowly defined, an approach which reflects the primacy generally afforded by English law to freedom of contract. Thus a line of decisions has recognized that a given economic effect may be achieved by more than one legal structure, and that parties are free to adopt whichever structure they choose. This applies, moreover, even where, by structuring their agreement in one way, the parties avoid being subject to statutory or other rules which would have applied if they had structured it in another. Many of the most important cases have concerned financing structures which achieved the same economic result as a secured borrowing of cash but which adopted a different legal structure such as sale (factoring or block discounting) or hire purchase. The courts follow the traditional rule that it is for parliament, not the courts, to decide whether the public policy objectives behind legislation such as the Bills of Sale Acts, the Moneylenders Acts and the provisions of the Companies Acts requiring registration of various company charges should be extended to other kinds of disposition.

Because of this restrictive approach, the risk of recharacterization arises in two relatively narrow cases. The first is where the transaction as documented is a sham - that is, it has been deliberately put forward to mask a different underlying understanding between the parties.[1] There should ordinarily be no question of repos or sell/buy-backs being attacked on this basis.

The second basis of recharacterization is where the substance of the transaction, as evidenced by the terms of the agreement between the parties (and not by the court's analysis of its economic effect), differs from the description which they have applied to it. The guiding principle applied by English law is expressed in a leading case as follows -

> *'I concede that the agreement must be looked at as a whole - its substance must be looked at. The parties cannot, by the insertion of any mere words, defeat the effect of the transaction as appearing from the whole of the agreement into which they have entered. If the words in one part of it point in one direction and the words in another part in another direction, you must look at the agreement as a whole and see what its substantial effect is. But there is no such thing, as seems to have been argued here, as looking at the substance apart from looking at the language which the parties have used. It is only by a study of the whole of the language that the substance can be ascertained."* [2]

It is therefore crucially important to use accurate and consistent terminology in the documentation of repo and sell/buy-back transactions. This is all the more so because traders and businessmen tend in practice to use terminology appropriate to a secured loan rather than to an outright sale; referring, for example, to "collateral" and "repo interest" rather than to "purchased securities" and "price differential" or "premium". Indeed the term "repurchase" is itself a misnomer; the securities purchased on the first leg of the transaction are not repurchased (a word which would imply that they have to be retained by the purchaser in the same way that a chargee retains charged property); the correct description of the second limb of the transaction, and that adopted in the GMRA, is a purchase of equivalent securities ("securities of the same issuer, forming part of the same issue and of an identical type, nominal value, description and amount as the purchased securities").

The GMRA includes a number of other instances of careful terminology, some of which are noted later in this chapter. It also includes a general provision[3] to the following effect - "Notwithstanding the use of expressions such as Repurchase Date", "Repurchase Price", "margin", "Net Margin", "Margin Ratio" and "substitution" which are used to reflect terminology used in the market for transactions of the kind provided for in this Agreement, all right, title and interest in and to Securities and money transferred or paid under this Agreement shall pass to the transferee upon transfer or payment, the obligation of the party receiving purchased

---

[1] See *Garnac Grain Co. Inc. -v- HMF Faure & Fairclough Ltd.* [1966] 1 Q.B. 650 and *Snook -v- London & West Riding Investments Ltd* [1967] 2. Q.B. 786.

[2] From the speech of Lord Herschell in *McEntire -v- Crossley Bothers* [1895] A.C. 457 at page 462-3. This passage was quoted in *Welsh Development Agency -v- Export Finance Co.* (1992) BCC 270, [1992] BCLC 148. Other important cases include *re: George Inglefield Ltd.* [1933] Ch1 and *Lloyds and Scottish Finance Ltd. -v- Cyril Lord Carpet Sales Ltd.* (a 1979 House of Lords decision reported at [1992] BCLC 609).

[3] Paragraph 6(f)

securities or Margin Securities being an obligation to transfer Equivalent Securities or Equivalent Margin Securities.".

Other features of repo transactions which could be regarded as supporting a recharacterization argument (because of their relatively artificial character and the extent to which they emphasise the character of the transactions as financing transactions) are the substitution and margin maintenance provisions. The relevant provisions of the GMRA are, once again, carefully drafted to avoid this risk (see 'The GMRA' below).

It is, therefore, quite possible to address concerns about recharacterization satisfactorily by the use of clear and consistent documentation. The GMRA has been drafted with an eye to eliminating recharacterization risk; the general view, which is supported by an opinion of leading Counsel (Richard Sykes Q.C.) obtained by ISMA, is that it succeeds in doing so.

## Close-Out Netting : Classic Repos and Sell/Buy-backs Documented under the GMRA

Classic repos and sell/buy-backs documented under the GMRA, in common with many derivative and foreign exchange transactions, rely upon contractual close-out netting rights as a method of reducing counterparty risk.

"Close-out netting" is a term which simply means, in the case of repo, accelerating outstanding obligations on the default of the other party and setting off (or 'netting out') the resulting obligations owed to each party by the other over the whole series of outstanding transactions. Close-out netting provides two important protections against counterparty exposure. The power of acceleration gives protection against the risk of an adverse movement in the market after it is clear that a counterparty will not be able to perform its obligations (typically because of insolvency). English law will not necessarily treat insolvency as itself a repudiation of a contract; a liquidator may choose to perform a contract if it is favourable at its contractual maturity date and the general principle of "wait and see" may be applied. In the absence of a power to accelerate obligations, therefore, the solvent party may see its exposure increasing after it is clear that its counterparty will not be in a position to perform its obligations.

In protecting against market risk, the power of acceleration is complemented by the requirements for provision of margin, which are described in more detail under 'The GMRA' below. These ensure that market movements do not cause significant exposures to arise before any default.

The second protection conferred by the power of close-out arises from the ability to combine ("net") the individual claims arising from the acceleration of each transaction outstanding at the time of default. This protects against the possibility of "cherry-picking", as described below.

In addition to reduced counterparty risk, there are other benefits of close-out netting as a result of increasing recognition of the effectiveness of the technique as a means of reducing exposure. International regulators will now permit parties relying on close-out netting to report their exposure on a net basis for capital adequacy purposes, with a consequent reduction in capital charges. Exposures may also be reported net on balance sheet under statutory accounting rules, resulting in an improved balance sheet. Net treatment is usually subject to conditions in either case, foremost of which will be the legal enforceability of the close-out netting arrangement in all relevant jurisdictions in the event of a party's default or insolvency, supported by appropriate legal opinions.

Under the **GMRA**, the mechanics of close-out netting are as follows: certain events of default are stipulated, including the insolvency of a counterparty, which if triggered entitle the non-defaulting party to serve notice of default (certain insolvency events trigger an automatic default without notice). At that time, the repurchase date for each outstanding transaction under the master agreement is deemed to occur immediately; the repurchase prices and the cash value of the securities to be redelivered are established for all such transactions, and the resulting amounts are set off with only the balance of the account being payable by the party which owes the higher amount.

In order to be fully effective as a tool for risk reduction, the close-out netting rights must stand up on the insolvency of the counterparty, as well as on a solvent default. It is usually only on insolvency that challenges may be made to these rights, since insolvency legislation will apply in place of the general law and policy considerations are brought to the fore. Few countries (if any) restrict the ability to close out on an ordinary default where solvency is not an issue.

The two elements of close-out netting, which must be considered separately, are the right to accelerate outstanding transactions and the right to set off the resulting exposures.

## Acceleration

In England, there is no objection to acceleration of obligations under classic repos on insolvency, and no freeze on these acceleration rights. Indeed, this appears to be the mainstream international view unless a specific bankruptcy statute has intervened.

Some other countries, however, mainly as a result of pro-debtor corporate rehabilitation insolvency statutes in the late 1970s and the 1980s, imposed freezes on the cancellation of contracts on insolvency so that the debtor would have the opportunity of continuing with contracts (such as essential supply or other contracts) so as to try and achieve the corporate debtor's survival. Unhappily, these statutes have the effect of preventing netting. Such statutes are to be found in various countries, including the United States, France and more recently Canada. In each of these countries it has been necessary to introduce a very complicated set of carve-outs, including carve-outs in favour of netting on certain markets. The result is a discriminatory and complicated system which is difficult for traders to follow. Fortunately, close-out of classic repos is covered by the carve-outs in the three countries mentioned, but in each case subject to conditions.

It is important to check the terms of these insolvency statutes and any other relevant insolvency laws carefully, not only to ensure that any conditions for the permission of netting apply, but as a first step to ascertaining whether the particular type of close-out specified in the **GMRA** is actually prohibited at all. There is, for example, a difference between cancellation or termination of a contract (which may be prohibited) and acceleration of obligations under a contract which is kept alive (which may not be prohibited).

## Set-off

So far as English law is concerned, set-off on insolvency is permitted and is an extremely strong English policy. Indeed the policy is so strong that the set-off of mutual debts on liquidation (whether solvent or insolvent) is mandatory.[4] The mandatory liquidation set-off applies regardless of the terms of any contract, and it is not possible to extend that set-off by contract.

The insolvency laws of different jurisdictions differ widely in their approach to the set-off of obligations owed by and to an insolvent institution. Some jurisdictions favour a wide set-off on the grounds that this produces a more just result as between the parties. These jurisdictions include England, where the set-off of mutual obligations in an insolvency is not only permitted but is actually mandatory. Other jurisdictions regard set-off as conflicting with the fundamental principle of the pari passu distribution of the assets of an insolvent entity for the benefit of all its creditors, since it has the effect of causing assets of the insolvent entity (debts or other obligations owed to it) to be applied for the benefit of particular creditors (those to whom it owes reciprocal debts or obligations).

As a matter of general insolvency policy, there is something to be said in favour of either view. From the narrower perspective of repo transactions, a wider set-off is clearly preferable, because it reduces counterparties' credit exposure to each other. An active participant in the repo market will typically have a number of transactions outstanding with another active participant at a given time. If its exposure on each "in-the-money" transaction has to be assessed individually, without any reduction for corresponding exposures of the counterparty to it under "out-of-the-money" transactions, its overall exposure will be higher, and perhaps substantially higher. This will be reflected in its policy on credit limits (which may therefore reduce both parties' ability to do business with each other) and its regulatory capital requirements.

Banking and other financial regulators have recognized this fact and have reflected the perceived benefits of netting in reducing counterparty exposure by reducing regulatory capital requirements in cases where a net approach is legally valid.[5] This has prompted many jurisdictions traditionally hostile to set-off to pass special legislation validating or imposing netting in the case of specified classes of contract, generally including repos and derivatives. Countries which have passed such legislation applicable to repos include Belgium, France, Germany, Italy, Portugal and the United States.

The close-out provisions of the GMRA closely follow those of the applicable English insolvency rules, with additional provisions to ensure that obligations for the delivery of securities are assigned a monetary value so as to be susceptible to set-off. These additional provisions operate by assigning a "Default Market Value" to securities due to be delivered. The definition allows the non-defaulting party a "window" within which it is able to fix the default market value by actually dealing in securities of the relevant kind, thereby guaranteeing that the value taken into account for purposes of close-out reflects the actual value and, therefore, that

---

[4] *Rule 4.90 Insolvency Rules 1986*
[5] *In most cases the parties must also have adopted an agreement, such as the GMRA, which includes provision for daily marking-to-market of outstanding transactions and the provision of margins against any exposures - see under 'The GMRA' below.*

the close-out figure reflects its actual loss. If the non-defaulting party does not deal within the specified period, the value is fixed at the market value at the end of the period (defined as the "Default Valuation Time"). Where the default occurs on a dealing day in the principal market for the relevant securities, the Default Valuation Time is the close of business on the next dealing day; where it occurs on a non-dealing day, the Default Valuation Time is the close of business on the second dealing day thereafter.

The dealing "window" was introduced as part of the 1995 update of the GMRA, and reflects experience gained on the collapse of Barings in February 1995. The 1992 version of the GMRA provided for default valuation by reference to the closing price on the dealing day preceding the default. Barings went into administration in London on a Sunday, and because of the difference in time zones the news of its collapse did not reach the markets in Asia, where many of its transactions had been entered into, until after they had closed on the Monday. This meant that counterparties found that their rights against Barings were quantified by reference to closing prices on the previous Friday, whereas they could only trade to close out or replace their positions on a Tuesday. In the light of this, it was generally agreed that the GMRA should be amended so as to permit non-defaulting parties to close out their positions and ensure that their actual exposure was reflected in the agreement.

## Limitations on set-off

Factors affecting rights of set-off include:

- MUTUALITY: In order for the insolvency set-off to operate, the reciprocal claims must be mutual in the sense that there are only two debtor-creditors and each debtor-creditor is personally liable on the claim it owes and beneficial owner of the claim owed to it. This means, for example, that a party could not set off claims owed to a counterparty acting as agent against claims owed to it by that counterparty in its capacity as principal, or claims owed to a parent against claims owed by a subsidiary. In each case, the infringement of mutuality would mean that one person's asset is used to pay another person's debt. For example, a parent's asset might be used to pay the debt of a subsidiary so that the parent is expropriated; this is not permitted on insolvency. All jurisdictions require mutuality in this sense. One of the main problems is that in broker or intermediary markets, the broker may be personally liable on debts it owes but may own the benefits of contracts for outside clients or customers, thereby destroying set-off mutuality on the broker's insolvency. Similar problems arise in dealings with trustees such as unit trusts or other trust funds. Conversely, where a party deals as agent for a single principal, there is mutuality between all claims owed to it, and by it, under transactions entered into with it in the same capacity.

The need for mutuality has an important impact on the provisions of the GMRA relating to agency transactions. The 1992 version of the Agreement did not permit agency transactions at all. The 1995 revision included for the first time Annex IV, which permits agency transactions, but only if it is made clear that each transaction is a transaction between the counterparty and the underlying principal. Mutuality is therefore preserved and the default provisions operate separately between the counterparty and each underlying principal. Annex IV is described further overleaf (see under 'Agency annex').

- **INTERVENERS**: The intervener risk is that an assignee, chargee, attaching creditor, undisclosed beneficiary or undisclosed principal may intervene on one side of the contract and take it over so that the question arises as to whether the other party can set off against the intervener. The simplest example is where the counterparty assigns one of the claims to a third party who then claims that from the debtor and the debtor would then wish to be able to diminish that claim in the third party assignee's hands by setting off a debt owed to the debtor by the original assignor. The same situation arises where a third party creditor attaches a claim owing by the debtor to the counterparty.

The basic rule in England is that a contractual set-off cannot be upset by an intervener provided that the claims both ways were incurred prior to notice of the intervener. They do not have to be accrued by the time of notice of the intervener. In other words, a set-off which would have arisen in the normal course in the absence of an intervention cannot be upset by a subsequently notified intervention as a matter of priority. But for various technical reasons there must be a contractual set-off since the enhanced insolvency set-off is not available (by reason of lack of mutuality). Hence it is possible in English law to protect against interveners by contract.

However, this is not the case in a number of other legal systems, notably in the Napoleonic camp. Here the intervener takes priority unless the set-off has actually accrued at the time of notice of the intervention; this is usually impossible to be sure about since the debtor does not know when the intervener is going to come out from the behind the arras.

The GMRA seeks to address this by prohibiting undisclosed agency transactions and requiring prior consent to any assignment, charging or other dealing with rights and obligations under the Agreement.

- **VULNERABLE TRANSACTIONS**: The Insolvency Act 1986 contains provisions for the reversal of transactions preferring creditors[6], transactions at an undervalue[7] and transactions defrauding creditors.[8] In principle these provisions could be applied to repo transactions. However, it seems unlikely that it will in any normal circumstances be possible to satisfy the test of preference (which includes a desire to place the creditor in a better position) or that of a transaction at an undervalue (because the transaction is entered into on arm's length terms and the economic value of the securities remains with the seller). The same applies in respect of transfers by way of margin: although they are not made for a cash consideration, their purpose is to comply with obligations imposed by the contract and to avoid the risk of default and close-out which would otherwise arise, and, again, the economic value of the securities transferred remains with the transferor.

[6] *section 239*
[7] *section 238*
[8] *section 423*

- **CURRENCIES:** There is no objection in English law to cross-currency insolvency set-off, although the valuation of the currencies for the purposes of the set-off may be the market rate prescribed by the insolvency rules at the relevant date, which may be different from the rate fixed by the **GMRA**. This is not generally considered a major commercial problem in practice. However, some other jurisdictions may not permit it, even if close-out netting is generally allowed there.

- **REHABILITATION PROCEEDINGS:** Under English law the appointment of an administrator does not result in a freezing of contracts or a freezing of set-off. A voluntary arrangement voted on by creditors may, however, have the effect of postponing the maturity of debts owed by the insolvent, thereby potentially harming the set-off (since the other party may be obliged to pay in the debt it owes). The **GMRA** therefore includes as an event of default the convening of a meeting for the purpose of considering a voluntary arrangement; this enables the non-defaulting party to exercise the right of close-out before the voluntary arrangement can become effective.

- **BUILD-UP:** Set-offs acquired after notice of a counterparty's imminent liquidation (such as notice of the presentation of a petition for winding-up, or of a creditors' meeting called to pass a resolution to wind up a counterparty) are not available. In practice, all creditors must receive notice of any such creditors' meeting and accordingly in practice one will be aware that trades with such a counterparty should cease. Where a winding-up petition is presented, no notice is given automatically but there is an obligation on the insolvent counterparty under the **GMRA** to notify the other party, as this is an event of default. The exclusion from set-off applies only to transactions actually entered into after notice of the relevant event; the fact that a repo may mature (or be closed out) after the notice is not a bar to inclusion.

- **CHERRY PICKING:** An English liquidator has the power to disclaim 'onerous property' which may include any 'unprofitable contracts'. This power may be used to disclaim the obligations of the defaulter under classic repos or sell/buy-backs, where for instance the market value of the securities to be repurchased is higher or lower than the repurchase price to the potential detriment of the liquidator. If the power is exercised, the non-defaulter will have an unsecured claim for damages which it may prove for in the liquidation. The risk is mitigated in the **GMRA** for classic repos and sell/buy-backs documented under the **GMRA** by specifying events of default which should enable acceleration and set-off to be exercised before liquidation. In addition, the single agreement clause (see the section on 'The **GMRA**' below) is intended to ensure that all classic repos and sell/buy-backs under the agreement are treated as forming part of a single agreement which must be disclaimed or honoured in full, although the enforceability of this clause has not yet been tested.

- **FOREIGN COUNTERPARTIES:** Insolvency procedures are usually determined by the law of the jurisdiction of the insolvent entity, regardless of the governing law of the contract. Even where insolvency is not an issue, the English conflicts of law rules on set-off are not fully resolved. This makes it essential when dealing with non-UK counterparties to take local advice as to whether the set-off rights described above would be upheld in the relevant jurisdiction, particularly in view of the policies involved in set-off and the jurisdictional differences on insolvency set-off discussed above. There is in any event a requirement to obtain legal opinions in order to obtain the benefits of netting for capital adequacy purposes and for balance sheet netting. The International Securities Market Association (ISMA) has obtained opinions in 28 jurisdictions[9], confirming that the close-out and netting provisions of the GMRA would be enforceable in an insolvency under the law of the relevant jurisdiction.

Where a counterparty enters into a repo through a branch office in a jurisdiction different from that of its incorporation, additional issues may arise. This is because it may be possible for the branch, or the counterparty as a whole, to be put into liquidation in the jurisdiction of the branch. Since such a liquidation would be conducted under the rules of that jurisdiction, this makes it desirable to confirm that the validity of netting would be recognized there also. For this reason, the requirements imposed by regulators as a condition of favourable regulatory capital treatment include a requirement to obtain a legal opinion on the validity of netting both in the jurisdiction of the branch and in the home jurisdiction of incorporation.

## *Close-Out Netting: Sell/Buy-backs without a master agreement*

Sell/buy-backs entered into on the traditional basis and documented simply by confirmations have no contractual close-out netting rights because there is no documentation giving them these rights, and no close-out rights are agreed in the telephone conversation between dealers. This gives classic repos a crucial advantage over sell/buy-backs from a legal perspective, which is reflected in their preferential capital treatment.

Without contractual close-out netting rights, parties who have several sell/buy-backs outstanding with a counterparty bear increased counterparty risk and market risk compared to classic repos in the event of a default by the counterparty. If the counterparty defaults on one deal, the other party must simply wait until the scheduled maturity dates of the other deals to see if the counterparty will perform them, unlike classic repos where all outstanding deals can be closed out.

In the event of the insolvency of the counterparty, it is not at all certain that the other party can terminate the outstanding deals, unless it can rely on an argument that the counterparty has repudiated the contracts by its insolvency. The outstanding contracts will also be vulnerable to cherry-picking by a liquidator, although the liquidator, if it chooses to perform, will have to perform the deal in full rather than insisting on the non-defaulting party performing its part of the bargain (payment of purchase price or delivery of securities) whilst reneging on the other side. This limits the risk of the non-defaulting party to the difference between the market value of the bonds at the date of performance or disclaimer by the liquidator and the buy-back price of the bonds.

[9] *At the time of writing (August 1999), there are opinions in relation to Australia, the Bahamas, Bahrain, Barbados, Belgium, Bermuda, the British Virgin Islands, Canada, the Cayman Islands, Denmark, England, Finland, France, Germany, Hong Kong, Ireland, Italy, Japan, Luxembourg, Malaysia, the Netherlands, the Netherlands Antilles, New Zealand, Singapore, South Africa, Sweden, Switzerland, and the United States (New York law). ISMA members may obtain copies of the opinions from ISMA. The opinions, are, naturally, subject to assumptions and qualifications and need to be reviewed in detail.*

It should be clear that it is preferable by far to document sell/buy-backs under a master agreement providing for events of default entitling the non-defaulting party to close out (see 'The GMRA' below).

## Capacity

Equally important is the question of capacity: does a counterparty have the requisite power to enter into the classic repo or sell/buy-back transaction? If the transaction is outside its powers ('ultra vires'), it may be void.

The importance of this issue was most vividly demonstrated in the swaps market in the Hammersmith and Fulham case[10], where the House of Lords found that local authorities had no power to enter into swaps; consequently all swaps with local authorities were void, and many of their counterparties were left facing huge losses. The consequences for innocent counterparties in the context of classic repos and sell/buy-backs should be less serious because each payment obligation is matched by a delivery obligation of the counterparty, but they could still be required to return any cash or securities received under the void transactions (presumably on redelivery of securities or purchase price) and consequently they would be exposed to market movements in cash rates or values of securities.

The powers of a counterparty will generally be found in its constitutional documents and any relevant legislation, and will vary from counterparty to counterparty.

A distinction must be made between UK companies incorporated under the Companies Acts, other UK entities which are not subject to those Acts and foreign entities.

## Companies incorporated under the Companies Acts

Parties dealing with companies formed and registered under the UK Companies Acts benefit from a statutory regime which has largely abolished the ultra vires risk.

Section 35 (1) of the Companies Act 1985 (as amended by the Companies Act 1989) provides that:

> 'the validity of an act done by a company shall not be
> called into question on the grounds of lack of capacity
> by reason of anything in the company's memorandum.'

It is widely accepted that omissions from a memorandum are also covered by this protection. In addition, those dealing with the company in good faith are entitled to assume that its board of directors has full power to bind the company or authorise others to do so. It will still be necessary to enquire that the board has actually exercised its power, and this is achieved by seeking certified copies of the relevant board resolution and specimen signatures. Note that the resolutions should be from the board and not (or in addition to) a committee of the board, since the statutory protection does not extend to committees.

Notwithstanding this protection, the law sometimes imposes restrictions on the power of some companies to enter into certain types of business, such as insurance companies which are

---

[10] *Hazell -v- Hammersmith & Fulham London Borough Council and others [1991] 1 All E.R. 545 (HL)*

prohibited by the Insurance Companies Act 1982 from carrying on any business other than insurance business.

## Other UK Entities

The position of UK entities which are not companies governed by the Companies Acts is more complicated. Each such counterparty will need to be considered separately, which will generally involve an examination of the constitutional documents and/or legislation relating to that particular entity. Particular care needs to be taken with these entities since the ultra vires principle will continue to apply.

Although most UK participants in classic repos and sell/buy-backs are Companies Act companies, the range of counterparties is substantially greater and may increase further. Building societies, pension funds, insurance bodies, trustees, partnerships, charities and others will all need special consideration. Those entities which are formed by statute will have only the powers which the relevant statute grants to it and these may be construed narrowly.

When construing constitutional or statutory powers, a view will need to be taken on the category to which classic repos and sell/buy-backs belong. If there is a power to borrow money, does this include power to repo and sell? Conversely, does a power to lend money cover reverses and buy-backs? Given the legal nature of the trades as outright sales and purchases, it is not thought that a power to borrow money will be sufficient but a power to "raise" money is likely to be more widely construed and should include a power to enter into a reverse repo. The position should in fact be much simpler since a power to purchase or sell securities should arguably cover this type of trading (particularly sell/buy-backs), but the absence of any power to raise finance (highly unlikely), or any limitations on any such power, should be investigated. Furthermore, any qualifications to the power, such as a requirement for such sales or purchases to be performed in the ordinary course of business or for full consideration, will need to be considered in the context of each transaction. In the case of trustees, the scope of the investment and other powers conferred by the trust instrument will need to be considered. Economically a reverse repo is the equivalent of a secured cash deposit, but it may not be regarded as an investment for trust purposes; specific examination of the trust instrument, or other confirmation of the trust's powers, may therefore be advisable.

## Foreign Entities

The powers of companies or other entities incorporated or organised outside the UK are governed by the laws of the relevant country of incorporation or organisation. This category includes UK branches and offices of foreign entities, which covers many participants currently operating in the UK classic repo and sell/buy-back market. Unfortunately, there is not always a quick and cheap answer for parties dealing with these entities and local legal advice should ideally be obtained for each foreign counterparty on this question.

## Documentation

### Sell/buy-backs

We have seen that a sell/buy-back arrangement is in fact comprised of two separate but linked deals, a spot and a forward. The first involves a sale of securities by one party to the other for immediate settlement and the second is the reverse (i.e. a resale of an equal amount of the relevant securities) for settlement at an agreed date in the future, the desired maturity of the overall transaction. The two deals are executed simultaneously.

Under a simpler sell/buy-back entered into on the traditional basis without a master agreement, each leg of the arrangement is documented by a simple exchange of telexes, faxes or electronic messages constituting the normal confirmations which follow any bond sale. These confirmations simply contain the essential terms agreed in the telephone deal and will typically include the names of the parties to each deal, the contract date, the type of security subject to the deal, the price, the settlement date and the account details. It would be unusual under such an agreement to include any additional terms for the protection of the parties such as default provisions, although the exact contents of the confirmation will vary from participant to participant and, in theory, can include any additional terms agreed between the parties at the time of dealing.

## Classic Repos

When a European market first began to develop, mainly in London, most active market participants sought to use their own form of master agreement. Such agreements were generally based on the standard forms prevalent in the United States, but were naturally tailored to the particular needs and commercial objectives of the particular firm. Often, therefore, they did not include fully reciprocal rights and obligations.

With documentation varying across the market, participants faced some difficulty, since their counterparties would want to negotiate the terms of the master agreement (if they were prepared to sign it at all) and this could be a time-consuming and expensive process. Trading and market development were impeded as internal procedures, particularly credit controls, often required documentation to be executed before trading commenced.

The solution naturally favoured by the market was to develop a market standard document. This was expected to reduce the need for negotiation, with its attendant cost and delay, and to reassure possible new entrants to the market with the knowledge that the standard agreement represented a market consensus on what was fair.

A committee of market participants was formed under the auspices of ISMA in conjunction with the Public Securities Association (PSA) of New York (now the Bond Market Association). The result was that in November 1992 a standard master agreement was produced by the PSA and endorsed by ISMA: the Global Master Repurchase Agreement (referred to in this Handbook as 'the GMRA'). The GMRA was issued in a revised form in November 1995. A copy of the GMRA is reproduced as an Appendix to this Handbook.

In 1999 a new master agreement covering derivatives and repo was produced by the European Banking Federation, principally to replace the plethora of European domestic repo, securities lending and derivatives master agreements. This Handbook concentrates on the GMRA as the standard master agreement in the international repo market.

## The GMRA

In November 1995 the GMRA was reissued with amendments following discussions with a group of market practitioners under the auspices of ISMA.

The GMRA was originally modelled on the standard agreement used in the US repo market, the PSA (now Bond Market Association (BMA)) Master Repurchase Agreement, but with variations to reflect English law and regulation and international practice which are substantial, particularly following the 1995 revision. It is governed by English law and is designed for use in both international and domestic transactions.

Since its introduction in 1992, the GMRA has become the market standard document in the international repo market. It has been promoted by ISMA, with considerable success, as the standard agreement in both domestic and cross-border transactions in a number of the world's major markets. Although ISMA focussed initially on the European markets, the promotion of the GMRA has now been extended and covers Australasia, Asia and emerging market jurisdictions in Latin America and Eastern Europe.

ISMA has promoted the GMRA in conjunction with local market participants, regulators and legal advisers in accordance with the following objectives -

> *wherever possible, the adoption of the GMRA for both the domestic and cross-border markets in a jurisdiction without making any changes;*
>
> *where this is not possible, the development of an annex adapting the GMRA for use in that jurisdiction;*
>
> *where there is apparent reluctance to adopt the GMRA in a jurisdiction, the use of promotional and educational meetings in conjunction with the local Isma committee.*
>
> *Jurisdictions in which, following these principles, the GMRA is used with or without a local annex include Australia, Belgium, Denmark, France, Ireland, Italy, the Netherlands, Sweden and Switzerland.*

The GMRA was designed for use with gross-paying securities. It was not originally intended for use for transactions in U.S. Treasuries or equities, and the head-note to the printed form continues to reflect this, but since the form was issued it has been established that it may be used for transactions in U.S. Treasuries and wording has been developed for transactions in net paying securities[11] and equities. Some of the provisions of the equity annex are described overleaf.

The structure of the GMRA documentation will be familiar to those involved in the swaps market, bearing a close resemblance to the Isda architecture. It consists of:

· the GMRA - a printed standard form master agreement containing provisions applicable to all classic repo trades between the parties to it;

---

[11] *Annex VIII (Net Paying Securities)*

- a series of annexes to the GMRA, including supplemental terms and conditions agreed between the parties, a specimen form of trade confirmation and the parties' contact details; and

- a confirmation sent out after each trade confirming the specific terms of that trade.

This structure has a number of practical advantages, not least of which is its flexibility. The annexes enable the parties to tailor particular provisions of the document to their own needs. Negotiation can be kept to a minimum, usually focusing only on the one or two pages of supplementary terms contained in Annex I to the agreement, most of which are commercial rather than legal issues.

Once the master agreement is in place, no further documentation needs to be exchanged when trading except for confirmations.

Some of the more significant provisions of the GMRA are summarised below:

## General

One general characteristic of this agreement which constitutes a significant advantage over participants' own standard forms previously used is its mutuality. The representations and warranties and events of default in particular are entirely reciprocal.

## Nature of trades

For the reasons explained above, the GMRA is carefully structured and worded to emphasise the character of the transactions as sales and purchases of securities. The buyer's obligation is to deliver equivalent securities at maturity, and the financing charge on the cash received by the seller (the economic equivalent of interest) is described as a price differential arrived at by the cumulative application of a specified "pricing rate" to the purchase price.

## Margin

An important element in the range of protections afforded by the GMRA is the system of marking outstanding transactions to market daily, with the power for either party to require the other to provide margin to eliminate any credit exposure. These provisions, which are set out in paragraph 4 of the GMRA, operate as follows.

First, a "transaction exposure" is calculated for each transaction. Each transaction has a "margin ratio" equal to the proportion which the value of the securities at the time of purchase bore to the purchase price[12]. The transaction exposure is calculated by applying this ratio to the repurchase price[13] at the relevant time and comparing the result with the current market price

---

[12] *This corresponds to what is sometimes referred to by traders as "initial margin" or "haircut". The 1992 version of the GMRA provided for it to be specified in the confirmation, but experience showed that this often was not done; under the 1995 version, the margin ratio is obtained simply by dividing the market value at the purchase date by the agreed purchase price.*

[13] *The repurchase price will, of course, be gradually increasing over the life of the transaction because of the daily application of the pricing rate (the equivalent of daily accrual of interest on the cash side of the transaction).*

of the equivalent securities due to be delivered by the buyer. If the value of the securities is higher, this constitutes a transaction exposure of the seller to the buyer (because what he is due to receive is worth more than what he is due to give); if it is lower, the buyer has a transaction exposure to the seller.

The transaction exposures arising from all outstanding transactions between the parties (whether as buyer or seller) are then aggregated and account is taken of any margin already provided (or, if both parties have provided margin, the net margin provided). If this calculation produces a "net exposure" of one party to the other, the exposed party is entitled to call for a "margin transfer". (In principle, this power arises however small the net exposure, though in practice parties often agree not to make margin calls, or simply refrain from making margin calls, if the net exposure is de minimis.)

A "margin transfer" is a payment or repayment of cash, a transfer of securities reasonably acceptable to the party calling for the margin transfer or the transfer of "equivalent margin securities" - that is, securities equivalent to securities previously transferred as margin.

As indicated by the expression "equivalent margin securities", a transfer of securities as margin constitutes an outright transfer of the entire ownership of the securities, rather than a mere charge or pledge. The basic position is that margin is calculated on an aggregate net basis, taking into account all outstanding transactions. The parties may however agree that some transactions are to be margined individually or left out of account altogether.

The GMRA provides an alternative method of eliminating net exposures. This is often referred to by traders as "repricing"; legally, it involves the premature termination, by agreement, of one or more current transactions, together with simultaneous entry into a new transaction on slightly amended terms. The resulting cash payments and deliveries of securities are then set off against each other, so that only a net difference is paid or transferred.

Repricing may be effected in two ways. Under the first method, the securities purchased under the new transaction are identical to those under the old transaction, but the purchase price is different, being derived from the application of the original margin ratio (or "haircut") to the current market value of the securities. The result is the payment of a cash difference equal to the transaction exposure.

Under the second method, the purchase price under the new transaction is equal to the current repurchase price under the new transaction, and the new transaction is in respect of securities agreed between the parties with the appropriate current market value.

Whichever method is adopted, the maturity date and pricing rate agreed under the original transaction apply to the new.

## *Manufactured payments*

If a repo spans an interest or dividend payment date in respect of the relevant securities, the seller will not receive the payment, since he will not be holding the securities. In order to preserve the seller's economic ownership, therefore, the GMRA requires the buyer to pay the seller an amount equal to the interest or dividend which he would have received but for the repo. This payment is often referred to as a "manufactured" payment, to distinguish it from the "real" dividend or interest payment. A corresponding requirement applies where margin securities are held over an interest payment date.

## Substitution

Many repos are primarily cash financing transactions - that is, their main motivation is to enable the seller to raise cash and to provide the buyer, as provider of cash, with acceptable "security". Provided that the purchased securities are of acceptable credit quality and not susceptible to abnormal market risk, their precise identity and composition will not be of great concern to the buyer. The seller will therefore tend to provide whatever securities meet the required criteria and are available when the repo is entered into.

However, where a repo extends over a significant period, the seller may find that it needs some of the securities back before the contractual repurchase date. The most obvious reason for this is where the seller has decided to sell the securities. It could also happen because the securities have become scarce and command a premium in the securities borrowing and reverse repo markets. Scarce securities of this kind are referred to as having "gone special" and a repo which is primarily driven by the buyer's desire to obtain the securities is referred to as a "special" repo (and is likely to be priced accordingly).

Sellers therefore seek to ensure that they have the ability to call securities back before the contractual repurchase date and to "substitute" for them other securities of similar value and quality. The GMRA contains a provision[14] conferring such a right, but only with the agreement of the buyer.

The term "substitution" is unfortunate, since it tends to suggest that the buyer is obliged to retain the particular securities purchased and therefore could be used to support an argument for recharacterization. For this reason the GMRA does not use the word outside the title of the paragraph, even though it is the one generally used by traders. The text instead provides for early termination of one transaction and the simultaneous initiation of a replacement transaction relating to other securities acceptable to the buyer, having a market value at least equal to that of the securities recalled. The terms of the replacement transaction (e.g. pricing rate and repurchase date) will otherwise replicate those of the original.

The right of substitution also applies where securities have been provided as margin.

## Representations and warranties

A fairly comprehensive set of mutual representations and warranties has been included, which are made on the execution of the agreement and are deemed to be repeated each time a trade is entered into and on each delivery of securities under the agreement.

Further representations and warranties may be sought in Annex I to the agreement in the event that a party feels it necessary because of the status of a particular counterparty or the nature of the dealing in question.

---

[14] *Paragraph 8*

## Events of default

The agreement contains various events of default, again on a reciprocal basis, which are designed to provide a remedy to the non-defaulting party in the event of a default, insolvency or possible insolvency of its counterparty.

The most common events of default are covered, although there is no cross-default (other than for classic repos between the same parties) and no material adverse change clause, and it is left to the parties, if they so wish, to include these and any other events deemed to be necessary in Annex I to the agreement. In practice, the events of default are not usually extended, but this may change as the range of participants in the market increases.

The consequences of an event of default are as follows:

(a) all outstanding classic repos are immediately due for repurchase;

(b) each party's obligations to the other are valued and converted into a monetary amount; and

(c) the resulting cash sums are set off and only the net balance is payable by the party owing the greater amount.

As a result there is a corresponding reduction in the non-defaulting party's exposure on a default or insolvency, provided that the set-off mechanism works on a default and insolvency and that adequate margin arrangements have been effected. Provided that margining has been monitored effectively and that the set-off is not open to challenge, the exposure of the non-defaulting party should in theory be zero or, at the most, the difference between the pre-agreed margin level and the purchase price. However, there is an additional market risk that between calling for margin and the payment or set-off, the market may move against the non-defaulting party and/or the relevant margin may not be delivered prior to insolvency.

## English law and jurisdiction

The agreement is governed by English law and both parties submit to the non-exclusive jurisdiction of the English courts.

## Single agreement

All trades under the master agreement form part of a single agreement between the parties. As noted earlier, the intention is to avoid the possibility of a liquidator 'cherry-picking' by repudiating some trades whilst enforcing others.

## Tri-Party Repo

The tri-party concept involves a third party offering services to the primary repo parties. The services may include custody of the securities, daily marking to market of the securities and making any necessary margin calls, arranging simultaneous delivery of securities against payment and controlling substitution rights (see Chapter 2 for a fuller explanation).

Although the documentation varies, the usual structure in the European market is for the main repo contract (the GMRA) to be put in place between the primary parties and for a service agreement to be entered into between all three parties. The service agreement is usually a standard form of the service provider, the principal providers in the market being Euroclear, Cedel Bank, Chase and Bank of New York. Accordingly, in addition to rights and obligations under the GMRA, the parties also have rights and obligations under the service agreement. It is important to remember that the rights and obligations under the GMRA remain unaffected, so that it continues to be the primary parties' obligations to make payments and to deliver securities. The consequences of a default by either counterparty are still those set out in the GMRA, although if a default is caused by the service provider, the parties may have a claim against it to recover their losses. Any liability of the service provider, however, is usually limited in the service agreement to liability for negligence or wilful misconduct.

## Annexes to the GMRA

A number of annexes may be used to supplement the GMRA. Seven annexes were published as part of the 1995 version of the Agreement; others have been produced subsequently. Some of the annexes are in the nature of "housekeeping", for example Annex I (additional agreed terms and conditions), Annex II (form of confirmation) and Annexes V, VI and VII (details of the parties' addresses and of any agents for service of legal process). Others add substantive provisions; perhaps the most important of these are the buy/sell back annex (Annex III) the agency annex (Annex IV), the gilts annex and the equities annex.

## Buy/sell back annex

As explained earlier, a "buy/sell back" or "buy/sell" transaction was originally a simple pair of matching purchase and sale transactions, with different maturity dates, documented only by confirmations. The main attraction of such "undocumented" buy/sell transactions is their simplicity; they do not require the sophisticated systems which in the case of a classic repo are necessitated by the mark to market and margin procedures.

The absence of a power of close-out, and of mark-to-market and margining provisions, is the main substantive difference between a classic repo and an undocumented buy/sell. As explained above, it represents a significant increase of risk and is the principal disadvantage of the undocumented buy/sell. This increased risk is reflected in the approach of regulators: entities subject to prudential supervision generally suffer a higher regulatory capital charge for such transactions.

In addition to these differences of substance, buy/sell back transactions are also priced differently from classic repos in two respects. First, prices are quoted as "clean" prices, without any allowance for accrued interest, which is paid separately; classic repos use "dirty" pricing - that is, accrued interest is treated as part of the price. Secondly, buy/sells do not incorporate "manufactured" dividends; if a buy/sell transaction spans an interest payment date, the "sell back" price (the agreed price for the forward dated purchase) will be adjusted to reflect the fact that the buyer will receive and retain the payment.

For some years before the publication of the 1995 version of the GMRA, there was much discussion of whether buy/sells should be superseded by classic repos, in order to encourage participants to subject their transactions to master agreements, with consequent reduction of risk. It was pointed out, however, that a number of counterparties preferred, for reasons of powers, policy or familiarity, to characterize transactions as buy/sells; the better way of encouraging more widespread use of the master agreement was therefore to produce a version which could be used for buy/sells. This argument prevailed and resulted in the production of Annex III.

The function of Annex III is, essentially, to adapt the close-out and margining provisions of the GMRA to reflect the special characteristics of buy/sell transactions. The main provision is an elaborate definition of "Sell Back Price". Normally when parties enter into a buy/sell back transaction, they will simply agree the prices for the spot and forward elements of the transaction. The forward price will be arrived at by using an implied interest rate to fix the financing charge, but this will not be expressly stated. Where the transaction spans an interest payment date, this will complicate the pricing further, and it may not be possible to derive the implied interest rate simply by applying a mathematical formula to the spot and forward prices. Annex III therefore requires the parties expressly to specify a pricing rate; this makes it possible to calculate the figures required to give proper effect to the margining and close-out provisions of the agreement.

## Agency annex

As explained above, the agency annex was first introduced in the 1995 version of the agreement. Its principal provisions are as follows -

(a) a transaction (an "agency transaction") may be entered into by one party (but not both) as agent;

(b) the transaction must be identified as an agency transaction;

(c) the principal must be a single person (that is, the transaction cannot be a "block transaction" allocated among several principals) and his identity must be disclosed to the counterparty (either by name or by the use of a code or identifier, the key to which will be disclosed to specified individual officers of the counterparty, for example senior management or the head of the credit department);

(d) the agent must have express authority to enter into the transaction on behalf of the principal;

(e) the representations and warranties are modified so that a party acting as agent warrants that the requirements of Annex IV will be complied with in respect of any agency transaction into which it enters;

(f) the events of default are modified so that a default by an agent entitles the counter party to give a default notice treating that event as an event of default in relation to the principal;

(g) generally, the GMRA applies separately as between the counterparty and each underlying principal. This means, in particular, that the mark-to-market and margining provisions are operated individually and not on an aggregate net basis in respect of all transactions with the agent - a point with important systems implications for firms which operate repo programmes for multiple principals.

## Gilts annex

The gilts annex was drafted by a working party under the auspices of the Bank of England as part of the preparations for the introduction of the liberalized market for repos in U.K. government securities ("gilts") in January 1996. It contains provisions facilitating the operation of the GMRA in connection with the Central Gilts Office Service, the settlement system for transactions in U.K. gilts.

## Equity annex

The equity annex is structured as a set of supplemental terms and conditions to be added as part of Part II of Annex I to the GMRA.

Its provisions mainly reflect the special taxation treatment of equities (see Chapter 9) and the need to deal with "corporate events" such as capital reorganizations, rights issues and takeover bids, and with the exercise of voting rights.

Where a dividend payment date is due to occur during the term of a repo, the seller is required to seek to effect a substitution, and in the absence of a substitution may give a notice terminating the repo, before the dividend payment date. If the buyer in facts holds the securities over the dividend payment date, it is obliged only to pass on to the seller what it actually receives, plus any amount which the buyer is entitled to recover from the source jurisdiction of the equities in respect of tax (i.e. there is no "grossing up" for any withholding on account of tax), unless the buyer has failed to make reasonable efforts to transfer equivalent securities in response to a termination notice given by the seller (in which case the buyer is required to indemnify the seller against loss). These provisions may all be varied by agreement between the parties.

The provisions relating to corporate events and voting reflect a compromise between the wish to preserve for the seller the economic ownership of the securities and the need to avoid any argument for recharacterization.

It would not be possible simply to empower the seller to direct the buyer how to respond to a rights issue or takeover offer or to exercise voting rights. To do so would be to court a recharacterization argument and, in any event, the buyer may not have retained the securities; it is fully entitled to dispose of them, either by outright sale or by way of securities loan or repo, and reacquire them in time to enable it to deliver equivalent securities when required.

The equity annex therefore provides as follows -

> (a) the buyer is required to notify the seller of the issue, by the issuer of any equities which are subject to a repo, of a notice relating to a prospective corporate event;
>
> (b) the seller has the right to give a notice terminating the repo before the corporate event is due to occur;
>
> (c) if the repo is not terminated -
>
> (i) in the case of a corporate event which happens without any choice on the part of the shareholder (e.g. a sub-division or consolidation), the definition of "equivalent securities" is modified so that the buyer is obliged to deliver the appropriate quantity of securities in the new form;

(ii) in the case of a corporate event which does require choice by the shareholder (e.g. a rights issue or takeover offer), the seller may give the buyer a noticespecifying inwhat form it wishes to receive securities at the repurchase date, and this notice has the effect of modifying the definition of "equivalent securities" appropriately.

Where the decision requires expenditure on the part of the shareholder (e.g. the taking up of rights on a rights issue), the seller must pay the buyer an amount sufficient to fund this expenditure;

(d) as regards voting rights, the seller may give a notice (which must be given at least seven business days in advance) requesting the buyer to exercise voting rights in a specified way. Provided that the buyer holds securities of the appropriate kind at the relevant time (and there is no obligation on the buyer to do so), the buyer is then obliged to use its best endeavours to arrange for the exercise of rights in the specified manner.

The provisions relating to dividend payments and those relating to corporate events and voting extend to equities provided as margin in the same way as to equities purchased under a repo.

# Chapter 8

# Accounting for Repos

## Introduction

Repo agreements are transactions involving the 'sale' of a security with a simultaneous agreement to repurchase the same or, in some cases, a substantially identical security at a specified future date. The main accounting issue is whether the repo should be accounted for as a sale (by the seller/borrower) or a financing transaction (i.e. the security acts as collateral for a loan). In most countries there is now a trend towards ensuring that the accounting treatment follows the commercial substance of a transaction, rather than the legal form. Increasingly, therefore, while a repo will transfer legal title to the securities from seller to buyer, the accounting treatment will depend on whether the risks and rewards of ownership have been transferred from the seller/borrower to the buyer/lender. In the current terminology it is necessary to determine whether or not the asset should continue to be recognised on the seller/borrower's balance sheet. The other key issue in repo accounting is the extent to which balances can be netted or offset.

## General Accounting Rules - recognition

In order to recognise the commercial substance of a transaction, it is necessary to analyse and assess the risks and rewards attaching to an asset (or liability). From the point of view of the seller/borrower (in a repo), in order to remove the securities from their balance sheet the conditions for the so-called derecognition of an asset must be satisfied. Where risk and reward are the determining factors then securities can only be removed (derecognised) from the balance sheet if substantially all of the risks and rewards associated with the asset have been transferred to others, and the fair value of any risks and rewards retained can be measured reliably.

A similar analysis applies from the point of view of the buyer/lender (in a reverse repo). Accordingly, securities can only be included on the balance sheet if substantially all of the risks and rewards associated with them have been transferred to the enterprise; and the cost or fair value of the asset to the enterprise can be measured reliably. The alternative approach to determine derecognition used in some accounting regimes considers which party has control over the underlying asset.

In most circumstances it is unlikely that a repo/reverse repo will satisfy the above derecognition/recognition criteria and the correct accounting treatment will be as a financing transaction and not a sale/purchase.

While the qualifying criteria and accounting detail can and does vary between accounting regimes as discussed later, the general effect is that the seller/borrower will:

- retain the securities on its balance sheet valued in accordance with the normal accounting policy for securities owned (for a financial institution, usually market value for trading securities and (amortised) cost for non-trading securities) - separately identified either on the balance sheet or in a note to the financial statements;

- include the obligation to repay the cash advanced by the buyer/lender as a liability, usually called 'securities sold under repurchase agreements' and often disclosed separately on the face of the balance sheet;

- accrue the interest expense (in whatever legal form) as a financing cost over the life of the agreement.

The buyer/lender will:

- usually not record the securities on its balance sheet or recognise any profits or losses arising from changes in the market value of the securities;

- include the cash advanced to the seller/borrower as an asset, usually called 'securities purchased under agreements to resell';

- accrue the interest income (in whatever legal form) over the life of the agreement.

For both the seller/borrower and the buyer/lender, the notes to the financial statements and the accounting policies would explain the treatment adopted.

It is also necessary to consider the accounting treatment of any additional collateral or return of collateral which passes between the seller/borrower and the buyer/lender as a result of changes in the market value of the securities underlying the repo. Collateral can take two forms: cash or securities. To the extent that cash is used for additional collateral, this may be added to or offset against the amount of the repo/reverse repo. Offset rules vary by country but, in general, offset is only permitted when there is a legally enforceable right to offset and there is an intention or an ability to settle on a net basis. If additional securities are used, then these will be treated consistently with those involved in the original repo/reverse repo (i.e. normally remaining on the balance of the seller/borrower and off the balance sheet of the buyer/lender).

For some more complex repo arrangements it is possible that the criteria for derecognition (or recognition) could be met, for example if the agreement incorporates terms whereby the buyer/lender assumes price risk, or in the case of repos to maturity where the maturity date of the repo coincides with that of the underlying securities. In such circumstances the transaction will be treated as a sale. However, the nature of the repurchase commitment will normally be disclosed, if material. Careful analysis will be required of the risks and rewards of such transactions to determine the accounting treatment.

Where repos/reverse repos are carried out in a 'trading book' (i.e. a portfolio held for dealing or trading purposes) then in some regimes the balances arising from repos and reverse repos may be 'marked-to-market' (i.e. recorded at fair value) for balance sheet purposes.

## United Kingdom

In the United Kingdom, the appropriate accounting treatment and disclosures in financial statements of repo/reverse repo transactions are within the scope of Financial Reporting Standard 5 - 'Reporting the Substance of Transactions' ('FRS 5') published by The Accounting Standards Board in April 1994. In addition, Statement of Recommended Accounting Practice - 'Securities' issued by The British Bankers' Association in September 1990 ('BBA SORP') also provides guidance for banks in the accounting and disclosure of repos, as does the Bank Accounts Directives of the European Union (incorporated into Schedule 9 of the Companies Act 1985).

## FRS 5

This states that

*'a reporting entity's financial statements should report the substance of transactions into which it has entered. In determining the substance of a transaction, all its aspects and implications should be identified and greater weight given to those more likely to have a commercial effect in practice'. [FRS 5 paragraph 14]*

FRS 5 details conditions necessary for recognising and ceasing to recognise assets, and also states that

*'Where a transaction involving a previously recognised asset results in no significant change in:*
*(a)the entity's rights or other access to benefits relating to that asset, or*
*(b)its exposure to the risks inherent in those benefits; the entire asset should continue to be recognised. In particular, this will be the case for any transaction that is in substance a financing of a previously recognised asset, unless the conditions for linked presentation given in paragraphs 26 and 27 are met in which case such a presentation should be used.'*
*[FRS 5 paragraph 21]*

FRS 5 also includes a number of 'Application Notes' designed to interpret how the requirements of the standard are to be applied to certain transactions. In particular, Application Note B deals with 'Sale and Repurchase Agreements'. This application note states that:

*'In a straightforward case, the substance of a sale and repurchase agreement will be that of a secured loan - i.e. the seller will retain all significant rights to benefits relating to the original asset and all significant exposure to the risks inherent in those benefits and will have a liability to the buyer for the whole of the proceeds received... The seller should account for this type of arrangement by showing the original asset on its balance sheet together with a liability for the amounts received from the buyer.' [FRS 5 paragraph 184]*

The application note provides guidance on the assessment of benefits and risks, as well as other features of the agreement such as the sale price, the nature of the repurchase provision and the provision for a lender's return and ability to use the asset. This guidance will assist in determining the nature of any more complex repo arrangements, for example if the buyer/lender is not assured of a lender's return then, in substance, a sale may have been made and the asset would be removed from the seller's balance sheet.

In most circumstances repo transactions will result in the continued recognition of the asset by the seller/borrower and will not constitute a sale. Such a treatment will recognise the economic substance of the transaction and not the legal form. Even when different securities can be returned which are substantially similar, since the risks and rewards are unchanged, the substance of the transaction will still be that of a financing. The buyer/lender will treat the transaction as secured lending and will not put the collateral into its balance sheet.

## BBA SORP

The BBA SORP on securities states that securities subject to repos should be

> 'retained in the books whenever substantially all the
> risks and rewards of ownership remain with the seller,
> as, for example, where the repurchase commitment
> is a predetermined price ..... Similarly, securities
> purchased subject to a commitment to resell should be
> treated as lending transactions if the bank does not
> acquire the risks and rewards of ownership'.
> [Paragraph 35 BBA SORP]

This treatment is consistent with FRS 5 which has, in effect, codified the SORP in this respect. FRS 5 is also the relevant guidance for more complex repo transactions.

### Schedule 9 Companies Act 1985

Schedule 9 of the Companies Act 1985 ('Schedule 9'), which incorporates the UK implementation of the European Union's Bank Accounts Directive, sets out the required treatment of sale and repurchase transactions in the financial statements of UK banks. Paragraph 13 of Part I of Schedule 9 requires that where a bank is party to a sale and repurchase transaction, the following treatment must be adopted:

> '(2) Where the company is the transferor of the assets
> under the transaction:
> (a)the assets transferred shall, notwithstanding the
> transfer, be included in its balance sheet;
> (b)the purchase price received by it shall be included
> in its balance sheet as an amount owed to the transferee; and
> (c)the value of the assets transferred shall be disclosed
> in a note to its accounts.
> (3) Where the company is the transferee of the assets
> under the transaction it shall not include the assets
> transferred in its balance sheet but the purchase price
> paid by it to the transferor shall be so included as an
> amount owed by the transferor.'

This is consistent with the requirements of FRS 5, albeit with the additional requirement to quantify, in a note to the accounts, the amount of securities held on the seller/borrower's balance sheet which are the subject of repo transactions.

The equivalent Schedule 4 rules for non-bank corporates do not deal specifically with repos, however there is a requirement to disclose the amount of borrowings secured on assets of the company.

## United States

The accounting for repo transactions in the US is governed by Statement of Financial Accounting Standards No. 125, 'Accounting for Transfers and Servicing of Financial Assets and Extinguishments of Liabilities' ('SFAS 125'). Paragraph 9 details the criteria to be met by a transaction recorded as a sale and paragraph 27 gives specific guidance for repos. In summary, SFAS 125 directs that an agreement that both entitles and obligates a transferor (seller/borrower) to repurchase transferred assets from the transferee (buyer/lender) is to be accounted for as a secured borrowing only if:

- The assets (securities) underlying the reverse leg of each repo agreement are the same or substantially the same (i.e. having the same obligor, maturity date, contractual interest rate and unpaid principal amount; and of identical form and type) as those transferred under the corresponding initial leg;

- The seller/borrower will be able to repurchase or redeem the assets (securities) transferred on substantially the agreed terms at all times, even in the event of the buyer/lender's default - this requires maintenance of adequate collateral by the seller/borrower;

- The reverse leg of the repo agreement will require that the transferred assets (securities) be repurchased before maturity, at a determinable price; and

- The seller/borrower enters into an agreement to reacquire the assets (securities) transferred concurrent with the original transfer.

Under SFAS 125, accounting for the underlying security by both the seller/borrower and the buyer/lender depends on whether the buyer/lender has taken control over the security and on the rights and obligations stemming from the related collateral arrangements. SFAS 125's requirements in this area can be complex. However, the Statement provides that the seller/borrower of the security (collateral) is to continue to report the security as its asset, and the buyer/lender (secured party) may not recognise the item in its financial statements, if certain conditions are present. One of these conditions is the seller/borrower's contractual right and ability to redeem the collateral on short notice, for example, by substituting other collateral or terminating the contract. If this condition is not met then the buyer/lender will record a purchase of the underlying security, although the seller/borrower can still show a secured borrowing (and a pledged asset).

Repos to maturity occur when the maturity date of the underlying securities coincides with the maturity of the repo contract. Under the SFAS rules above, repos/reverse repos to maturity are treated as purchases and sales of securities rather than financing transactions provided the seller/borrower is isolated from the underlying security in all situations, including bankruptcy., In essence, the securities ultimately will not be repurchased or resold and therefore it is not a financing.

137

SEC Regulation S-X 4-08(m) requires that repos and/or reverse repos, including accrued interest payable, be separately disclosed on the balance sheet, if the carrying amount (or market value of the underlying collateral for repos, if higher) exceeds 10% of total assets. In the case of reverse repos, additional disclosure is required concerning policies regarding possession of assets purchased and provisions ensuring the sufficiency of the collateral.

If an entity does not mark its collateral to market, additional disclosures may be warranted. Such disclosures include the type of securities sold under the agreement; the maturities of the agreements grouped into overnight, term up to 30 days, term of 30 to 90 days, term 90 days and over and demand; and, for each maturity group, the carrying amount and market value of the assets sold under a repo, including accrued interest, and any cash or other assets on deposit under the agreements and the repurchase liability associated with such transactions and the interest rates thereon.

In all cases, if the amount at risk under a repo or reverse repo with any counterparty or group of related counterparties exceeds 10% of stockholders' equity, SEC Regulation S-X 4-08(m) requires disclosure of the name of each counterparty, the amount at risk and the weighted average maturity of the agreements with each counterparty.

The amount at risk as defined by the SEC regulation is:

- under repurchase agreements:

the excess of the carrying amount (or market value, if higher than the carrying amount or if there is no carrying amount) of the securities or other assets sold under agreement to repurchase, including accrued interest plus any cash or other assets on deposit to secure the repurchase obligation, over the amount of the repurchase liability (adjusted for accrued interest);

- under reverse repurchase agreements:

the excess of the carrying amount of the reverse repurchase agreements over the market value of assets delivered pursuant to the agreements by the counterparty to the registrant (or to a third party agent that has affirmatively agreed to act on behalf of the registrant) and not returned to the counterparty, except in exchange for their approximate market value in a separate transaction.

## International accounting standards

The International Accounting Standard (IAS) dealing with accounting for repo agreements is IAS 39 - 'Financial Instruments: Recognition and Measurement'. This is based on control, similar to US accounting, rather than access to risks and benefits as in UK accounting, although in practice the two approaches often (but not always) give the same result.

Under IAS 39 the security sold is not removed from the balance sheet of the seller/borrower because the seller has retained control through its right and obligation to re-acquire the security on terms which give the buyer/lender a lender's return on the cash received in exchange. Instead, the seller/borrower should reclassify the security as 'securities given as collateral' and treat the cash received as collateralised borrowing. Similarly, the buyer/lender should treat the cash paid as a collateralised loan. The buyer/lender would not recognise the security if the seller/borrower has the right to substitute other collateral at short notice.

Although IAS 39 is not effective until 2001, in the absence of other guidance, it can be regarded as best practice for measurement and recognition of repos in financial statements prepared under IAS. It is also generally consistent with accounting principles and industry practice in many jurisdictions.

## General Accounting Rules - Netting

Where an entity enters into several repo and reverse repo contracts with the same counterparty then, as described above, the entity will record a series of assets (collateralised loans - from reverse repos) and liabilities (borrowings - from repos) on its balance sheet. The question arises as to whether the assets and liabilities can be offset in the balance sheet - sometimes referred to as 'balance sheet netting'.

A pre-requisite for such netting in most jurisdictions will be a legal right of set-off between the counterparties which is enforceable in all situations, including liquidation.

Where the repo/reverse repo trades are settled through a clearing system such that the clearing entity acts as the counterparty to all repo/reverse repo contracts then there may be scope for significant offsets across an entire repo book.

## UK

Under rules in FRS 5, in the UK, debit and credit balances must be combined where, and only where, all of the following apply:

    (a) The reporting entity and another party owe each other determinable monetary amounts, denominated either in the same currency, or in different but freely convertible currencies (note that one impact of this requirement is that repos in some emerging market currencies will not be eligible for cross-currency balance sheet netting);

    (b) The reporting entity has the ability to insist on a net settlement. In determining this, any right to insist on a net settlement that is contingent should be taken into account only if the reporting entity is able to enforce net settlement in all situations of default by the other party; and

    (c) The reporting entity's ability to insist on a net settlement is assured beyond doubt. It is essential that there is no possibility that the entity could be required to transfer eco nomic benefits to another party whilst being unable to enforce its own access to economic benefits. For this to be the case it is necessary that the debit balance matures no later than the credit balance. It is also necessary that the reporting entity's ability to insist on a net settlement would survive the insolvency of the other party. [FRS 5 paragraph 29]

Although the entity must have the ability to settle net, it does not need an intention to do so. FRS 5 (in Paragraph 21 of Appendix III) makes it clear that a contingent right to settle net is sufficient provided (a) the right can be invoked in all situations of default; and (b) the entity's debit balance matures no later than its credit balance. Where balances mature on the same day this requires that a credit balance is not paid away before funds to cover a debit balance are received, which may also be accomplished by actual net settlement. The latter proviso is consistent with condition (c) above which states there should be no possibility that the reporting entity could be required to transfer economic benefit to another party whilst being unable to enforce its own access to economic benefits. FRS 5 considers that this requires debit balances to mature no later than credit balances.

However, given the collateralised nature of repo business and provided settlement arrangements are on a delivery versus payment basis, then in reality there will be no transfer of economic benefit (i.e. settlement of repo borrowings) without immediate receipt of economic benefit (i.e. return of collateral securities) even though repo borrowings may mature before receivable amounts under reverse repos. Therefore for fully collateralised amounts the order of maturity of debits and credits is not a relevant issue in protecting the economic benefit of the reporting entity and amounts covered by appropriate legal right to offset must be offset across freely convertible currencies for all maturities.

In the case of amounts subject to a legal right of offset but which are not fully collateralised, then the order of maturity of debits and credits remains relevant for offset purposes. The ability to offset matched book repo transactions with the same counterparty will also be determined using the above principles.

## US

Offset under US GAAP is a particularly complex area and is dependent on the precise nature of the transaction and method of settlement. Only an overview can be provided here. In considering offset of repo balances under US GAAP, two documents are particularly relevant: FASB Interpretation No. 39, 'Offsetting of Amounts Related to Certain Contracts' ('FIN 39'), and FASB Interpretation No. 41, 'Offsetting of Amounts Related to Certain Repurchase and Reverse Repurchase Agreements' ('FIN 41').

Under FIN 39, a debtor having a valid right of setoff may offset a related asset and liability and report only the net amount in its balance sheet in certain limited circumstances. A right of setoff exists when only all of the following conditions, required by paragraph 5 of FIN 39, are met:

(a) Each of two parties owes the other determinable amounts;

(b) The reporting party has the right to set off the amount owed with the amount owed by the other party;

(c) The reporting party intends to set off (FIN 39 generally requires actual net settlement in all circumstances to meet this requirement. Gross settlement can rarely occur without violating FIN 39's provisions.); and

(d) The right of setoff is enforceable at law.

Amounts arising from repo/reverse repo transactions that are due in different currencies can be offset for reporting purposes if they are settled with a single payment. If they are settled on a gross basis on the same day with a single banking institution the offset may still apply, provided the requirements of FIN 41 also are met.

FIN 41 clarifies the circumstances in which amounts recognised as payables under repurchase agreements may be offset against amounts recognised as receivables under reverse repurchase agreements and reported net. This interpretation was written because, under the Fedwire Securities Transfer System in the United States, the record of security ownership and the associated cash payments can be made on only a gross basis for each transaction. Accordingly, the Fedwire system does not permit transactions to be settled on a net basis.

So FIN 41 establishes certain additional conditions that, if met, permit a reporting entity to setoff receivables and payables stemming from repurchase transactions settled through a centralised clearing system, even though the transactions may not actually occur on a net basis as required by FIN 39, paragraph 5.c. These conditions are set forth in paragraph 3 of FIN 41:

(a) The repurchase and reverse repurchase agreements are executed with the same counterparty;

(b) The repurchase and reverse repurchase agreement have the same explicit settlement date specified at the inception of the agreement;

(c) The repurchase and reverse repurchase agreement are executed in accordance with a master netting arrangement;

(d) The securities underlying the repurchase and reverse repurchase agreements exist in 'book entry' form and can be transferred only by means of entries in the records of the transfer system operator or securities custodian;

(e) The repurchase and reverse repurchase agreements will be settled on a securities transfer system, and the enterprise must have associated banking arrangements in place, both as further described in FIN 41; and

(f) The enterprise intends to use the same account at the clearing bank or other financial institution at the settlement date in transacting both the cash inflows resulting from the settlement of the reverse repurchase agreement(s) and the cash outflows in settlements of the offsetting repurchase agreement(s).

The Financial Accounting Standards Board initially considered limiting the scope of FIN 41 to transactions that settle on the Fedwire system; however, the FASB ultimately concluded that such a scope limitation was not warranted and thus permitted FIN 41 to apply to any settlements made through a transfer system having the required attributes.

Within the above very strict conditions it is possible to achieve offset of repo balances across currency and with matching maturity.

Transactions under Master Repo Agreements have been used by brokers and dealers for matched book repo transactions. Generally, matched book transactions with the same customer and identical maturity dates under such a master agreement cannot be netted as they are each settled on a delivery-versus-payment basis (i.e. gross) and this does not qualify for netting (under FIN 39) unless the additional FIN 41 criteria are met.

## IAS

Under IAS, the criteria for offsetting financial assets and financial liabilities are contained in IAS 32, 'Financial instruments: disclosure and presentation'. Specifically, under IAS 32, a financial asset and a financial liability should be offset and the net amount reported in the balance sheet when an enterprise:

(a) has a legally enforceable right to set off the recognised amounts; and

(b) intends either to settle on a net basis, or to realise the asset and settle the liability simultaneously.

The requirements are not based solely on credit risk but also on the timing of expected future cash flows. When a legal right of set-off exists, but settlement in practice is normally gross, debit and credit balances are not netted, but the effect of the reduced credit risk exposure is disclosed in the financial statements.

Offsetting of debit and credit balances under IAS 32 is based on the intention to settle either net or simultaneously. This does not necessarily mean that every possible contract is settled net or simultaneously, but it does imply a general rule that netting is the usual form of settlement. The concept of simultaneous settlement is applied restrictively in IAS 32. Simultaneous settlement includes settlement through the operation of a clearing house in an organised financial market. Otherwise settlement is considered simultaneous only when transactions occur at the same moment. Therefore under IAS the repo amounts should be offset where there is net or simultaneous settlement, including across currencies. Offset between different maturities will not be appropriate.

# Chapter 9

# Tax Treatment of Repo

## Introduction

The current basic UK tax position on the sale and repurchase of securities reflects to a considerable extent the economic substance of the transaction as a collateralised loan of cash. To achieve this, the enactment of specific legislation has been necessary, as without it the tax treatment would follow the underlying legal form of a repo as a sale and reacquisition of the securities which are the subject matter of the repo. The dilemma over whether to follow legal form or economic substance is not confined to the UK: the treatment of repo transactions under other tax systems, though outside the scope of this chapter, varies from jurisdiction to jurisdiction according to the tax authorities' level of sophistication and the tendency of the particular jurisdiction to characterise transactions for tax purposes by reference to legal form or economic substance. It should never be assumed, in the case of a cross-border repo, that the two tax systems of seller and buyer (let alone the jurisdiction of the issuer of the securities) will treat the repo in the same way. Anomalies can arise, which represent an opportunity for tax planning as often as the potential for unanticipated cost.

In the UK a repo seller, if acting as a trader, will not generally recognise any accounting profit on the sale of securities under a repo if the sale price under the repo exceeds their acquisition cost or their carrying cost in his accounts, if different. Since a trader's taxable profits are based on his accounts, this means that no special tax provision is necessary to prevent a repo artificially triggering taxable profits on securities that have grown in value in the trader's hands. The same is not true, however, for taxpayers for whom the securities are a capital asset rather than a trading asset. The sale of securities under a repo is prima facie a disposal and a special legislative provision is needed to prevent capital gains occurring. Section 263A of the Taxation of Chargeable Gains Act 1992 represents such a provision. Repos on conventional market terms will fall within section 263A, but any non-arm's length features could cause section 263A to be disapplied and gains recognised, as could the assumption by the repo purchaser of any price risk on the securities during the repo term.

## Price Differential

Following the statutory logic that a repo deserves to be treated for tax purposes as a collateralised loan, the differential between the purchase price and repurchase price, which functions economically as the charge made by the buyer to the seller for the finance represented by the purchase price, is for tax purposes treated by virtue of section 730A of the Income and Corporation Taxes Act 1988 (the "Taxes Act") as an amount of interest, paid at the maturity date of the repo. The normal tax consequences of payments of interest flow from this. Withholding is required if, exceptionally, the repo represents funding which is intended to have a term of a year or more so that the section 730A interest is "annual" or "yearly" interest:

no UK withholding is required for interest on shorter-term obligations, nor, normally, if the interest is paid by or to a UK bank. A deduction for the section 730A deemed interest is available where a true interest payment would have attracted relief. For corporate taxpayers this takes the form of a debit under the provisions in the Finance Act 1996 dealing with "loan relationships" and is required to be deducted on an accruals basis (section 730A(3)). The "deemed interest" treatment also carries with it the consequence that no deduction will be available if a real payment of interest would have been recharacterised as a non-deductible distribution under certain of the provisions of section 209 of the Taxes Act, for example on the grounds that the "interest" represents excessive debt funding of a thinly-capitalised UK repo seller by an overseas affiliate.

Section 730A will not apply to confer the quality of interest on the price differential if the repo contains any non-arm's length features or if the repo purchaser assumes the entirety of the price risk on the securities during the repo term (section 730A(8)). Note that the test here is rather different from that which applies to the disapplication of section 263A of the Taxation of Chargeable Gains Act 1992 (see above), which in determining whether the seller has made a disposal asks the question whether any (rather than all) of the price risk of the securities is assumed by the repo buyer.

Repos on buy/sell terms, where the repo buyer retains for his own account any income payments arising on the securities during the repo term, present their own difficulties here. Economically the retention by the buyer of the income payment contributes to the financing return he makes and the UK tax logic extends to recognising these economics by adjusting upwards the amount of repo interest that the repo seller is deemed by section 730A to be paying (section 730A(9)).

## *Manufactured Dividends*

When securities are transferred, there will always be income rights attached to them in terms of interest or dividend rights. The seller will wish to be compensated for the income which has been paid on the securities during the repo term, effectively so as to place him in the same position he would have been in had he not sold the securities. This is generally achieved in one of two ways. First, the repurchase price of the securities can be adjusted to take account of any income which has been paid by the issuer on the securities; this is commonly referred to as the "roll-up" procedure and is, as mentioned above, common in "buy/sell" agreements. Secondly, it is possible for the buyer actually to pay to the seller an amount representative of the income paid by the issuer, known as a manufactured dividend.

The UK tax rules generally approach this area by treating a manufactured dividend for tax purposes in a way that is so far as possible analogous to the real dividend it represents, with various withholding consequences discussed below. The withholding rules are to be found in Schedule 23A to the Taxes Act. And where the "roll-up procedure" is adopted, a system of deeming manufactured dividends to have been paid even though in reality they are not prevents the parties from avoiding the withholding tax consequences that would have arisen if manufactured dividends had actually been paid.

The provisions relating to deemed manufactured dividends are contained in section 737A of the Taxes Act. Section 737A provides that where under a repo agreement:

- a (real) dividend which becomes payable is not received by the seller;

- there is no requirement under the agreement to pay a manufactured dividend to the seller on or before the date the repurchase price becomes due; and

- it is reasonable to assume that in arriving at the repurchase price, account was taken of the fact that the seller did not receive the real dividend;

the buyer shall, on the date the repurchase price becomes due, be treated as if he were required to pay a manufactured dividend representative of the real dividend to the seller, and did in fact make a payment of that amount. Thus to the extent that a withholding tax obligation arises under Schedule 23A, the buyer must account for the tax due to the Inland Revenue. Whilst in more highly structured transactions it can sometimes be difficult to be certain that all of the conditions (particularly the last) are fulfilled, it is beyond doubt that section 737A extends to cases where the receipt and retention of dividends by the repo buyer is demonstrably reflected in the repurchase price, such as a normal "buy/sell" agreement.

The withholding rules differ as between three types of securities: UK equities (shares of UK resident issuers), other UK securities (debt securities of UK resident issuers) and overseas securities (shares and securities of non-UK resident issuers). One important feature of this categorisation is that quoted bearer eurobonds issued by UK resident entities which are held in a recognised clearing system count as overseas securities, rather than UK securities, for this purpose. The Inland Revenue has produced a set of guidance notes for each category of securities which provide a helpful general treatment of the legislation as well as indication of how the Inland Revenue expect the withholding rules to be operated in practice.

## UK equities

Where a real dividend is paid on a UK equity, there is no withholding tax and, since April 1999, no obligation on the UK company to make a payment of advance corporation tax. The payment nonetheless carries a tax credit for UK recipients of an amount equal to one-ninth of the dividend. Accordingly a dividend of 90 represents, for a UK taxpayer, income of 100 on which tax of 10 has been paid. Recipients of UK dividends who are resident in jurisdictions whose tax treaties provide for them to have an entitlement to a payment in respect of the tax credit on UK dividends which they receive will generally find their entitlement to such a payment fully, or virtually fully, extinguished by the withholding tax for which the treaty provides.

On paying manufactured dividends representing dividends on UK equities, a repo buyer will not need to account for any withholding tax (Schedule 23A, paragraph 2 Taxes Act). The manufactured dividend will not be deductible for UK tax purposes unless the repo buyer is a dealer in securities for the purposes of section 95 of the Taxes Act. This is logical, since such taxpayers are themselves by virtue of section 95 taxable on the actual dividends on the UK equities which the manufactured payments represent. A non-trading corporate taxpayer would not however be taxable on the real dividend on the UK equities (section 208 of the Taxes Act), and so cannot be surprised to find a manufactured payment representing UK dividend income non-deductible.

One interesting feature arises in relation to repos of UK equities where the repo buyer retains the dividends under the "roll-up procedure". As described above, the dividend amount forms the basis of an adjustment to the amount of interest which is deemed to have been paid by the repo seller. For UK equities, the adjustment operates by reference to the dividend plus the one-ninth tax credit (sections 730A(9) and 737C(3)(b)), and this is apparently so even if, for example, neither the repo buyer nor the repo seller is or would have been in a position to turn the tax credit to account in any way. This is perhaps a surprisingly generous result for repo sellers who are entitled to deductions for repo interest they are deemed to pay.

A series of anti-avoidance provisions prevents repo transactions from manipulating the incidence of tax credits on dividends arising on UK equities. Section 231B, although not specifically targeted at repo transactions, inhibits certain arrangements to pass on the value of tax credits in respect of UK dividends to persons who would not have been entitled to them if they had received the dividends direct. Section 231AA will generally inhibit a repo buyer from obtaining tax credit where UK equities have been the subject of a repo. Finally, section 231BB will prevent a repo seller from obtaining a tax credit where a manufactured dividend on UK equities is paid, or deemed to be paid, to him by the repo buyer but the seller has transferred ex-div shares to the buyer.

Before October 1997 the sale and repurchase of equities of UK incorporated companies was likely to incur stamp duty or stamp duty reserve tax on both the sale and repurchase at the rate of ½% each (in practice UK transfer taxes are not usually a constraint with equities issued by companies incorporated outside the UK). This acted as a significant discouragement to repos over UK equities. However, parallel reliefs from stamp duty and stamp duty reserve tax (sections 80C and 89AA of the Finance Act 1996) now enable repos of UK equities to be accomplished without stamp duty/stamp duty reserve tax cost. The conditions for the relief include a requirement that the repo buyer should not take any price risk on the equities during the repo period and that the transaction is otherwise on arm's length terms. It is also a requirement that the transaction be effected on a stock exchange fulfilling various characteristics: typically this will be the London Stock Exchange. In practice this condition is designed to enable the Inland Revenue to track that the conditions for relief are met properly in all cases.

## UK securities

The withholding rules in Schedule 23A paragraph 3 relating to UK debt securities also attempt to arrive at a treatment of the manufactured payment which reflects the treatment of the real interest payment. A withholding on account of income tax is required on the part of a repo buyer who makes (or is deemed by section 737A to make) a manufactured payment on UK securities if the real interest payment would itself have been paid under deduction of income tax. Where, however, the interest payment would itself have been made gross, a manufactured payment which represents that interest can similarly be paid gross: paragraph 3A of Schedule 23A. In fact, however, it will be rare for income tax to fall to be deducted under these provisions. Most UK resident companies will, if they are planning to raise funds through the issue of longer-term securities, do so by issuing quoted eurobonds which will predominantly be held in a recognised clearing system. And, if they do so, those securities will as mentioned above count as "overseas securities" rather than "UK securities" for Schedule 23A withholding purposes. Gilts issued by HM Treasury are UK securities, but they also generally pay interest gross and in any event manufactured interest on gilts is specifically carved out from Schedule 23A withholding by paragraph 3A of Schedule 23A.

Paragraph 3 withholding may however occasionally be encountered, for example in relation to long term registered debenture stock or local authority debt. Where it is, a UK resident corporate repo buyer which received the real underlying interest payment would be able to take credit for income tax suffered on that payment in computing the amount of tax to be accounted for to the Inland Revenue. As with manufactured overseas dividends (see below), a "reverse charge" operates in circumstances where the interest manufacturer (repo buyer) does not have any UK tax presence and will accordingly not in practice be likely to operate any UK withholding procedures even if he was within their theoretical scope. In such a case the recipient of the manufactured interest has to operate the withholding tax as a surrogate for the manufacturer (Schedule 23A paragraph 3(5)).

A tax deduction is available for the amount of any interest paid or deemed by virtue of section 737A to have been paid in respect of United Kingdom securities which is not otherwise deductible: paragraph 3(2)(c) of Schedule 23A. However, a deduction in respect of manufactured interest will normally be available to corporate taxpayers in any event under the terms of section 97 of the Finance Act 1996, as part of the self contained code applicable to a company's "loan relationships".

## *Overseas securities*

Overseas securities form perhaps the most frequently encountered category of securities to which the Schedule 23A withholding rules apply: a dividend or interest payment on an overseas security is often termed a MOD. Importantly, however, the rules relating to withholding on account of UK tax have been significantly relaxed by the removal of any obligation to apply UK withholding in any case where the MOD is an interest payment on debt securities. Under paragraph 2B of the applicable regulations (the Income Taxes (Manufactured Overseas Dividends) Regulations 1993 SI 1993 no. 2004), MODs on debt securities may generally (except where a UK collecting agent is involved) be paid gross, leaving the withholding rules in Schedule 23A described below applicable only to transactions involving equities.

The effect of Schedule 23A is to impose an obligation on the payer of a MOD relating to overseas equities to deduct "relevant withholding tax" on the payment of a MOD (para 4(2)). Relevant withholding tax means, broadly speaking, tax equal to the amount of the overseas tax which would have been deducted from the gross amount of the real dividend. Alternatively, if the payer of the MOD is neither UK resident nor makes the payment through a UK branch, it is the recipient of the MOD who, as with UK securities as described above, is liable to account for the same tax for which the payer would have been liable had he been UK resident under a "reverse charge" procedure. If tax is withheld pursuant to these provisions, the recipient will, if UK resident or carrying on a trade through a UK branch or agency, be treated as having received a real overseas dividend (rather than a MOD) from which an amount of overseas tax has been deducted and for which a tax credit is available.

It therefore follows that if dividends on the overseas equities can be paid by the issuer without deduction of tax at source, the rate of relevant withholding tax will be nil. Such securities are referred to as "gross-paying" securities and standard form documentation common in the market provides for the MOD to be paid by the buyer to the seller on the security's coupon date (see Chapter 7). It also follows that if the repo does not cross a dividend payment date the buyer will not be required to pay a MOD (because the Schedule 23A obligation arises only on actual payment) and the associated withholding tax problems are, therefore, avoided.

The applicable regulations (SI 1993 no. 2004) make detailed provision for mitigating the rates of withholding tax which would otherwise be applicable as a result of paragraphs 4(2) and 4(3) of Schedule 23A.

As a result of the regulations, the withholding tax obligation imposed by the primary legislation in Schedule 23A may be extinguished where the real dividend is paid net, but the relevant interest or dividend article in any treaty concluded between the country of the issuer and the UK either reduces the withholding tax on the real dividend to nil or provides for a full repayment or refund of the tax withheld. In these circumstances, the relevant withholding tax on the MOD is likewise reduced to nil.

There is also a further exemption, known as the "domestic-to-domestic" exemption. This applies to exempt or reduce the relevant withholding tax charge where the MOD2 procedure (see below) cannot be used and the rate of tax on the overseas securities, if paid to a beneficial owner resident in the same jurisdiction as the issuer, would have been either nil or less than that provided for in the relevant treaty with the UK. The "domestic" rate can then be taken as the rate of relevant withholding tax.

## The MOD2 Procedure

There is also a procedure under the Regulations, based on the UK's network of double tax treaties, which enables MODs on net-paying overseas equities to be paid gross. The procedure is known as the MOD2 procedure. This is a certification exercise which requires:

- the seller to be resident in a country with a double tax treaty with the UK;

- the treaty to contain an "other income" article. In some treaties, such as the UK/Germany treaty, the article requires the beneficial owner to be "subject to tax", which precludes the use of the MOD2 procedure for certain tax-exempt bodies;

- the seller to certify its tax residence and beneficial entitlement to the MOD on a prescribed form (a MOD2);

- the seller's "home" fisc also to certify the seller's tax residence.

The MOD2 procedure was developed with the securities lending regime very firmly in mind and, for a number of reasons, is less helpful in the case of repo, which is different in certain respects. For example, the range of counterparties is not only vastly more extensive in the repo markets but the relationships between sellers and buyers are considerably more tenuous and a repo may sometimes be concluded on a "one-off" basis only. The MOD2 procedure would be unworkable in these circumstances. Repo transactions are also typically of much shorter duration than securities loans and this inevitably increases the overall volume of administration. Furthermore, repo deals, unlike securities loans, do not require "matching" of counterparties and can be agreed almost instantaneously, so the opportunity is not always there to obtain requisite documentation in advance.

The 1993 regulations also make specific provision in relation to various other important matters, including the ability to claim double tax relief for tax withheld under the Schedule 23A system insofar as applied to MODs. A particular category of taxpayer is the "approved UK intermediary" or AUKI. Applying for AUKI status enables an entity to obtain greater flexibility in the use of credits for tax withheld on real overseas dividends and MODs received, at the cost of exposure to an Inland Revenue audit procedure to check that the rules are properly being complied with. "Approved UK collecting agents" are another category of persons with particular responsibilities under the Schedule 23A scheme in relation to MODs.

A tax deduction is available in respect of MODs paid under the Schedule 23A withholding procedure on the grounds that they represent "annual payments" for tax purposes. Where withholding is not required, the payment will not rank as an annual payment but tax relief will in appropriate cases be available for the amount as a trading expense. In relation to debt securities, a special provision in the "loan relationships" provisions in the Finance Act 1996 (section 97) will normally enable corporate taxpayers to obtain relief for manufactured interest payments made (or deemed by section 737A to be paid) on overseas securities.

## *Anti-avoidance provisions*

Although repo transactions can in principle be used to obtain tax advantages, the statutory framework is now such that the basic rules generally afford enough control over the tax treatment of the transactions, without the need for specific anti-avoidance provisions. Indeed, some specific anti-avoidance provisions are specifically disapplied in the case of most repo transactions, such as the anti-bondwashing provisions of sections 731 to 735 (see section 731(2A) to (2E).

Some specific provisions designed to check abuses in relation to tax credits on UK dividends on UK equities are mentioned above. As for overseas securities, insofar as repo transactions can be used to affect the incidence of tax credits for overseas tax suffered, the general rules prevent repos from manipulating the tax rules to an unacceptable degree. For example, in the case of debt securities, section 807A of the Taxes Act will prevent credit being taken for overseas tax on interest to the extent the interest accrues outside a taxpayer's period. And in the case of overseas equities, a system of "matching" under the 1993 regulations ensures that tax credits flow through to the person who can be regarded as the ultimate recipient of the dividend: in a straightforward repo case, normally the repo seller rather than the repo buyer.

# Chapter 10

# UK Regulation of Repo

## Introduction

This chapter reviews the regulatory framework within which the international repo market operates. As the international market is concentrated in London, we have limited our coverage to the UK regulatory system. If you are familiar with the UK regulatory system and are interested only in the end calculations for capital charges, you should go straight to the final section of this chapter.

## The Regulatory System in the UK

The pattern of financial regulation in the UK, as elsewhere, is fairly complex. Regulatory requirements differ depending on:

- whether an institution is a credit institution (e.g. a commercial bank, merchant bank or building society) or an investment firm (e.g. a securities house);

- whether the business being conducted is classed as banking (e.g. deposit-taking and lending) or trading (buying and selling of securities and derivatives for short-term gain, including the underwriting of new issues);

- the nature of the institution's counterparty (e.g. another wholesale market participant or a professional investor).

There are also different areas of regulatory requirement, covering:

- **authorisation** to conduct business, both initial authorisation and ongoing prudential supervision;

- **conduct of business** rules; and

- **capital adequacy** requirements (strictly speaking, capital adequacy is one of the criteria for initial authorisation and a requirement of ongoing prudential supervision, but for convenience it has been tackled separately here).

The current regulatory framework is in the process of being revised and major changes will be brought about by new legislation which is expected to come into force during 2000 (to be known as the Financial Services and Markets Act and related secondary legislation). The most significant change is the introduction of a single regulator, the Financial Services Authority (the FSA) (formerly the Securities and Investments Board (SIB)) which will replace the existing self-regulating organisations (the Securities and Futures Authority (SFA), the Investment Management Regulatory Organisation (IMRO) and the Personal Investment Authority (PIA)). The FSA will regulate all investment and banking activity in the UK. Some of these changes have already been enacted: in June 1998 responsibility for the supervision of banks and for the wholesale market supervision regime was transferred from the Bank of England to the FSA under the Bank of England Act 1998.

Repo activity will continue to be subject to a requirement for authorisation under the new legislation. We have been able to describe the major changes which are impending but, at the time of going to press, a number of largely technical issues remained to be resolved.

## Authorisation to Conduct Repo Business in the UK

### Overview

In the UK, financial institutions must be authorised to conduct repo business under one of four regimes:

### The Financial Services Act 1986 (FS Act)

The FS Act lays down the general requirement that anyone conducting investment business, including repo, in the UK must be authorised by one of the self-regulating organisations or the FSA, unless they fall within an exemption. There are exemptions for participants covered by each of the three other regimes outlined below.

### Wholesale Markets Supervision Regime (WMS)

Financial institutions, whether investment firms or credit institutions, can apply for inclusion on a list maintained by the FSA under Section 43 of the FS Act in respect of their wholesale business, including repo. In respect of that business, such listed institutions will then be exempt from the need for authorisation under the FS Act, subject to certain conditions and limitations, and that business will instead be regulated by the FSA under the Wholesale Markets Supervision regime.

### EU Banking Co-ordination Directives (BCD)

Since January 1, 1993, **credit institutions** authorised by a competent authority in another European Union (EU) country to conduct repo business, whether they are incorporated in that country or outside the EU, can rely on that single authorisation without requiring further authorisation for that business in any other EU country. They are subject to the supervisory regime of the EU country in which they have been authorised rather than the EU country in or into which they are operating. This right is contained in the European First and Second Banking Co-ordination Directives[1] as implemented into English law by statutory instrument[2].

### Investment Services Directive (ISD)

Since January 1, 1996, a similar regime has applied to **investment firms**. Under the ISD[3], investment firms authorised by a competent authority in another EU country to conduct repo business, whether they are incorporated in that country or outside the EU, are able to rely on that single authorisation to conduct that business in any other EU country without further authorisation. As in the case of credit institutions they are subject to the supervisory regime of the EU country in which they have been authorised rather than the EU country in or into which they are operating.

[1] *First and Second EC Council Directives on the co-ordination of laws, regulations and administrative provisions relating to the taking up and pursuit of the business of credit institutions. (Nos. 77/780/EEC and 89/646/EEC).*
[2] *Banking Coordination (Second Council Directive) Regulations 1992 (SI 1992/3218)*
[3] *Council Directive on investment services in the securities field (No. 93/22/EEC)*

Major financial institutions conduct a wide range of business, some of which inevitably crosses the boundaries of the different pieces of legislation. For this reason, it is very common for institutions to be subject to more than one regulator. In order to avoid duplication of financial reporting and capital adequacy requirements, procedures have been agreed between the various regulators to select one of them as the lead regulator for each institution subject to more than one set of prudential rules. The rest of this section looks in greater detail at each of the regimes outlined above.

## The Financial Services Act 1986 (FS Act)

### Scope of the FS Act

The FS Act enacts the regulatory framework for the financial services industry. This legislation was intended to establish a comprehensive framework of protection for retail investors in the UK. Section 3 of the FS Act prohibits any person from carrying on 'investment business' in the UK unless he is an 'authorised person' or an 'exempted person' (including listed institutions under the WMS regime) or authorised pursuant to the BCD or ISD regimes (see below).

### Definition of Investment Business

The relevance of the FS Act prohibition to those entering into repo business arises from the definition of 'investment business' in Schedule 1 to the FS Act. Although the FS Act was intended primarily to protect retail investors, the definition of investment business is wide enough to encompass some largely professional markets such as the repo market. Investment business includes buying and selling investments (as principal or agent), arranging deals in investments, managing investments and giving investment advice. 'Investments' are defined in turn to include bonds, CDs, government or local authority securities, and other debt instruments.

From this it would seem that anybody transacting repo business would need to be authorised or exempt. However, the FS Act prohibition is not intended to catch 'end-users', but instead only those for whom repo is an integral part of their business. Accordingly, a participant dealing as principal is only required to be authorised or exempt if:

> '(a) he holds himself out as willing to enter into transactions of that kind [buying or selling investments] at prices determined by him generally and continuously rather than in respect of each particular transaction; or
>
> (b) he holds himself out as engaging in the business of buying investments with a view to selling them, and those investments are or include investments of the kind to which the transaction relates; or
>
> (c) he regularly solicits members of the public for the purpose of inducing them to enter as principals or agents into transactions [buying or selling investments] and the transaction is, or is to be, entered into as a result of his having solicited members of the public in that manner.'[4]

The position has been complicated by the implementation of the ISD. Even if a repo participant's activities do not constitute investment business because the firm does not fall within paragraphs (a), (b) or (c) above, it will still require authorisation if it is providing an

---

[4] *FS Act Schedule 1 Part III, paragraph 17(1)*

investment service for third parties on a professional basis. Investment services include dealing in transferable securities (which includes most equities and bonds which are likely to be repoed) and money market instruments[5].

The result of all this is that the regular participants in the repo market, other than end-users, are likely to be conducting investment business for the purposes of the FS Act and will need to be authorised or exempt.

## Initial Authorisation

Authorisation to conduct investment business may be (and usually is) obtained by joining a recognised self-regulating organisation (SRO). The FSA and the SROs are financed and run by market practitioners. Other means of obtaining authorisation are specified in the FS Act but these are less common for the participants in this market and will not be considered further here.

There are a number of SROs which may be relevant and the decision of which one to join will largely be determined by the general nature of the business which the relevant entity intends to conduct. The most relevant one for repo participants in the UK will be the Securities and Futures Authority (SFA) which regulates securities and derivatives business.

## Ongoing Prudential Supervision

In order to obtain authorisation, an applicant must demonstrate that it is a fit and proper person to carry on investment business of the kind and scale in respect of which it seeks authorisation.[6] In assessing whether an applicant is fit and proper, SFA will take into account the following matters -

- the firm's proposed activities and roles;
- the directors, management and staff of the firm and the structure of the group of which the firm is a member;
- the integrity, competence and financial soundness of the firm and its controllers;
- any matter which may have harmed or may harm the SFA's good standing and reputation.

On joining an SRO, an institution becomes subject to prudential supervision by that body and must comply with its financial, conduct of business, client money and custody rules, which are designed to protect investors using that institution's services.

The financial rules applicable to an SFA member firm depend on whether or not the firm is an "investment firm" for the purposes of the ISD. Most repo participants will be investment firms, since their regular occupation or business will be the provision of investment services for third parties on a professional basis[7] and we will therefore only consider the rules applicable to investment firms.[8]

---

[5] *ISD, Article 2(2)*          [6] *SFA rule 2-2*
[7] *ISD, Article 2(2)*          [8] *contained in Chapter 10 of the SFA rules*

These rules require firms to:

- maintain adequate capital to cover the risks of their business;
- operate proper systems of internal control over their financial risks and their clients' assets;
- maintain adequate and up-to-date accounting records;
- submit financial reporting statements to the SFA and notify important financial matters to the SFA immediately; and
- have an audit by an independent accountant of the annual financial report submitted to the SFA.

Conduct of business rules are discussed in a later section.

## Sanctions for breach of FS Act

Carrying on investment business without the required authorisation under the FS Act is a criminal offence and can be penalised by imprisonment, fines, orders for compensation or the return of profits. In addition, any agreement relating to unauthorised business will be unenforceable against the counterparty (although will be enforceable by the counterparty against the offending firm).

## Wholesale Markets Supervision Regime (WMS)
### Overview

The Wholesale Markets Supervision regime and the exemption it confers from the need to seek authorisation under the FS Act was intended to preserve the Bank of England's traditional role as supervisor of the foreign exchange and money markets. This reflected the importance of such markets to the commercial banks which, prior to the transfer of supervisory responsibility to the FSA, fell within the Bank of England's area of statutory responsibility, as well as the authority and experience which the Bank of England had acquired in such markets and the need to keep such professional markets free of regulation which is intended to protect retail investors only.

Responsibility for the WMS regime was transferred from the Bank of England to the FSA under the Bank of England Act 1998.

## Legal Status of the WMS

As noted earlier, the WMS regime is non-statutory. The FSA therefore has to enforce the regime by a combination of suasion, the threat of withdrawing exemption from the FS Act and use of its powers under banking supervision legislation.

## Listed Institutions

The WMS exemption from the requirement to obtain authorisation under the FS Act is granted to 'listed money market institutions', which are those institutions appearing on a list maintained by the FSA for the purposes of Section 43 of the FS Act. The institutions eligible for admission to the list, subject to FSA approval, are primarily banks (and potentially building societies), financial institutions requiring authorisation under the FS Act, money brokers and others whose main business involves operations on the wholesale money markets.

## Scope of Exemption

The exemption from FS Act authorisation for listed institutions is not absolute. Only those transactions specified in Schedule 5 to the FS Act benefit from the exemption. Under Schedule 5, repo (including sell/buy-backs) will generally be exempt from transactions where the maturity is within a year. However, it is also necessary that the sale price of the securities in a repo should be at least £100,000 or its equivalent in other currencies, if:

- the counterparty is unlisted; or
- the listed institution is acting as an agent for an unlisted person; or
- the listed institution is merely arranging a repo, where the repo being arranged is not between two listed counterparties.

It is apparent that the vast majority of repos entered into by a listed institution are eligible to benefit from exemption from the FS Act.

A listed institution proposing to enter into a transaction falling outside the exemption will require separate authorisation under the FS Act if that transaction constitutes the carrying on of investment business in the UK. Of course, most if not all listed institutions will be conducting a wide range of business, some of which will inevitably extend beyond the boundaries of the exemption. For this reason, it is very common for listed institutions to be members of an SRO and subject to that SRO's regulation in addition to FSA supervision under the WMS regime. As already noted, the concept of lead regulation is utilised to avoid overlapping prudential rules.

Listed institutions are required to warn their counterparties of the loss of FS Act protection if the transactions will be exempt from the FS Act, and that the transactions will be subject to the London Code of Conduct (see below) instead. If a transaction is entered into with a counterparty above the minimum size, the exempt status will apply to all further transactions with that counterparty, whether above or below the minimum size, over the following 18 months.

## Initial Authorisation

In order to be supervised by the FSA under the WMS regime and gain exemption from the FS Act, all that is required in formal terms is for an institution to be entered by the FSA on a list maintained for the purposes of identifying who is exempt from the FS Act under Section 43 of that Act.

In order to obtain admission to the list, the applicant must satisfy the FSA that it is financially sound and has appropriate ownership and structure, and managerial and operational resources to undertake the relevant activity on a regular basis.[9] In the case of an EEA institution which is seeking to rely on the ISD passport, the FSA may not take into account any factor relating to the applicant's fitness for inclusion in the list, financial standing or any other matter which is the responsibility of the home supervisor under the BCD or ISD.

---

[9] *Section B of the regulation of wholesale cash and OTC derivative markets under section 43 of the FS Act (known as the "Grey Paper") published by the FSA in June 1999*

### Ongoing Prudential Supervision

Listed institutions become subject to FSA regulation under the WMS regime in respect of that part of their business which is exempt from the FS Act authorisation requirement. The relevant regulation is contained in the Grey Paper. This lays down capital adequacy and financial reporting requirements and, in the London Code of Conduct[10] incorporated in the Grey Paper, conduct of business rules (such as dealing procedures and requirements relating to the sending of confirmations, recording of telephone trades and the use and prompt execution of standard form documentation). The conduct of business rules are discussed in the next section.

## EC Banking Co-ordination Directives (BCD) and Investment Services Directive (ISD)

### Scope of the BCD and ICD

In addition to those entities which are exempt from the requirement to obtain FS Act authorisation, certain EU institutions are excluded from the requirement by virtue of the BCD and ISD which form part of a package of European Directives designed to facilitate the creation of a single market in financial services in the EU. The BCD covers banking business and the ISD covers investment business. Both terms are explained below.

This legislation creates the concept of a single authorisation (or 'passport') for credit institutions and investment firms which enables them to establish branches or provide services throughout the EU. The authorisation is sought from the institution's **home** country, which will generally be the Member State in which it is incorporated or has its head office. All other Member States are required to recognise the authorisation, so that separate authorisation is not required to conduct business or establish branches in any other Member State. In addition to authorisation of the institution, a home State is solely responsible for the capital adequacy and prudential supervision of the authorised business, leaving the **host** country (in which the relevant services are to be provided or branch established) responsible only for certain conduct of business rules.

In the UK, this has the effect that the FS Act requirement for authorisation or exemption will not apply to European institutions carrying on investment activities which are subject to home authorisation by another Member State.

### Credit Institutions and Banking Business

The Second Banking Co-ordination Directive (2BCD) on "credit institutions" (broadly, banks and building societies) provides the single passport for banking activities. The 2BCD was implemented in the UK by regulations which came into force on January 1, 1993.[11]

The passport extends only to the activities specified in the Directives, although the range of those activities is broader than simply traditional banking business and would seem to cover

---

[10] *The London Code of Conduct for principals and broking firms in the wholesale markets, published by the FSA in June 1999*

[11] *The Banking Coordination (Second Council Directive) Regulations 1992*

most repo business by credit institutions: the list of eligible activities includes 'trading for own account or for account of customers in money market instruments [and] transferable securities'; 'money broking'; and 'portfolio management and advice'.

Provided, therefore, that a credit institution is authorised to enter into repo business in its home State, the FSA will not prohibit it from carrying on those activities in the UK. It will still, however, be subject to UK conduct of business rules - either the SRO rules or, if the transactions fall within the WMS regime (see above), the FSA Grey Paper.

## Investment Firms and Investment Business

The equivalent passport was conferred on investment firms by the ISD which was required to be implemented throughout the EU by January 1, 1996. The ISD was implemented in the UK by regulations[12] which came into force on January 1, 1996. The passport entitles an investment firm to carry on business on a cross-border basis, either through the establishment of a branch or by the provision of investment services from its home member state into another. An investment firm is a firm which provides an "investment service" to third parties on a professional basis. Investment service is broadly defined and covers dealing as principal, agent or broker in transferable securities and money market instruments and consequently includes repo business.

## Initial Authorisation

Under both the 2BCD and the ISD, an institution seeks authorisation from the competent authority in its home country (see above) to conduct specified banking or investment business. Each EU country is required to designate an authority which is competent for this purpose. Where authorisation is granted and the institution intends to conduct the same business in other EU countries, it only has to notify the competent authorities in its home country, naming the country in which it proposes to operate, describing the business to be conducted and, if it wishes to establish branches, the branch management and organisational structure. The competent authorities in the home country have three months in which to notify the competent authorities in the host country if branches are going to be established, or one month if business is going to be conducted cross-border. The home country authorities can veto the establishment of an overseas branch on the grounds of doubts about the institution's financial position or administrative structure, subject to judicial review. The host country authorities have up to two months in which to prepare to regulate the new branch and notify the firm of the rules to which it will be subject.

## Ongoing prudential supervision

The responsibility for ongoing prudential supervision rests with the competent authorities in the home country, leaving the host country responsible only for certain conduct of business rules.

There are a number of points worth emphasising about the scope of the BCD and ISD. The passport is only available to institutions which are incorporated or established in the EU.

---

[12] *The Investment Services Regulations 1995*

Therefore, for example, a UK branch of a US-incorporated institution cannot benefit from the passport. Secondly, even if an activity falls within the scope of the relevant Directive, it will not benefit from the passport unless it is specifically authorised by the home EU country. Finally, if an activity falls outside the scope of the Directive, it will not generally benefit from the passport and a credit institution or investment firm must continue to seek authorisation in EU countries in which it wishes to operate.

## Conduct of Business Rules in the UK

### Current rules

The conduct in the UK of the wholesale business activities (including repo) of a financial institution is governed by one of two regimes:

- Wholesale Markets Supervision regime of the FSA, which covers listed investment firms and credit institutions (see above). The WMS conduct of business rules are set out in the FSA's London Code of Conduct;

- for investment firms and credit institutions not subject to the WMS regime, conduct of business is governed by the SRO from which they have sought authorisation under the FS Act (see above), which in the repo market will usually be the SFA.

In addition, certain rules of the FSA apply to all participants whether listed institutions under the WMS, credit institutions or investment firms.

### Wholesale Markets Supervision Regime

The conduct of business rules which apply under the WMS regime were originally set out in the London Code of Conduct included within the Bank of England's 1988 Grey Paper. The Code is a consolidation of a set of rules which were drawn up over some two decades by the representatives of London banks and money brokers under the informal guidance of the Bank of England and communicated to the market in the form of letters to members from the British Bankers' Association (BBA) and the various associations which have represented money brokers. These rules were originally known as the 'O'Brien Letters' after the original letters from the BBA which were signed by the then chairman of the BBA, Lord O'Brien.

The London Code of Conduct has subsequently been revised and reissued in May 1990 and May 1992, to incorporate responses to criticism of money brokers in the wake, first, of the local authority swaps fiasco and then of the closure of the Bank of Credit and Commerce International (BCCI), in July 1995 following the implementation of the ISD and, most recently, in June 1999 by the FSA following the transfer of responsibility for the WMS regime to the FSA.

When the London Code was revised in July 1995, as well as introducing changes required by the ISD, the Bank of England used the opportunity to make broader revisions to the Code. The principal revisions were to the section on controls, with a new and detailed set of requirements under the heading 'Know your Counterparty'. The Code strikes a balance between, on the one hand, ensuring that market professionals have sufficient control procedures to minimise risks associated with dealing with customers of the wholesale markets (other than market professionals) and, on the other hand, emphasising the responsibility of those customers for their own actions, including for any losses which they may have incurred in transactions in wholesale market products. The current edition (June 1999) of the London Code sets out 'best practice' in the wholesale markets in matters such as general standards, controls, dealing procedures, the sending of deal confirmations, the recording of telephone trades and the use of standardised documentation. The 1999 edition of the London Code replaced the Bank of England's 1995 version but did not include substantial changes.

## Gilt and Equity Repo

The London Code of Conduct endorses the Code of Best Practice for gilt repo and the Code of Best Practice for equity repo, recently issued by the Stock Lending and Repo Committee (see Chapter 3). The FSA has also made it clear in the London Code that for all types of repo, it expects the same standards to be adhered to as those set out in the Code for gilt repo, whether or not it involves gilts.

## Self-Regulating Organisations (SRO)

On joining an SRO, an institution becomes subject to prudential supervision by that body and must comply with its rules, which include conduct of business rules designed to protect investors using that institution's services.

Many of the conduct of business rules will be disapplied or relaxed where the relevant institution is dealing with a market 'professional', on the basis that such counterparties do not need the same protection as investors as they are aware of the risks being taken and are equipped to manage them. The rules of each SRO determine which categories of counterparty can be treated as 'professional' in which market.

## SFA

The SFA's Conduct of Business Rules cover all aspects of a firm's relationship with its clients. However, the applicability of the rules varies depending on the sophistication of the client. There are broadly three classes of client:

- market counterparties;
- private customers; and
- non-private customers.

It is the responsibility of the firm to decide in which category the client falls at the time of dealing.

## Market Counterparties

Market counterparties are clients who can be deemed to have the same level of sophistication as the firm dealing with them. They are defined as professionals carrying on investment business of the same description as that of the firm. Another member of the SFA can automatically be treated as a market counterparty, as can a member of an exchange in respect of any business instrument traded on that exchange and a non-UK person which regularly deals in the relevant investments off-exchange.

In view of their professional nature, market counterparties receive very little protection under the rules of the SFA.

## Private Customers

Private customers may be individuals who are not acting in the course of investment business, and may be small businesses. They can also be businesses which do not meet certain size requirements stipulated by the SFA (which are outlined in the section on non-private customers). These clients are deemed to be unsophisticated and therefore receive the maximum protection of the SFA's Conduct of Business Rules.

## Non-Private Customers

Non-private customers are governments, local authorities or public authority trusts with gross assets of GBP10 million or more, any authorised persons or listed money market institutions and companies, partnerships or unincorporated associations who meet certain size requirements. That is, if it is a company with more than 20 members it must have share capital or net assets of GBP 500,000 or more, otherwise it must have net assets of GBP 5 million or more. Non-private customers are deemed to be more sophisticated than private customers, and therefore many of the protections of the Conduct of Business Rules do not apply.

Individuals who would normally be deemed to be private customers can be treated as non-private customers if the firm believes with reasonable grounds that the individual has sufficient experience and understanding to waive the protections of the SFA's rules for private customers. Such customers are known as "experts". The individual must agree to this in writing.

Examples of the Conduct of Business Rules include:

- best execution - requiring firms to obtain the best possible price for a client;

- timely execution - requiring the prompt execution of a client's order;

- suitability - requiring the firm to consider the suitability of a transaction for a client in the light of the firm's knowledge of that client;

- customer understanding - requiring steps to be taken to enable the client to understand the risks of a transaction;

(The foregoing requirements apply only to private customers)

- advertising - requiring investment advertisements to be prepared carefully and not to be misleading, and to include risk warnings in certain circumstances; and

- unsolicited calls - restricting firms from calling clients without prior invitation.

As noted above, the application of these rules will vary depending on the category into which the client falls.

In addition to the Conduct of Business Rules, firms are bound by a set of 10 general principles which were laid down by the FSA. These general principles are there to emphasise adherence to the spirit as well as the letter of the rules.

# Financial Services Act (FS Act)

For the guidance of market practitioners, it may be worth highlighting some key provisions of the FS Act which apply in addition to the rules of the SROs and which may be relevant to the conduct of business in the repo market:

## Misleading statements and practices

Section 47 of the FS Act makes it a criminal offence to make statements intentionally or recklessly to induce a person to enter into an investment agreement. The provision also extends to creating a false impression in the market as to the price or value of the investments. This provision applies whether or not an institution is authorised, exempt or an EU credit institution acting under a single passport.

Potentially, this provision has extra-territorial effect, since it applies to statements or conduct made outside the UK if they are capable of having an effect in the UK or the false or misleading impression is created in the UK.

## Unsolicited Calls

Section 56 restricts the ability of a person to enter into investment agreements with a counterparty made in consequence of an unsolicited call made from the UK or on a person in the UK. Circumstances where unsolicited calls are permitted include calls made on various categories of professional counterparties and large corporates. Again, the restriction applies whether or not an institution is authorised, exempt or an EU credit institution acting under a single passport.

## Investment Advertisements

Section 57 restricts the issue of advertisements in the UK inviting parties to enter into investment agreements or to buy or sell investments unless the advertisement has been issued or approved by a person authorised under the FS Act, but there are exceptions for advertisements only going to professionals and large corporates. This restriction does not apply to authorised institutions, including EU credit institutions acting under a single passport, or to exempt institutions in respect of activities covered by their exemption.

A breach of section 56 or section 57 is a criminal offence and will render any investment agreement (which would include a repo agreement) entered into as a result of the unsolicited call or unauthorised investment advertisement unenforceable by the offending party (although not against the offending party).

## Impact of the ISD

The single passport available under the ISD (and BCD) does not apply to conduct of business rules. Although the home country is responsible for the ongoing prudential supervision, including the capital adequacy of any institution it has authorised, host countries continue to be responsible for supervising the conduct of that institution's business in their own domestic market. Moreover, the ISD requires EU countries to have rules which govern the conduct of business in their domestic markets by investment firms. It requires that such rules be applied in a way which takes account of the 'professional nature of the person for whom the service is provided'. Specifically, the ISD allows the host country to impose those rules which are deemed to be 'in the interest of the general good', which means that they should not:

- be discriminatory; or

- duplicate home country requirements; or

- be disproportionate to the ends to which they are directed.

The ISD requirement that the competent authorities in EU countries have conduct of business rules which are for the 'general good' and are applied in a way which takes account of the 'professional nature of the person for whom the service is provided' is seen as being fulfilled in the UK wholesale money market by the London Code of Conduct.

The key principles laid down in the ISD are those in Article 11:

- firms must act honestly and fairly in the interests of clients and the integrity of the market; they must act with due skill and diligence;

- firms must have and employ effectively the resources and procedures necessary for the proper performance of their business activities;

- firms must seek from clients information on their financial situation, investment experience and objectives;

- firms must make adequate disclosure of relevant information material to clients with whom they are dealing;

- firms must try to avoid conflicts of interest and, where these cannot be avoided, ensure fair treatment for clients; and

- firms must comply with regulatory requirements applicable to conduct of business so as to promote clients' interests and the integrity of the market.

Failure to meet any of these standards will be deemed a breach of the Code of Conduct and the conditions for listing under the WMS regime.

## The Financial Services and Markets Act

When the Financial Services and Markets Act (the FSMA) comes into force it will, as noted above, bring radical changes to the UK regulatory regime.

## Authorisation

Repo activity (including dealing, arranging advising or as part of investment management) will continue to be regulated as it will be a "regulated activity" under the FSMA. There will be a "general prohibition" on conducting a regulated activity unless the person is authorised or exempt. Breach of the general prohibition will be a criminal offence and, as under the FS Act, agreements entered into in breach of the prohibition will be unenforceable.

Authorisation will be obtained by obtaining a "permission" from the FSA to carry on one or more regulated activities.

## Wholesale Market Supervision Regime

The WMS regime will not be continued under the FSMA with the consequence that wholesale market participants cannot rely on an exemption to the requirement for authorisation. However, the FSA proposes to introduce a separate conduct of business regime for inter-professional business. It is proposed that the regime will apply to all regulated investment activities and will therefore encompass the SFA's market counterparty regime as well as the WMS regime. The conduct of business rules applicable to inter-professional business will be contained in a new code which, it is expected, will be based on the current London Code.[13]

## Conduct of business rules

The SROs' conduct of business rules will be replaced by a new set of rules to be contained in a conduct of business sourcebook[14] which will be published by the FSA.

## Market Abuse

The FSMA will introduce a new civil regime prohibiting market abuse. This is designed to protect the integrity of the financial markets and their users. The regime applies to "qualifying investments" traded on a market designated by the Treasury. "Market abuse" is defined as behaviour which is likely or (if the circumstances were known or the behaviour became commonplace) would be likely to damage the confidence of informed participants that the market in question is a true and fair market.

The new regime supplements the existing criminal law in respect of the offences of insider dealing and misleading statements and practices. The FSA is required to publish a Code of Market Conduct which will assist in determining whether particular behaviour is or is not market abuse.

The proposals for the new regime have attracted a great amount of comment and criticisms, although a detailed discussion of the proposed regime is beyond the scope of this work.

## Financial Promotion

The current investment advertisement and unsolicited calls regimes will be replaced by a single set of rules which will apply to all "financial promotion". Broadly, the FSMA will prohibit the communication of an invitation to enter into investment agreements or to buy or sell investments unless the advertisement has been issued or approved by a person authorised under the FSMA. It is expected that there will be exemptions similar to those which currently apply.

---

[13] *At the time of going to press, it is expected that a consultation draft of the new code will be published in the fourth quarter of 1999.*

[14] *At the time of going to press, it is expected that a consultation draft of the business sourcebook will be published in the fourth quarter of 1999.*

164

# Capital Adequacy Requirements in the UK

## Capital Adequacy Regimes

Capital adequacy requirements in the UK vary between institutions and depend on the legislation under which they have been authorised to conduct their business:

- investment firms operating in the UK must satisfy capital adequacy requirements set under the FS Act by the SFA;

- credit institutions based in the UK must satisfy capital adequacy requirements set out under the Banking Act by the FSA; and

- credit institutions and investment firms authorised by a competent authority in another EU country, and therefore subject to the capital adequacy requirements of their home EU country, have been permitted to offer banking services, including investment services, in the UK under the EU single passport.

The minimum capital adequacy requirements for credit institutions operating within the EC, on which the FSA and other EC banking regulators rules are based, are set out in the Solvency Ratio Directive (SRD) and Own Funds Directive (OFD).

Minimum capital requirements for investment firms are prescribed in the EU Capital Adequacy Directive (the CAD), which was introduced at the same time as the ISD. The CAD was required to be implemented throughout the EU by January 1, 1996 and is implemented in the UK through the FSA's and SRO's capital adequacy rules. The CAD was amended in 1998 by a further directive known as CAD2.[15]

Capital requirements for banks' and investment firms' trading activities, including repo, are based on the CAD (as amended by CAD2).

As with the SRD and OFD for banks, one of the aims of the CAD was to prescribe minimum capital requirements for all investment firms in the EU so as to prevent regulatory arbitrage through exploiting differences in different capital regimes in the member states. A further objective was to establish a level playing field between banks and investment firms so that banks would not be penalised by higher capital costs for performing the same activities as their investment firm competitors. However, at least in the UK, the directive has been implemented separately by the SFA and the FSA and there are some discrepancies between the two regimes. The capital treatment of repo trading for both credit institutions and investment firms depends on whether a transaction falls within the "trading book" or the "banking book".

As its name suggests, the trading book covers an institution's short term trading and related hedging activities, including normal repo activities.

The banking book includes traditional banking activities such as deposit-taking and long term investment, but would also include a repo which does not fall in the trading book, e.g. a transaction which was not entered into for trading purposes.

---

[15] European Parliament and Council Directive 98/31/EC of 22 June 1998

A repo transaction will give rise to a potential counterparty risk charge to reflect the risk of counterparty default and, for the seller, a position risk charge to reflect the market risk to which it is subject in the event of a fluctuation in the value of the securities which it has sold on repo terms.

## A. FSA capital adequacy rules for banks

## Trading book: counterparty risk

The trading book of a bank includes:[16]

> exposures due to repurchase agreements and securities and commodities lending which are based on securities or commodities included in the trading book; and

> exposures due to reverse repos and securities and commodities borrowing transactions.

Within the trading book, there is a distinction between documented and undocumented transactions. If the FSA considers that the nature of a bank's repo business is such that risks are significant, the FSA reserves the right to impose a higher capital requirement, which may take the form of treating all such transactions as undocumented repos or reverse repos.

### (i) Documented transactions

Special treatment is given to counterparty risk for repos or reverse repos in the trading book, provided that the documentation includes both:

> • a netting agreement which provides for the claims of the bank to be set off automatically and immediately against the claims of the counterparty in the event of the latter's default; and

> • a variation margin provision, i.e. a right for the bank to call for variation margin daily when there is a material adverse move against the counterparty.

If both of these requirements are not met, the forward leg of the contract is treated as an undocumented repo/reverse repo (see (ii) below).

If these requirements are met, the capital charge for counterparty risk is calculated as follows:

repo: the higher of:

zero; and

(the market value of securities sold minus the market value of collateral taken) x the counterparty risk weight x 8%

reverse repo: the higher of:

zero; and

(the market value of collateral given minus the market value of securities bought) x the counterparty risk weight x 8%

---

[16] *FSA Guide to Banking Supervisory Policy, Ch. CB*

Where a bank has entered into a series of transactions with a single counterparty, the counterparty risk requirements may be calculated on a portfolio basis as long as the bank complies with the requirements on netting of counterparty risk (see (iii) below).

The charge may be calculated in this manner regardless of the terminology used (i.e. the arrangements may be called repo/reverse repo or stock lending/stock borrowing or sell-buy/buy-sell).

## (ii) Undocumented transactions

For repos or reverse repos which do not meet the netting and variation margin requirements set out above (e.g. where the transaction is an undocumented buy-sell) a higher capital charge will generally result.

Where the bank is receiving securities in exchange for cash (or collateral), the capital requirement for the counterparty risk is calculated as follows:

- (the replacement cost of the contract plus the potential future credit exposure) x counterparty risk weight x 8%.

The replacement cost for the receipt of securities is the higher of zero and the difference between -

- the market value of the securities to be received; and
- the market value of collateral.

The potential future credit exposure is the contracted value for forward delivery multiplied by a risk cushion factor (RCF) applicable to the securities (which varies from 0.25% to 6% according to the type and maturity of the securities), or to the collateral if its RCF is higher.

Where the bank is receiving cash in exchange for securities, the capital requirement for the counterparty risk is calculated as:

- (the replacement cost of the contract plus the potential future credit exposure) x counterparty risk weight x 8%.

The replacement cost for the receipt of cash equals the higher of zero and the difference between:

- the market value of collateral and
- the market value of the securities to be delivered.

The potential future credit exposure equals the RCF applicable to the securities (or to the collateral if its RCF is higher) multiplied by the contracted value for forward delivery.

## (iii) Portfolio basis/netting

Where a bank enters into a series of transactions with the same counterparty, it may report its counterparty risk exposure on a net basis provided that certain requirements are met.

The principal requirement is that the bank must use a netting agreement which contains close-out netting provisions (such as the GMRA[17]) which are enforceable in the event of the counterparty's and the bank's insolvency. This must be supported by a written, reasoned and independent legal opinion which states that, in the event of termination of the agreement due

[17] See Chapter 7

to the default, liquidation or bankruptcy (or other similar circumstances) of either the counterparty or the bank, or the member of the bank's group which is party to that agreement, the relevant courts and administrative authorities would find that the bank's claims and obligations would be limited to the net sum under:

- the law of the jurisdiction in which the counterparty is incorporated and, if a foreign branch of an undertaking is involved, also under the law of the jurisdiction in which the branch is located;

- the law that governs the individual transactions included; and

- the law that governs any contract or agreement necessary to effect the contractual netting.

ISMA has obtained legal opinions on the GMRA which satisfy these requirements in 28 jurisdictions.

The bank must also have adequate systems in place and fulfil the FSA's notification requirements.

An agreement will not constitute a netting agreement if it contains a "walk away" clause, i.e. a provision which enables a non-defaulting party to make limited payments or no payments at all to the defaulting party, even if the defaulting party is a net creditor.

## (iv) Examples[18]

### Case 1: properly documented transaction

A lends £100 cash to B, and receives a five-year bond (current mark-to-market value: £102) from B.

A and B each have a 20% counterparty risk weight.

Counterparty risk requirement for each bank to include in its capital adequacy calculation -

$$A \quad \max [\ 0,(£100 - £102)\ x\ 20\%\ x\ 8\%] = nil$$
$$B \quad \max [\ 0,(£102 - £100)\ x\ 20\%\ x\ 8\%] = £0.032$$

### Case 2: properly documented transactions calculated on portfolio basis

A lends five-year bonds (current mark-to-market valuation: £100) and US equities (current mark-to-market valuation: £100) to B and receives UK equities (current mark-to-market valuation: £97) and two-year bonds (current mark-to-market valuation: £105) from B.

A and B each have a 20% counterparty risk weight.

Counterparty risk requirement -

A    Securities and collateral paid away:

£100 + £100 = £200

Securities and collateral received: £97 + £105 = £202

Received > paid away

---

[18] taken from the FSA Guide to Banking Supervisory Policy, Ch TC

Therefore no counterparty risk requirement applies.

    B    Securities and collateral paid away:

        £97 + £105 = £202

        Securities and collateral received: £100 + £100 = £200

        Received < paid away

Therefore a counterparty risk requirement applies of

(£202 - £200) x 20% x 8%= £0.032

**Case 3: inadequate documentation** (or business of a type or volume which leads the FSA to insist on this treatment)

A lends a five-year bond (current mark-to-market value: £102) to B and receives £100 cash from B.

A and B each have a 20% counterparty risk weight.

Risk Cushion Factors:  for bond = 1.5%

                  for cash = 0%

Contracted value for forward delivery = £100

Counterparty risk requirement-

    A    Replacement cost: max [ 0,(£102 - £100)]

        Potential future exposure £100 x 1.5%

        Capital charge = (£2 + £1.50) x 20% x 8%= £0.056

    B    Replacement cost: max [ 0,(£100 - £102)]

        Potential future exposure    £100 x 1.5%

        Capital charge = £1.50 x 20% x 8%= £0.024

## *Trading book: position risk*

The repo seller is required to carry capital against market risk because of its contractual obligation to purchase equivalent securities on the repurchase date. Different rules apply to equities and debt securities reflecting the different risks (changes in the price of the equities and in interest rates respectively).

### (i) Debt securities

Debt securities are subject to a general interest rate risk charge (which reflects the risk of losses which may arise from price changes in instruments caused by parallel and non-parallel shifts in the yield curve, as well as to reflect the difficulty of constructing perfect hedges) and a specific interest rate risk charge which is charged against the individual instruments which may change in value for reasons other than movements in the yield curve of a given currency (primarily the perceived creditworthiness of the issuer).

The general market risk charge is based on net positions in the same instrument and is calculated according to the maturity, coupon and jurisdiction of the issuer.

The specific interest rate risk charge is calculated according to the type of security, e.g. government bond and its residual maturity.

## (ii) Equities

Equities are similarly subject to a general and specific risk charge. The general risk charge is intended to protect against moves in the market as a whole while the specific risk charge is against movements in particular shares.

The general market risk charge is calculated for each country on the basis of net long and short positions and is, broadly, 8% of the net position for each country.

Under the specific market risk charge, portfolios are assigned to particular bands according to a dual liquidity and diversity test and ascribed a weighting of 4% or 8%. The bank is then required to calculate a gross position for each country.

## *Banking book*

For transactions which do not fall within the trading book, different rules apply. In the banking book, assets of the bank are ascribed a risk weighting according to the perceived credit risk of the borrower (e.g. 0% for an OECD government; 20% for an OECD bank; 100% for a corporate). The value of the asset is multiplied by this risk weighting factor and then by 8% to give the capital charge.

An off-balance sheet item must be converted into a "credit equivalent amount" using an ascribed credit conversion factor. In the case of repos and reverse repos, the credit conversion factor is 100%. The credit equivalent amount is then multiplied by the appropriate risk weighting and 8%.

A repo is treated as a collateralised deposit and so no counterparty risk charge is required. However the seller must continue to report the securities as if they were still held by it. The securities are weighted according to the category of the issuer of the security and not according to the counterparty with whom the transaction has been entered into.

The treatment of a reverse repo is different to that of a repo. Reverse repos are treated as collateralised loans, with the risk being measured as an exposure to the counterparty. Where the security temporarily acquired attracts a preferential risk weighting (e.g. a Zone A government security) this is recognised as collateral and the risk weighting of the loan accordingly reduced.

# B. SFA rules

As in the case of banks, different rules apply to repos which fall in the trading book and the non-trading book.

## Trading book: counterparty risk

SFA rules define the trading book to include[19] -

"(a)  proprietary positions in financial instruments, physical commodities and commodity derivatives, which are held for resale and/or are taken on by the firm with the intention of benefiting in the short term from actual and/or expected differences between their buying and selling prices, or from other price or interest-rate variations;

(b)  positions in financial instruments, physical commodities and commodity derivatives, arising from matched principal broking;

(c)  positions taken in order to hedge other elements of the trading book;

(d)  exposures due to unsettled securities or physical commodities transactions, free deliveries, derivative transactions, repurchase, sale and buy back and securities and physical commodities lending agreements based on securities or physical commodities included in (a) to (c) above, reverse repurchase, buy and sale back and securities borrowing and physical commodities borrowing agreements based on securities or physical commodities included in (a) to (c) above; and

(e)  fees, commissions, interest and dividends which are directly related to the items included in (a) to (d) above."

SFA member firms are required to calculate a capital charge for counterparty risk and position risk.

### (i) Documented transactions

As in the case of banks, more favourable treatment applies to documented transactions than to those which are undocumented. For this purpose, a repo will be treated as documented only if:

- the securities, or physical commodities, and collateral are marked to market daily;

- the collateral may be adjusted in order to take account of material changes in the value of the securities, or physical commodities, or collateral;

- the agreement provides for the claims of the firm (collateral) to be immediately set off against the claims of the counterparty (securities/physical commodities) in the event of the latter's default; and

- such agreements are confined to their accepted and appropriate use, and are not artificial transactions, (especially those not of a short term nature).

---

[19]  SFA Rules, Chapter 9

Alternatively, if the agreement does not provide for the provision of margin, repos may nevertheless fall within the trading book if the agreement is an inter-professional one[20] provided that the other criteria set out above are satisfied.

In the case of a repo, the charge is the excess of the mark to market value of the securities over the value of adequate collateral[21] under the agreement, if the net figure is positive.

In the case of a reverse repo the capital charge is the excess of the amount paid or collateral given for the securities or physical commodities over the mark to market value of the securities or physical commodities received under the agreement, if the net figure is positive.

In either case, the counterparty exposure figure is then multiplied by the counterparty risk weighting which in turn is multiplied by 8%[22].

### (ii) Undocumented transactions

An undocumented transaction (i.e. one which does not comply with the requirements explained above) will lead to a charge which is double that which is applicable to a documented transaction.

### (iii) Netting

As in the case of banks, SFA member firms are permitted to calculate exposures on a net basis if a netting agreement is used which contains close-out netting provisions and that agreement is supported by independent legal opinions.

## Trading book: position risk

SFA member firms are required to calculate a general and specific position risk charge for securities sold on repo terms. The charge is calculated in a similar way to the equivalent FSA rules (see above).

## Non-trading book

The capital charge for a repo which does not fall within the trading book is based on the value of the securities multiplied by the counterparty risk weighting multiplied by 8%. The charge will be reduced by the amount of the purchase price, which will be "acceptable collateral"[23].

The charge for a reverse repo which does not fall within the trading book will be the amount of the purchase price multiplied by the counterparty risk weighting multiplied by 8%. The charge will be reduced by the value of the securities if they are "acceptable collateral".

---

[20] *i.e., broadly, the counterparty is a credit institution or investment firm*
[21] *"adequate collateral" includes cash and securities*
[22] *If the firm has not granted the counterparty a credit line under an approved credit management policy (ACMP), an additional charge may arise if the exposure exceeds 5% or 10% of the value of the securities (depending on the type of securities)*
[23] *broadly, cash and OECD government securities*

172

# Collateral Management, the Future of Repo?

Question: what are the similarities between the following transactions and finance facilities: repo, bonds borrowed, Target payments, derivative trading, FX margin trades, equity finance, securities lending and credit lines for securities settlement?

Possible answers include:

1. Each of them requires collateralisation;

2. They generally have an industry approved master agreement;

3. They have similar operations and settlement flows;

4. They have similar collateral administration functions.

It is partly in recognition of the last two factors that forward-thinking institutions are beginning to re-group traditional business lines that use collateral - equity, fixed income, OTC derivatives, repo - into something called "collateral trading". Instead of having fragmented business units, defined by product and geographical location, each independently managing collateral with no overall view or idea of what is available and how best to use it, the forward thinkers are creating "collateral centres of excellence." Such institutions are developing a central hub for all short-term money and capital market products. At the time of writing this, one highly rated European bank had already started calling its repo and equity finance dealers "collateral traders".

Recent headlines in the leading industry journals and magazines have captured precisely the trend toward multi-product, multi-market collateral trading and management. At the macro level, an integrated clearing and settlement infrastructure is finally being created in Europe.

Deciding which collateral should be used where can be best understood along the two dimensions of collateral usage: structural and trading. The latter's use of collateral is variable and opportunistic. The repo and securities lending markets best exemplify this. Structural use of collateral happens when securities are placed within a clearing system to obtain credit lines for timely securities settlement or for RTGS payment purposes. The skill required of collateral managers is the ability to allocate collateral sufficiently and optimally between these two activities; ensuring that the firm has sufficient eligible collateral for its structural needs but freeing up the rest for the front office to profit from. And there are numerous tools to "objectively" allocate this. For example, relative-value performance and potential lending/repo returns.

## Benefits of integrating collateral management

The first and foremost benefit of integrating collateral management activities is fundamental to any type of collateralised relationship - the ability to hedge credit risk. The problems in 1998 with emerging markets and exposures to leveraged players like hedge funds highlighted the importance of collateralised trading. The second driver for this type of trading was the introduction of the euro. The single currency gave many institutions the economies of scale necessary to look at more markets. Regional pockets of collateral began to consolidate into balance sheet positions that could be dynamically substituted on a pan-European basis. Thirdly, shrinking margins have forced aggressive institutions to 'sweat' all their assets to obtain the maximum efficiency for funding. Every asset is put to the most efficient use possible; collateral received is used again. It is estimated that effective collateral management can achieve an overall balance sheet saving of between 10 and 15 basis points, enabling firms to expand their business and handle more volume. The last benefit is for external customers who are requesting a single, composite collateralised relationship across multiple products, with the potential of cross product margining.

The development of collateral trading cannot be divorced from the macro-level consolidations in the European financial services industry. This decade has seen unprecedented merger activity within the European banking market. One of the direct effects of this on collateral trading will be the consolidation of liquidity in the dozen or so 'bulge bracket' investment banks and large European banks. They aim to become "collateral clearers" to their institutional clients and to medium to small-sized broker dealers. At the same time, the alliance of European stock exchanges is working towards a common trading platform. This will demand an integrated clearing and settlement infrastructure to replace the multiple national securities depositories and two international central securities depositories. A number of different options have been put forward as solutions to this obstacle to the continuing growth of Europe's equity and fixed-income markets.

There are, however, parts of the collateral-trading infrastructure that are proving to be difficult to harmonise. The main one for an industry that is strongly dependent on a proper legal framework is the lack of harmony between the laws of different jurisdictions for enforcement of cross-border collateral arrangements. Only three countries in the EU - Belgium, France and Luxembourg - are known to have enacted legislation specific to the use of pledged collateral or repo. A recent study under the European Union's DG11 unit concluded that the current laws and rules in the EU relating to the use of collateral are complex, inconsistent, impractical and, in important respects, out-of-date. The study disappointingly concludes that it would indeed be an ambitious undertaking to harmonise such laws throughout the EU. An alternative to forcing domestic parliamentarians to make changes in their legislation for the sake of European-wide consistency would be the development of a single master agreement to cater for the greatly expanded product range. The new European Banking Federation master agreement may assist this objective.

| Situation Today | The Future |
|---|---|
| Collateral split among different business lines each with own P&L | Centralised, cross-product and cross-market collateral business unit |
| Separate systems keep track of collateral available/pledged | A collateral data warehouse |
| Muddled settlement infrastructure in Europe | A consolidated settlement infrastructure for both bonds and equities. |
| Fragmented legal infrastructure | A multi-product master agreement and harmonised national laws in the EU |
| Standards for communication non-existent | Specific Swift message standards for collateral management available by year-end 2000. |

## From repo to collateral trading

Despite the benefits, developing an integrated collateral management business is a tough objective to achieve. This is especially difficult for those firms with well-established but separate financing desks using legacy systems. It is probably easier for a new firm either entering the business, being merged or taken over. But there are a number of options and halfway houses towards the goal of an integrated collateral trading business.

Collateral should be treated as the "hidden currency", managed and optimised on a firm-wide basis. One objective could be to establish a centre for firm-wide collateral management staffed by a mix of experienced personnel - credit, documentation, legal and repo traders. The repo desk is often positioned at the centre of a firm's trading activities - like an octopus with its tentacles reaching out to the fixed income traders, the derivatives traders, treasury and settlement. Repo traders were leveraging the firm's assets long before concepts like "asset optimisation" became known. Therefore one option is to build a firm-wide integrated collateral management business around the repo desk.

The new collateral trading group would require clearly-documented policies and procedures for management of credit risk and gathering good data. The latter is key to the success of the collateral trading desk. Pulling this data across disparate geographical locations, systems and business lines can be onerous, if not prohibitively costly. But without such a data warehouse, it would be impossible for the firm to allocate the assets optimally.

Firms for whom a centralised collateral management business is unfeasible can use a halfway house approach. This involves establishing strong links and service level agreements between the different collateral users of the firm. Such an approach demands, for example, firm-wide agreement on how the firm will source and place fixed-income collateral. It should include regular meetings between the traders and sales from the different units to leverage new and existing relationships with the firm's collateral consumers and providers.

## The out-sourcing option

The final and low-cost option for an integrated collateral management business would be to out-source it to a third party settlement and collateral agent. International central securities depositories Cedelbank and Euroclear have built sophisticated and real-time collateral management and optimisation engines for their customers. The advantage of these engines is the ability of the depository to view "all" the customer's assets in real-time - what's coming in and what needs to be delivered out. The net balance is then used to select appropriate and sufficient assets to collateralise each trade that the firm wants to settle. Users of such facilities can establish rules under which their assets can be automatically selected and delivered covering such aspects as prioritising the allocation of collateral between different deals, or rules for collateralising specific counterparts e.g. the type and quality of securities agreed with the counterpart, the minimum or maximum size of each collateral piece, the agreed haircuts and the concentration limits for different types of collateral for that counterpart.

# Chapter 12

# *Glossary of Repo Terminologies*

all-in price    The price of a bond including any accrued interest. Also known as the *dirty price.*

ask    *See offer.*

bid    The repo rate which the supplier of cash in a classic repo - who is said to be 'bidding' for collateral (not cash) - is demanding from the supplier of collateral. The lower the bid rate, the more expensive it is to acquire collateral through a repo. The opposite to *offer.*

bond borrowed    *See securities lending.*

Bond Market Association (BMA)    An American organisation representing certain sectors of the US bond market. The BMA (formerly known as the Public Securities Association or PSA) produced the standardised contract documentation (the Master Repurchase Agreement) which is used in the US domestic market following the Lombard Wall failure. This was used as a template for the GMRA which the BMA and ISMA produced for international repo.

borrower    The counterparty taking collateral and supplying cash in classic repos and sell/buy-backs, or taking a specific security and supplying collateral in securities lending. Also known as the buyer in classic repos and sell/buy- backs.

box    A bond dealer's central account with a clearing bank.

buy/sell-back    A sell/buy-back from the point of view of the counterparty who supplies cash and takes collateral.

calling the mark    The process of calling for margin to be reinstated following a mark-to-market revaluation of a repo transaction.

Capital Adequacy Directive (CAD)    One of the seven European Union directives underpinning the single passport concept, this directive substantially reduces the capital charges for most repo and reverse repo transactions (see Chapter 10).

Cedelbank    A major book-entry clearing facility for Eurocurrency and foreign securities. It is jointly owned by a large number of European banks.

Central Gilts Office    A function within the Bank of England responsible for the electronic settlement system for gilts (CGO)

classic repo    A name originated by ISMA to describe a US-style repo. A contract which commits one party to sell, and the other to buy, securities and to subsequently reverse the exchange at an agreed future date or on demand. Classic repos are carried out under a written master agreement, providing increased rights compared to undocumented sell/buy-backs. The counterparty supplying the collateral pays an agreed return to the counterparty supplying the cash (see Chapter 2). *See repo rate.*

| clearing bank | A bank holding securities on behalf of bond dealers. |
|---|---|
| closing leg | A repo is an initial sale of securities and a simultaneous agreement to repurchase them at a later date. The second transaction in a repo, the repurchase of the securities, is called the closing leg. *See opening leg.* |
| collateral | The assets supplied under the leg of a repo considered to be the least important and which effectively secure the performance of the obligations of the supplier of collateral under the other leg. In classic repo and sell/buy-backs, the collateral is considered to be the securities side of the transaction. In securities lending, the collateral will be the cash or securities supplied in exchange for the specific borrowed securities. |
| Council of Reporting Dealers Repo Sub-Committee of ISMA | The group which represents the principal dealers in the international repo market and produced the GMRA in cooperation with the Bond Market Association (BMA) (formerly the Public Securities Association (PSA)) of the US. |
| cross-border repo | *See international repo.* |
| cross-currency repo | A repo in which the cash or specific securities on one side of the exchange and the collateral on the other side are denominated in different currencies. |
| customer repo | A Fed repo in which the Federal Reserve Bank of New York invests cash in the market on behalf of its customers (other central banks and official bodies). *See system repo, Fed repo.* |
| day-to-day repo | *See open repo.* |
| deliver-out repo | A repo in which collateral is physically delivered to the supplier of cash *cf hold-in-custody (HIC) repo.* |
| delivery-against-collateral, receipt-against-payment (DAC-RAP) | A name used in the international repo market for delivery-versus-payment (DVP). |
| delivery-versus-payment (DVP) | The simultaneous exchange of securities and cash. DVP eliminates delivery risk, which is the possibility of loss because a counterparty fails to honour its side of an exchange. |
| demand repo | *See open repo.* |
| dirty price | The price of a bond including any accrued interest. Also known as an *"all-in"* price. |
| dollar repo | A repo agreement whereby the collateral given back at maturity does not have to be the same as the original one, but it can differ within certain agreed limits. It is designed to give greater flexibility to the supplier of collateral and is often used in longer-term transactions. Dollar repo is also often arranged as a repo-to-maturity. Variants are: fixed-coupon repo, yield maintenance agreement. |

178

| | |
|---|---|
| double-dipping | The fraudulent pledging or allocation of the same collateral to more than one counterparty at the same time. This is technically a risk whenever collateral is not delivered to the buyer or a custodian, such as in hold-in-custody (HIC) repo. An example occurred in March 1985, when ESM Government Securities, a dealer in the US domestic repo market, failed owing US$300 million. ESM specialised in HIC repo and would reverse in collateral which it would pledge several times over in repos to raise cash. Tri-party repo was developed following the failure of ESM. |
| equivalent securities | A term denoting that the securities returned must be of the identical issue and nominal value to those repoed, but not necessarily the very same identically-numbered securities. |
| Euroclear | A book-entry clearing facility for most Eurocurrency and foreign securities, many domestic securities and for international equities. |
| failed trade | An agreed sale of a security which is not honoured by the seller, usually because it does not possess the security and cannot acquire it in time to deliver. Also known as fail. |
| Fed repo | A repo between the Federal Reserve Bank of New York (Fed) and US Treasury market primary dealers in which the Fed supplies cash to the market. Fed repos are administered by the manager of the System Open Market Account and are executed by the Domestic Trading Desk of the Fed. Fed repos are for periods of up to 15 days and are against collateral in the form of US Treasury or Federal agency securities. *See customer repo, system repo, matched sale-purchase.* |
| fixed-coupon repo | A variant of a dollar repo in which the collateral returned by the supplier of the cash to the supplier of collateral at the maturity of the repo does not have to be exactly the same as the original, but must have the same coupon. |
| flat repo | A repo transacted with no margin. Valuing collateral to be exchanged through a classic repo using its 'clean price', ie without accrued interest *(cf full-accrual pricing).* |
| flex repo | A classic repo with a definite maturity and a fixed repo rate, but allowing the supplier of cash to draw down the cash outstanding under the repo on an agreed schedule. |
| full-accrual pricing | Valuing collateral to be exchanged through a classic repo using its 'dirty price', ie with accrued interest *(cf flat repo).* |
| general collateral | Collateral which will meet the 'general' requirements of suppliers of collateral in the repo market where specific collateral has not been requested. *See stock collateral.* |
| Gensaki | Japanese domestic repo. |
| GMRA | The term used in the market and this book to describe the Global Master Repurchase Agreement: standardised contract documentation for classic repos in the international repo market which was drafted by the BMA and the Council of Reporting Dealers Repo Committee of ISMA, first published in the UK in |

| GMRA continued/... | November 1992 and updated in November 1995. It is based on the standardised contract documentation produced for the US domestic market by the **BMA**, but is governed by English law. The Agreement has been endorsed by the Bank of England and the Inland Revenue. Also known as the **PSA-ISMA** Agreement, or the **ISMA** Agreement. |
|---|---|
| gross-paying security | Securities on which coupons are paid gross of withholding tax (ie without income tax being deducted at source). cf *net-paying security*. |
| haircut | Another name for an initial margin. |
| hard stock | A security for which demand exceeds supply. If there is a strong demand in the repo market, the security will also be said to be 'on special' or simply 'special'. Also known as *hot stock*. |
| hold-in-custody (HIC) repo | A classic repo in which collateral is not physically delivered to the supplier of cash. Instead, the supplier of collateral simply segregates it internally in a customer account or delivers it to a bulk segregation account at its clearing bank *(cf deliver-out repo)*. The collateral may remain in the supplier's name. Also known as *letter repo*. |
| hot stock | *See hard stock.* |
| icing stock | *See putting stock on hold.* |
| implied repo rate | The rate of return for the supplier of cash in a sell/buy-back. The rate is not quoted separately but is incorporated into the buy-back price. |
| indexed repo rate | A classic repo where the repo rate is periodically reset as a function of a money market interest rate index e.g. LIBOR, Fed funds, etc. |
| initial margin | A percentage difference between the amount of cash and the market value of the collateral for which it is to be exchanged in a classic repo or sell/buy-back. Its purpose is to provide the supplier of the cash with protection against a reduction in the market value of collateral due to price volatility, and so the initial margin is usually taken by the supplier of cash. Also known as a haircut. cf *overcollateralisation*. |
| inter-dealer broker (IDB) | In the repo markets, these are brokers which arrange repos and reverse repos between active dealers. |
| international repo | A term used to describe the international and European domestic repo markets. Also known as non-dollar repo, cross-border repo, multi-currency repo. |
| investor | The supplier of cash and taker of collateral. |
| ISDs | International Securities Depositories |
| ISMA | The International Securities Market Association, a body comprising most of the banks and other financial institutions active in the international securities market. ISMA's rules govern all trading in international securities, including repo, between its members. |

| | |
|---|---|
| *continued/...* | Formerly known as the Association of International Bond Dealers. |
| lender | The counterparty supplying collateral and taking cash in classic repos and sell/buy-backs, or supplying a specific security and taking collateral in securities lending. Also known as the buyer in classic repos and sell/buy-backs. |
| letter repo | See *hold-in-custody (HIC) repo.* |
| London interbank offered rate (LIBOR) | The rate at which prime banks offer to make deposits with other prime banks for a given maturity, which can range from overnight to five years in London. |
| manufactured dividends | Payments made to suppliers of collateral in order to recompense them for coupons which have been paid on collateral securities during the term of a repo transaction. The payment is of an amount equal to the gross coupon and is usually a contractual obligation. |
| margin call | A demand for variation margin. |
| market value | The value of an asset at its current market price. In repo, the market value of collateral securities includes accrued interest. |
| mark-to-market | The process of redetermining the market value of an asset during the term of a transaction. In classic repo and securities lending, the securities are marked to market. Also known as remarking, repricing, revaluing. See *variation margin.* |
| matched book | A trading book of repos and matching reverse repos, or sell/buy-backs and matching buy/sell-backs (often used, paradoxically, as another name for mismatched book when taking a position on interest rates). |
| matched sale-purchase | A reverse repo between the Federal Reserve Bank of New York (Fed) and US Treasury market primary dealers in which the Fed takes cash from the market. The opposite of a *Fed repo.* |
| mismatched book | A number of repos and reverse repos that do not complement each other and that would result in a loss or profit. Also known as *open book (cf matched book). See tail.* |
| multi-currency repo | See *international repo.* |
| net-paying security | Securities on which coupons are paid net of withholding tax *cf gross-paying security.* |
| non-dollar repo | See *international repo.* |
| offer | The repo rate which the supplier of collateral in a classic repo - who is said to be 'offering' collateral - is willing to pay on cash received in exchange for the collateral being offered. Note that the offer is made in respect of the collateral, not the cash. The lower the offer rate, the more expensive it is to acquire collateral through a repo. Also known as *ask.* The opposite to *bid.* |
| on-side date | The value date at the start of a repo trade. |
| open book | See *mismatched book.* |

| | |
|---|---|
| opening leg | A repo is an initial sale of securities and a simultaneous agreement to repurchase them at a later date. The initial sale is called the opening leg. *See closing leg.* |
| open repo | Classic repos which are entered into with no fixed term. They are automatically rolled over every day until one of the counterparties terminates the agreement. Two day's notice is often required. At each rollover, the repo rate is refixed and the supplier of cash has the right to vary the amount. On the other hand, the supplier of collateral has the unconditional right to substitute it. A series of overnight repos that expose the counterparties to interest rate risk. Also known as *demand repo, day-to-day repo. See recall.* |
| overcollateralisation | The practice of requiring the value of the collateral in a transaction to be greater than the value of the other leg (cash in a classic repo or sell/buy-back, and specific borrowed securities in securities lending). The purpose of overcollateralisation is to provide the overcollateralised party with protection against a reduction in the market value of collateral due to the volatility of its price. *cf initial margin.* |
| overnight repo | A classic repo which matures on the business day following its value date. The most common form in the international repo market. |
| pay for hold | A commitment fee paid to the supplier of collateral to hold particular securities back for a securities lending transaction *cf hold-in-custody (HIC) repo.* |
| pension | The French domestic equivalent of the classic repo which succeeded the *réméré.* Enshrined in French law since December 1993. Formerly known as pension livrée. |
| prêt de titres | The name for securities lending in the French domestic market. |
| price differential | The term used in the **GMRA** to describe the accrued return on cash for the supplier of cash in a classic repo. *See pricing rate, repo rate.* |
| pricing rate | *See repo rate.* |
| prime brokerage | Clearing, custody, securities lending and financing services offered by securities houses to customers such as hedge funds. |
| principal | A party to a repo transaction which acts on its own behalf, or which authorises an agent to act on its behalf. |
| putting stock on hold | The practice of reserving securities at the request of a party planning to acquire that security through a repo. Also known as *icing stock.* |
| rebate | A securities lending transaction fee. This is deducted by the supplier of the special security from the interest earned on the cash collateral before it is repaid to the supplier of collateral. |
| rebooking | *See rollover.* |
| recall | A demand by one of the counterparties to an open repo to terminate the transaction. |
| remarking | *See mark-to-market.* |

| | |
|---|---|
| réméré | Once a common form of repo in the French domestic market. The seller of securities has an option to repurchase the securities. In practice, the option is expected to be exercised, but after a notable failure of one counterparty to do so, the market has largely abandoned the réméré in favour of the newer *pension*, which commits the supplier of collateral to reverse the initial exchange of cash and collateral. |
| repo | See *sale and repurchase agreement*. |
| repo rate | The rate of return earned by the supplier of cash in a classic repo. A repo rate is similar to an interest rate but also reflects factors relating to the demand for the purchased securities. The interest analogy is inaccurate, however, because the cash in a classic repo is a purchase or repurchase price and not a loan. |
| repo-to-maturity | A repo which matures on the maturity of the collateral securities. |
| repricing | See *mark-to-market*. |
| revaluing | See *mark-to-market*. |
| reverse repo | A repo from the point of view of the counterparty which supplies cash and takes collateral. |
| reverse-to-maturity | A reverse repo which matures on the maturity of the collateral securities. |
| reversing | Transacting a reverse repo. One is said to 'reverse in' securities. |
| rollover | An extension of the maturity of a sale and repurchase agreement. Also known as *rebooking*. |
| safe custody repo | See *safekeeping repo*. |
| safekeeping repo | A classic repo in which collateral is not physically delivered to the supplier of cash. Instead, it is segregated in an account established at the supplier's clearing bank or at a depository in the name of the counterparty. Also known as *trust account repo, safe custody repo*. |
| sale and repurchase agreement (repo) | A contract which commits two counterparties to sell securities for cash and to repurchase them on an agreed future date or on demand. The counterparty taking the cash pays an agreed return to the counterparty supplying the cash. The term 'repo' is used generically to describe three different types of transaction: classic repo, sell/buy-back, and occasionally securities lending, which is not technically a sale and repurchase agreement. |
| securities lending | A contract which commits two counterparties to exchange agreed securities against collateral and to subsequently reverse the exchange at an agreed future date or on demand. The counterparty borrowing the agreed securities pays an agreed fee to the other counterparty. Also known as *stock lending* or, in the US, a *bond borrowed* transaction. |
| sell/buy-back | A type of sale and repurchase agreement. This contract commits two counterparties to sell securities for cash and to repurchase them on an agreed future date or on demand. International repos |
| sell/buy-back | have traditionally been sell/buy-backs rather than classic repos. |

| | |
|---|---|
| *continued/...* | Sell/buy backs differ from classic repos in several ways, including the treatment of coupon payments, the use of documentation, the practice of margining and marking-to-market. |
| seller | The counterparty taking cash and supplying collateral in classic repos and sell/buy-backs. Equivalent to the borrower in these types of repo. |
| set-off | The legal right to net opposite obligations (to deliver securities or pay cash) between two counterparties in the event of default by one of them. |
| specials | Collateral which is in heavy demand and is said to be 'on special' or to 'go special'. The repo rate on specials will be low; in other words, the counterparty seeking special collateral will accept a lower repo rate on the cash it supplies in exchange for the collateral. |
| specific collateral | Collateral which is required in the form of a specific issue of a security. |
| spread trade | Employing lower-yielding securities as collateral in a repo and using the cash which is received in exchange to buy higher-yielding securities in order to achieve a yield pick-up, while minimising the extra risk. |
| stock collateral | Also known as general collateral in the US domestic market. |
| stock lending | A name used in the UK to describe securities lending. |
| substitution | The replacement of collateral during the term of a repo by the supplier of collateral. The right of substitution is at the discretion of the counterparty who holds the collateral, who will insist on substitute collateral being of equivalent value and quality to the original. Substitution may occur more than once in a repo transaction and a number of substitutions is normally agreed prior to trading. |
| system repo | A Fed repo in which the Federal Reserve Bank of New York (Fed) invests cash in the market in order to boost the level of reserves held by the banking system and thereby influence very short-term interest rates. |
| tail | The mismatch between the maturity of a repo and the maturity of a reverse repo. It represents an exposure to interest rate risk. The intermediary is said to be running a mismatched book. |
| termination date | The date on which a repo transaction terminates (i.e. the initial exchange of cash and collateral is reversed). |
| term repo | Repo with a maturity which is more than one business day after its value date. In theory, repos go out to one year, but they have been made available for longer in special circumstances. |
| third-party lending | Securities lending where the administration of the transaction is handled by an independent third-party agent such as a global custodian. The securities lending equivalent of *tri-party repo*. |
| third-party repo | *See Tri-party repo.* |

| | |
|---|---|
| tri-party repo | Collateral is held by an independent (third party) agent acting as a custodian, which transfers it internally between accounts established for each of the counterparties and only against a payment of cash. A type of *safekeeping repo*. Also known as *third-party repo*. |
| trust account repo | *See safekeeping repo.* |
| variation margin | An amount of collateral which the supplier of collateral through a classic repo is required to deliver to, or is entitled to retrieve from, its counterparty in order to maintain the initial margin. Either the market value of the collateral has decreased and the initial margin has been eliminated, or the market value of the collateral has increased and the initial margin has been widened too much. If the initial margin is eliminated, the supplier of cash becomes exposed to the risk of default by the taker of cash. If the initial margin is widened, the supplier of collateral becomes unduly exposed to the risk of default by the taker of collateral. In order to establish whether a variation margin is required, the market value of collateral must be recalculated regularly, usually daily. The process of revaluation is called marking to market. *See margin call.* |

# *Appendix 1*

ISMA CRD REPO SUB COMMITTEE

ACCEPTABLE GENERAL COLLATERAL LIST

Amended Version as on 22nd February, 1999

The following security types were deemed to be acceptable as collateral by the **ISMA CRD** Repo Sub Committee on 22nd February, 1999 on general collateral repo and buy/sell transactions unless specifically indicated otherwise prior to engaging in transactions

GERMAN BONDS

    German Unity Fund **DBRUF**

    Bund **DBR**

    Bobl **OBL**

    Tobl **TOBL**

    Treuhand (bonds only) **THA**

    Schatz **BKO**

    BuBill **BUBILL**

    World Bank Global (2bn +)

    All other bond types such as Bundesbahn or Bundespost are currently excluded as acceptable collateral on general collateral transactions unless otherwise agreed by the counterparties prior to the transaction.

FRENCH BONDS

    OATS, BTANS (fixed coupon securities only)

    BTF (Index linked are excluded unless specifically agreed by both counterparties)

ITALIAN BONDS

    CCT

    CTO

    BTP

    BOT

    CTZ

SPANISH BONDS

    Bonos

    NB The seller must specify if the securities go over record date 30 days prior to the trade being consummated.

SWEDISH, DANISH, NORWEGIAN

    Government guaranteed bonds and bills only

BELGIAN BONDS

    Phillipe Bonds

    Government guaranteed bonds and bills (including any non redenominated securities)

## DUTCH BONDS

Dutch State loans and bills

## JAPANESE BONDS

'Clean' bonds only

## CANADIAN BONDS

Government guaranteed bonds and bills only

## AUSTRALIAN BONDS

Government guaranteed bonds and 'semi' government guaranteed (i.e. New South Wales, Queensland Treasury Corp) and bills

## AUSTRIAN BONDS

Government guaranteed bonds and bills

In addition, the **buyer** must specify if securities constituting general collateral and paying gross coupon will go over a record date prior to the trade being consummated. For securities which pay coupon net, the **seller** must specify if securities will pay coupon over a record date prior to the trade being consummated. The only exception to this would be in the case of Spanish Bonos. Here the **seller** must specify if the securities go over record date 30 days prior to the trade being consummated.

# *Appendix 2*

Day count conventions

The day count convention to be applied to the cash is that prevailing in the domestic money market of the currency traded, eg A/365 in sterling, A/360 in Euro. The day count convention of the bonds supplied as collateral is used only to calculate accrued interest on the securities. In those countries where the day count convention of the bond and money markets differ, the domestic money market convention is used.

| Country | Repo Rate | Bond day count |
|---|---|---|
| Australia | 365 | Act / Act |
| Belgium | 360 | Act / Act |
| Canada | 365 | Act / Act |
| Denmark | 360 | ISMA 30/360 |
| France | 360 | Act / Act |
| Germany | 360 | Act / Act |
| Italy | 360 | Act / Act |
| Japan | 360 /365 | NL/365 |
| Netherlands | 360 | Act / Act |
| Spain | 360 | Act / Act |
| Sweden | 360 | ISMA 30/360 |
| United Kingdom | 365 | Act / Act |
| United States | 360 | Act / Act |

d

I S M A

INTERNATIONAL SECURITIES MARKET ASSOCIATION

Public Securities Association
40 Broad Street, New York, NY 10004-2373

Rigistrasse 60, P.O. Box, CH-8033 Zürich

**VERSION 1**

**GROSS PAYING SECURITIES**

**GLOBAL MASTER REPURCHASE AGREEMENT**

This agreement is to be used for repos or reverse repos and buy/sell backs of securities
other than equities, U.S. Treasury instruments and Net Paying Securities

Dated as of _____

**Between:**

_____ ("Party A")

and

_____ ("Party B")

**1. Applicability**

(a) From time to time the parties hereto may enter into transactions in which one party, acting
through a Designated Office, ("*Seller*") agrees to sell to the other, acting through a Designated
Office, ("*Buyer*") securities and financial instruments ("*Securities*") (other than equities, U.S.
Treasury instruments and Net Paying Securities) against the payment of the purchase price by
Buyer to Seller, with a simultaneous agreement by Buyer to sell to Seller Securities equivalent to
such Securities at a date certain or on demand against the payment of the purchase price by Seller
to Buyer.

(b) Each such transaction (which may be a repurchase transaction ("*Repurchase Transaction*") or a
buy and sell back transaction ("*Buy/Sell Back Transaction*")) shall be referred to herein as a
"*Transaction*" and shall be governed by this Agreement, including any supplemental terms or
conditions contained in Annex I hereto, unless otherwise agreed in writing. If this Agreement may
be applied to Buy/Sell Back Transactions, this shall be specified in Annex I, and the provisions of
Annex III shall apply to such Buy/Sell Back Transactions. If Transactions are to be effected under this
Agreement by either party as an agent, this shall be specified in Annex I, and the provisions of
Annex IV shall apply to such Agency Transactions.

**2. Definitions**

(a) "*Act of Insolvency*" shall occur with respect to any party hereto upon:

(i)   its making a general assignment for the benefit of, or entering into a reorganisation,
arrangement, or composition with creditors; or

(ii)  its admitting in writing that it is unable to pay its debts as they become due; or

(iii) its seeking, consenting to or acquiescing in the appointment of any trustee,
administrator, receiver or liquidator or analogous officer of it or any material part of its
property; or

(iv)  the presentation or filing of a petition in respect of it (other than by the counterparty to
this Agreement in respect of any obligation under this Agreement) in any court or

before any agency alleging or for the bankruptcy, winding-up or insolvency of such party (or any analogous proceeding) or seeking any reorganisation, arrangement, composition, re-adjustment, administration, liquidation, dissolution or similar relief under any present or future statute, law or regulation, such petition (except in the case of a petition for winding-up or any analogous proceeding, in respect of which no such 30 day period shall apply) not having been stayed or dismissed within 30 days of its filing; or

    (v)    the appointment of a receiver, administrator, liquidator or trustee or analogous officer of such party or over all or any material part of such party's property; or

    (vi)    the convening of any meeting of its creditors for the purposes of considering a voluntary arrangement as referred to in section 3 of the Insolvency Act 1986 (or any analogous proceeding);

(b)    *"Agency Transaction"*, the meaning specified in paragraph 1 of Annex IV hereto;

(c)    *"Base Currency"*, the currency indicated in Annex I hereto;

(d)    *"Business Day"*:

    (i)    in relation to the settlement of any Transaction which is to be settled through Cedel or Euroclear, a day on which Cedel or, as the case may be, Euroclear is open to settle business in the currency in which the Purchase Price and the Repurchase Price are denominated;

    (ii)    in relation to the settlement of any Transaction which is to be settled through a settlement system other than Cedel or Euroclear, a day on which that settlement system is open to settle such Transaction;

    (iii)    in relation to any delivery of Securities not falling within (i) or (ii) above, a day on which banks are open for business in the place where delivery of the relevant Securities is to be effected; and

    (iv)    in relation to any obligation to make a payment not falling within (i) or (ii) above, a day other than a Saturday or a Sunday on which banks are open for business in the principal financial centre of the country of which the currency in which the payment is denominated is the official currency and, if different, in the place where any account designated by the parties for the making or receipt of the payment is situated (or, in the case of ECU, a day on which ECU clearing operates);

(e)    *"Cash Margin"*, a cash sum paid to Buyer or Seller in accordance with paragraph 4;

(f)    *"Cedel"*, Cedel Bank, société anonyme;

(g)    *"Confirmation"*, the meaning specified in paragraph 3(b);

(h)    *"Contractual Currency"*, the meaning specified in paragraph 7(a);

(i)    *"Defaulting Party"*, the meaning specified in paragraph 10;

(j)    *"Default Market Value"* with respect to any Securities on any date:

    (i)    in the case of Securities to be delivered to the Defaulting Party,

        (aa)    if the non-Defaulting Party has between the occurrence of the relevant Event of Default and the Default Valuation Time (as defined below) sold Securities forming part of the same issue and being of an identical type and description to those Securities and in substantially the same amount as those Securities, the net proceeds of sale (after deducting all reasonable costs, fees and expenses incurred in connection therewith) and

        (bb)    failing such sale before the Default Valuation Time, the Market Value of such Securities at the Default Valuation Time;

    (ii)    in the case of Securities to be delivered by the Defaulting Party,

        (aa)    if the non-Defaulting Party has between the occurrence of the relevant Event of Default and the Default Valuation Time purchased Securities forming part of the same issue and being of an identical type and description to those Securities and in substantially the same amount as those Securities, the cost of such purchase (including all reasonable costs, fees and expenses incurred in connection therewith) and

(bb) failing such purchase before the Default Valuation Time, the amount it would cost to buy such Securities at the Default Valuation Time at the best available offer price therefor (and where different offer prices are available for different delivery dates, such offer price in respect of the earliest available such delivery date) on the most appropriate market, together with all reasonable costs, fees and expenses that would be incurred in connection therewith (calculated on the assumption that the aggregate thereof is the least that could reasonably be expected to be paid in order to carry out the Transaction),

in each case as determined by the non-Defaulting Party; and for this purpose the *"Default Valuation Time"* means, with respect to any Securities

(A) if the relevant Event of Default occurs during normal business hours on a day which is a dealing day in the most appropriate market for Securities of the relevant description (as determined by the non-Defaulting Party), the close of business in that market on the following dealing day;

(B) in any other case, the close of business on the second dealing day in that market after the day on which the relevant Event of Default occurs;

Where the amount of any Securities sold or purchased as mentioned in (i)(aa) or (ii)(aa) above is not identical to that of the Securities to be valued for the purposes of this definition, the Default Market Value of those Securities shall be ascertained by dividing the net proceeds of sale or cost of purchase by the amount of the Securities sold or purchased so as to obtain a net unit price and multiplying that net unit price by the amount of the Securities to be valued;

(k) *"Default Notice"*, a written notice served by the non-Defaulting Party on the Defaulting Party under paragraph 10 stating that an event shall be treated as an Event of Default for the purposes of this Agreement;

(l) *"Designated Office"*, with respect to a party, a branch or office of that party which is specified as such in Annex I hereto or such other branch or office as may be agreed to by the Parties;

(m) *"Distributions"*, the meaning specified in sub-paragraph (s) below;

(n) *"Equivalent Margin Securities"*, Securities equivalent to Securities previously transferred as Margin Securities;

(o) *"Equivalent Securities"*, with respect to a Transaction, Securities equivalent to Purchased Securities under that Transaction. If and to the extent that such Purchased Securities have been redeemed the expression shall mean a sum of money equivalent to the proceeds of the redemption;

(p) Securities are *"equivalent to"* other Securities for the purposes of this Agreement if they are: (i) of the same issuer; (ii) part of the same issue; and (iii) of an identical type, nominal value, description and (except where otherwise stated) amount as those other Securities;

(q) *"Euroclear"*, Morgan Guaranty Trust Company of New York, Brussels office, as operator of the Euroclear System;

(r) *"Event of Default"*, the meaning specified in paragraph 10 hereof;

(s) *"Income"*, with respect to any Security at any time, all interest, dividends or other distributions thereon (*"Distributions"*);

(t) *"Income Payment Date"*, with respect to any Securities, the date on which Income is paid in respect of such Securities, or, in the case of registered Securities, the date by reference to which particular registered holders are identified as being entitled to payment of Income;

(u) *"LIBOR"*, in relation to any sum in any currency, the one-month London Inter Bank Offered Rate in respect of that currency as quoted on Page 3750 on the Telerate Service (or such other page as may replace Page 3750 on that service) as of 11:00 a.m., London time, on the date on which it is to be determined;

(v)  "*Margin Ratio*", with respect to a Transaction, the Market Value of the Purchased Securities at the time when the Transaction was entered into divided by the Purchase Price (and so that, where a Transaction relates to Securities of different descriptions and the Purchase Price is apportioned by the parties among Purchased Securities of each such description, a separate Margin Ratio shall apply in respect of Securities of each such description), or such other proportion as the parties may agree with respect to that Transaction;

(w)  "*Margin Securities*", in relation to a Margin Transfer, Securities reasonably acceptable to the party calling for such Margin Transfer;

(x)  "*Margin Transfer*", any, or any combination, of the payment or repayment of Cash Margin and the transfer of Margin Securities or Equivalent Margin Securities;

(y)  "*Market Value*", with respect to any Securities as of any time on any date, the price for such Securities at such time on such date obtained from a generally recognised source agreed to by the parties (and where different prices are obtained for different delivery dates, the price so obtainable for the earliest available such delivery date) (provided that the price of Securities that are suspended shall (for the purposes of paragraph 4) be nil unless the parties otherwise agree and (for all other purposes) shall be the price of those Securities as of close of business on the dealing day in the relevant market last preceding the date of suspension) plus the aggregate amount of Income which, as of such date, has accrued but not yet been paid in respect of the Securities to the extent not included in such price as of such date, and for these purposes any sum in a currency other than the Contractual Currency for the Transaction in question shall be converted into such Contractual Currency at the Spot Rate prevailing at the relevant time;

(z)  "*Net Exposure*", the meaning specified in paragraph 4(c);

(aa)  the "*Net Margin*" provided to a party at any time, the excess (if any) at that time of (i) the sum of the amount of Cash Margin paid to that party (including accrued interest on such Cash Margin which has not been paid to the other party) and the Market Value of Margin Securities transferred to that party under paragraph 4(a) (excluding any Cash Margin which has been repaid to the other party and any Margin Securities in respect of which Equivalent Margin Securities have been transferred to the other party) over (ii) the sum of the amount of Cash Margin paid to the other party (including accrued interest on such Cash Margin which has not been paid by the other party) and the Market Value of Margin Securities transferred to the other party under paragraph 4(a) (excluding any Cash Margin which has been repaid by the other party and any Margin Securities in respect of which Equivalent Margin Securities have been transferred by the other party) and for this purpose any amounts not denominated in the Base Currency shall be converted into the Base Currency at the Spot Rate prevailing at the relevant time;

(bb)  "*Net Paying Securities*", Securities which are of a kind such that, were they to be the subject of a Transaction to which paragraph 5 applies, any payment made by Buyer under paragraph 5 would be one in respect of which either Buyer would or might be required to make a withholding or deduction for or on account of taxes or duties or Seller would or might be required to make or account for a payment for or on account of taxes or duties (in each case other than tax on overall net income) by reference to such payment;

(cc)  "*New Purchased Securities*", the meaning specified in paragraph 8(a) of this Agreement;

(dd)  "*Price Differential*", with respect to any Transaction as of any date, the aggregate amount obtained by daily application of the Pricing Rate for such Transaction to the Purchase Price for such Transaction (on a 360 day basis or 365 day basis in accordance with the applicable ISMA convention, unless otherwise agreed between the parties for the Transaction), for the actual number of days during the period commencing on (and including) the Purchase Date for such Transaction and ending on (but excluding) the date of calculation or, if earlier, the Repurchase Date;

(ee)  "*Pricing Rate*", with respect to any Transaction, the per annum percentage rate for calculation of the Price Differential agreed to by Buyer and Seller in relation to that Transaction;

(ff)  "*Purchase Date*", with respect to any Transaction, the date on which Purchased Securities are to be sold by Seller to Buyer in relation to that Transaction;

h

(gg) *"Purchase Price"*, on the Purchase Date, the price at which Purchased Securities are sold or are to be sold by Seller to Buyer;

(hh) *"Purchased Securities"*, with respect to any Transaction, the Securities sold or to be sold by Seller to Buyer under that Transaction, and any New Purchased Securities transferred by Seller to Buyer under paragraph 8 of this Agreement in respect of that Transaction;

(ii) *"Repurchase Date"*, with respect to any Transaction, the date on which Buyer is to sell Equivalent Securities to Seller in relation to that Transaction;

(jj) *"Repurchase Price"*, with respect to any Transaction and as of any date, the sum of the Purchase Price and the Price Differential as of such date;

(kk) *"Spot Rate"*, where an amount in one currency is to be converted into a second currency on any date, unless the parties otherwise agree, the spot rate of exchange quoted by Barclays Bank PLC in the London inter bank market for the sale by it of such second currency against a purchase by it of such first currency;

(ll) *"Term"*, with respect to any Transaction, the interval of time commencing with the Purchase Date and ending with the Repurchase Date;

(mm) *"Termination"*, with respect to any Transaction, refers to the requirement with respect to such Transaction for Buyer to sell Equivalent Securities against payment by Seller of the Repurchase Price in accordance with paragraph 3(f), and references to a Transaction having a *"fixed term"* or being *"terminable upon demand"* shall be construed accordingly;

(nn) *"Transaction Exposure"*, with respect to any Transaction at any time during the period from the Purchase Date to the Repurchase Date (or, if later, the date on which Equivalent Securities are delivered to Seller or the Transaction is terminated under paragraph 10(e) or 10(f)), the difference between (i) the Repurchase Price at such time multiplied by the applicable Margin Ratio (or, where the Transaction relates to Securities of more than one description to which different Margin Ratios apply, the amount produced by multiplying the Repurchase Price attributable to Equivalent Securities of each such description by the applicable Margin Ratio and aggregating the resulting amounts, the Repurchase Price being for this purpose attributed to Equivalent Securities of each such description in the same proportions as those in which the Purchase Price was apportioned among the Purchased Securities) and (ii) the Market Value of Equivalent Securities at such time. If (i) is greater than (ii), Buyer has a Transaction Exposure for that Transaction equal to that excess. If (ii) is greater than (i), Seller has a Transaction Exposure for that Transaction equal to that excess; and

(oo) except in paragraphs 14(b)(i) and 18, references in this Agreement to *"written"* communications and communications *"in writing"* include communications made through any electronic system agreed between the parties which is capable of reproducing such communications in hard copy form.

### 3. Initiation; Confirmation; Termination

(a) A Transaction may be entered into orally or in writing at the initiation of either Buyer or Seller.

(b) Upon agreeing to enter into a Transaction hereunder Buyer or Seller (or both), as shall have been agreed, shall promptly deliver to the other party written confirmation of such Transaction (a *"Confirmation"*).

The Confirmation shall describe the Purchased Securities (including CUSIP or CINS or other identifying number or numbers, if any), identify Buyer and Seller and set forth-

   (i)   the Purchase Date;

   (ii)   the Purchase Price;

   (iii)   the Repurchase Date, unless the Transaction is to be terminable on demand (in which case the Confirmation will state that it is terminable on demand);

   (iv)   the Pricing Rate applicable to the Transaction;

(v)   in respect of each party the details of the bank account[s] to which payments to be made hereunder are to be credited;

(vi)   where Annex III applies, whether the Transaction is a Repurchase Transaction or a Buy/Sell Back Transaction;

(vii)   where Annex IV applies, whether the Transaction is an Agency Transaction and, if so, the identity of the party which is acting as agent and the name, code or identifier of the Principal; and

(viii)   any additional terms or conditions of the Transaction;

and may be in the form of Annex II hereto or may be in any other form which the parties agree.

The Confirmation relating to a Transaction shall, together with this Agreement, constitute prima facie evidence of the terms agreed between Buyer and Seller for that Transaction, unless objection is made with respect to the Confirmation promptly after receipt thereof. In the event of any conflict between the terms of such Confirmation and this Agreement, the Confirmation shall prevail in respect of that Transaction and those terms only.

(c)   On the Purchase Date for a Transaction, Seller shall transfer the Purchased Securities to Buyer or its agent against the payment of the Purchase Price by Buyer.

(d)   Termination of a Transaction will be effected, in the case of on demand Transactions, on the date specified for Termination in such demand, and, in the case of fixed term Transactions, on the date fixed for Termination.

(e)   In the case of on demand Transactions, demand for Termination shall be made by Buyer or Seller, by telephone or otherwise, and shall provide for Termination to occur after not less than the minimum period as is customarily required for the settlement or delivery of money or Equivalent Securities of the relevant kind.

(f)   On the Repurchase Date, Buyer shall transfer to Seller or its agent Equivalent Securities against the payment of the Repurchase Price by Seller (less any amount then payable and unpaid by Buyer to Seller pursuant to paragraph 5).


## 4.   Margin Maintenance

(a)   If at any time either party has a Net Exposure in respect of the other party it may by notice to the other party require the other party to make a Margin Transfer to it of an aggregate amount or value at least equal to that Net Exposure.

(b)   A notice under sub-paragraph (a) above may be given orally or in writing.

(c)   For the purposes of this Agreement a party has a Net Exposure in respect of the other party if the aggregate of all the first party's Transaction Exposures plus any amount payable to the first party under paragraph 5 but unpaid less the amount of any Net Margin provided to the first party exceeds the aggregate of all the other party's Transaction Exposures plus any amount payable to the other party under paragraph 5 but unpaid less the amount of any Net Margin provided to the other party; and the amount of the Net Exposure is the amount of the excess. For this purpose any amounts not denominated in the Base Currency shall be converted into the Base Currency at the Spot Rate prevailing at the relevant time.

(d)   To the extent that a party calling for a Margin Transfer has previously paid Cash Margin which has not been repaid or delivered Margin Securities in respect of which Equivalent Margin Securities have not been delivered to it, that party shall be entitled to require that such Margin Transfer be satisfied first by the repayment of such Cash Margin or the delivery of Equivalent Margin Securities but, subject to this, the composition of a Margin Transfer shall be at the option of the party making such Margin Transfer.

(e)   Any Cash Margin transferred shall be in the Base Currency or such other currency as the parties may agree.

(f)   A payment of Cash Margin shall give rise to a debt owing from the party receiving such payment to the party making such payment. Such debt shall bear interest at such rate, payable at such times, as may be specified in Annex I in respect of the relevant currency or otherwise agreed between the parties, and shall be repayable subject to the terms of this Agreement.

(g)  Where Seller or Buyer becomes obliged under sub-paragraph (a) above to make a Margin Transfer, it shall transfer Cash Margin or Margin Securities or Equivalent Margin Securities within the minimum period specified in Annex I or, if no period is there specified, such minimum period as is customarily required for the settlement or delivery of money, Margin Securities or Equivalent Margin Securities of the relevant kind.

(h)  The parties may agree that, with respect to any Transaction, the provisions of sub-paragraphs (a) to (g) above shall not apply but instead that margin may be provided separately in respect of that Transaction in which case -

   (i)  that Transaction shall not be taken into account when calculating whether either party has a Net Exposure;

   (ii)  margin shall be provided in respect of that Transaction in such manner as the parties may agree; and

   (iii)  margin provided in respect of that Transaction shall not be taken into account for the purposes of sub-paragraphs (a) to (g) above.

(i)  The parties may agree that any Net Exposure which may arise shall be eliminated not by Margin Transfers under the preceding provisions of this paragraph but by the repricing of Transactions under sub-paragraph (j) below, the adjustment of Transactions under sub-paragraph (k) below or a combination of both these methods.

(j)  Where the parties agree that a Transaction is to be repriced under this sub-paragraph, such repricing shall be effected as follows -

   (i)  the Repurchase Date under the relevant Transaction (the "*Original Transaction*") shall be deemed to occur on the date on which the repricing is to be effected (the "*Repricing Date*");

   (ii)  the parties shall be deemed to have entered into a new Transaction (the "*Repriced Transaction*") on the terms set out in (iii) to (vi) below;

   (iii)  the Purchased Securities under the Repriced Transaction shall be Securities equivalent to the Purchased Securities under the Original Transaction;

   (iv)  the Purchase Date under the Repriced Transaction shall be the Repricing Date;

   (v)  the Purchase Price under the Repriced Transaction shall be such amount as shall, when multiplied by the Margin Ratio applicable to the Original Transaction, be equal to the Market Value of such Securities on the Repricing Date;

   (vi)  the Repurchase Date, the Pricing Rate, the Margin Ratio and, subject as aforesaid, the other terms of the Repriced Transaction shall be identical to those of the Original Transaction;

   (vii)  the obligations of the parties with respect to the delivery of the Purchased Securities and the payment of the Purchase Price under the Repriced Transaction shall be set off against their obligations with respect to the delivery of Equivalent Securities and payment of the Repurchase Price under the Original Transaction and accordingly only a net cash sum shall be paid by one party to the other. Such net cash sum shall be paid within the period specified in sub-paragraph (g) above.

(k)  The adjustment of a Transaction (the "*Original Transaction*") under this sub-paragraph shall be effected by the parties agreeing that on the date on which the adjustment is to be made (the "*Adjustment Date*") the Original Transaction shall be terminated and they shall enter into a new Transaction (the "*Replacement Transaction*") in accordance with the following provisions -

   (i)  the Original Transaction shall be terminated on the Adjustment Date on such terms as the parties shall agree on or before the Adjustment Date;

   (ii)  the Purchased Securities under the Replacement Transaction shall be such Securities as the parties shall agree on or before the Adjustment Date (being Securities the aggregate Market Value of which at the Adjustment Date is substantially equal to the Repurchase Price under the Original Transaction at the Adjustment Date multiplied by the Margin Ratio applicable to the Original Transaction);

   (iii)  the Purchase Date under the Replacement Transaction shall be the Adjustment Date;

(iv)   the other terms of the Replacement Transaction shall be such as the parties shall agree on or before the Adjustment Date; and

(v)   the obligations of the parties with respect to payment and delivery of Securities on the Adjustment Date under the Original Transaction and the Replacement Transaction shall be settled in accordance with paragraph 6 within the minimum period specified in sub-paragraph (g) above.

## 5.   Income Payments

Unless otherwise agreed -

(i)   where the Term of a particular Transaction extends over an Income Payment Date in respect of any Securities subject to that Transaction, Buyer shall on the date such Income is paid by the issuer transfer to or credit to the account of Seller an amount equal to (and in the same currency as) the amount paid by the issuer;

(ii)   where Margin Securities are transferred from one party ("the first party") to the other party ("the second party") and an Income Payment Date in respect of such Securities occurs before Equivalent Margin Securities are transferred by the second party to the first party, the second party shall on the date such Income is paid by the issuer transfer to or credit to the account of the first party an amount equal to (and in the same currency as) the amount paid by the issuer;

and for the avoidance of doubt references in this paragraph to the amount of any income paid by the issuer of any Securities shall be to an amount paid without any withholding or deduction for or on account of taxes or duties notwithstanding that a payment of such Income made in certain circumstances may be subject to such a withholding or deduction.

## 6.   Payment and Transfer

(a)   Unless otherwise agreed, all money paid hereunder shall be in immediately available, freely convertible funds of the relevant currency. All Securities to be transferred hereunder (i) shall be in suitable form for transfer and shall be accompanied by duly executed instruments of transfer or assignment in blank (where required for transfer) and such other documentation as the transferee may reasonably request, or (ii) shall be transferred through the book entry system of Euroclear or Cedel, or (iii) shall be transferred through any other agreed securities clearance system, or (iv) shall be transferred by any other method mutually acceptable to Seller and Buyer.

(b)   Unless otherwise agreed, all money payable by one party to the other in respect of any Transaction shall be paid free and clear of, and without withholding or deduction for, any taxes or duties of whatsoever nature imposed, levied, collected, withheld or assessed by any authority having power to tax, unless the withholding or deduction of such taxes or duties is required by law. In that event, unless otherwise agreed, the paying party shall pay such additional amounts as will result in the net amounts receivable by the other party (after taking account of such withholding or deduction) being equal to such amounts as would have been received by it had no such taxes or duties been required to be withheld or deducted.

(c)   Unless otherwise agreed in writing between the parties, under each Transaction transfer of Purchased Securities by Seller and payment of Purchase Price by Buyer against the transfer of such Purchased Securities shall be made simultaneously and transfer of Equivalent Securities by Buyer and payment of Repurchase Price payable by Seller against the transfer of such Equivalent Securities shall be made simultaneously.

(d)   Subject to and without prejudice to the provisions of sub-paragraph 6(c), either party may from time to time in accordance with market practice and in recognition of the practical difficulties in arranging simultaneous delivery of Securities and money waive in relation to any Transaction its rights under this Agreement to receive simultaneous transfer and/or payment provided that transfer and/or payment shall, notwithstanding such waiver, be made on the same day and provided also that no such waiver in respect of one Transaction shall affect or bind it in respect of any other Transaction.

(e)   The parties shall execute and deliver all necessary documents and take all necessary steps to procure that all right, title and interest in any Purchased Securities, any Equivalent Securities, any

Margin Securities and any Equivalent Margin Securities shall pass to the party to which transfer is being made upon transfer of the same in accordance with this Agreement, free from all liens, claims, charges and encumbrances.

(f) Notwithstanding the use of expressions such as *"Repurchase Date"*, *"Repurchase Price"*, *"margin"*, *"Net Margin"*, *"Margin Ratio"* and *"substitution"* which are used to reflect terminology used in the market for transactions of the kind provided for in this Agreement, all right, title and interest in and to Securities and money transferred or paid under this Agreement shall pass to the transferee upon transfer or payment, the obligation of the party receiving Purchased Securities or Margin Securities being an obligation to transfer Equivalent Securities or Equivalent Margin Securities.

(g) Time shall be of the essence in this Agreement.

(h) Subject to paragraph 10, all amounts in the same currency payable by each party to the other under any Transaction or otherwise under this Agreement on the same date shall be combined in a single calculation of a net sum payable by one party to the other and the obligation to pay that sum shall be the only obligation of either party in respect of those amounts.

(i) Subject to paragraph 10, all Securities of the same issue, denomination, currency and series, transferable by each party to the other under any Transaction or hereunder on the same date shall be combined in a single calculation of a net quantity of Securities transferable by one party to the other and the obligation to transfer the net quantity of Securities shall be the only obligation of either party in respect of the Securities so transferable and receivable.


## 7.  Contractual Currency

(a) All the payments made in respect of the Purchase Price or the Repurchase Price of any Transaction shall be made in the currency of the Purchase Price (the *"Contractual Currency"*) save as provided in paragraph l0(c)(ii). Notwithstanding the foregoing, the payee of any money may, at its option, accept tender thereof in any other currency, provided, however, that, to the extent permitted by applicable law, the obligation of the payer to pay such money will be discharged only to the extent of the amount of the Contractual Currency that such payee may, consistent with normal banking procedures, purchase with such other currency (after deduction of any premium and costs of exchange) for delivery within the customary delivery period for spot transactions in respect of the relevant currency.

(b) If for any reason the amount in the Contractual Currency received by a party, including amounts received after conversion of any recovery under any judgment or order expressed in a currency other than the Contractual Currency, falls short of the amount in the Contractual Currency due and payable, the party required to make the payment will, as a separate and independent obligation, to the extent permitted by applicable law, immediately transfer such additional amount in the Contractual Currency as may be necessary to compensate for the shortfall.

(c) If for any reason the amount in the Contractual Currency received by a party exceeds the amount of the Contractual Currency due and payable, the party receiving the transfer will refund promptly the amount of such excess.


## 8.  Substitution

(a) A Transaction may at any time between the Purchase Date and the Repurchase Date, if Seller so requests and Buyer so agrees, be varied by the transfer by Buyer to Seller of Securities equivalent to the Purchased Securities, or to such of the Purchased Securities as shall be agreed, in exchange for the transfer by Seller to Buyer of other Securities of such amount and description as shall be agreed (*"New Purchased Securities"*) (being Securities having a Market Value at the date of the variation at least equal to the Market Value of the Equivalent Securities transferred to Seller).

(b) Any variation under sub-paragraph (a) above shall be effected, subject to paragraph 6(d), by the simultaneous transfer of the Equivalent Securities and New Purchased Securities concerned.

(c) A Transaction which is varied under sub-paragraph (a) above shall thereafter continue in effect as though the Purchased Securities under that Transaction consisted of or included the New

Purchased Securities instead of the Securities in respect of which Equivalent Securities have been transferred to Seller.

(d)   Where either party has transferred Margin Securities to the other party it may at any time before Equivalent Margin Securities are transferred to it under paragraph 4 request the other party to transfer Equivalent Margin Securities to it in exchange for the transfer to the other party of new Margin Securities having a Market Value at the time of transfer at least equal to that of such Equivalent Margin Securities. If the other party agrees to the request, the exchange shall be effected, subject to paragraph 6(d), by the simultaneous transfer of the Equivalent Margin Securities and new Margin Securities concerned. Where either or both of such transfers is or are effected through a settlement system in circumstances which under the rules and procedures of that settlement system give rise to a payment by or for the account of one party to or for the account of the other party, the parties shall cause such payment or payments to be made outside that settlement system, for value the same day as the payments made through that settlement system, as shall ensure that the exchange of Equivalent Margin Securities and new Margin Securities effected under this sub-paragraph does not give rise to any net payment of cash by either party to the other.

## 9.   Representations

Each party represents and warrants to the other that -

(a)   it is duly authorised to execute and deliver this Agreement, to enter into the Transactions contemplated hereunder and to perform its obligations hereunder and thereunder and has taken all necessary action to authorise such execution, delivery and performance;

(b)   it will engage in this Agreement and the Transactions contemplated hereunder (other than Agency Transactions) as principal;

(c)   the person signing this Agreement on its behalf is, and any person representing it in entering into a Transaction will be, duly authorised to do so on its behalf;

(d)   it has obtained all authorisations of any governmental or regulatory body required in connection with this Agreement and the Transactions contemplated hereunder and such authorisations are in full force and effect;

(e)   the execution, delivery and performance of this Agreement and the Transactions contemplated hereunder will not violate any law, ordinance, charter, bye-law or rule applicable to it or any agreement by which it is bound or by which any of its assets are affected;

(f)   it has satisfied itself and will continue to satisfy itself as to the tax implications of the Transactions contemplated hereunder;

(g)   in connection with this Agreement and each Transaction:

(i)     unless there is a written agreement with the other party to the contrary, it is not relying on any advice (whether written or oral) of the other party, other than the representations expressly set out in this Agreement;

(ii)    it has made and will make its own decisions regarding the entering into of any Transaction based upon its own judgment and upon advice from such professional advisers as it has deemed it necessary to consult;

(iii)   it understands the terms, conditions and risks of each Transaction and is willing to assume (financially and otherwise) those risks;

(h)   at the time of transfer to the other party of any Securities it will have the full and unqualified right to make such transfer and that upon such transfer of Securities the other party will receive all right, title and interest in and to those Securities free of any lien, claim, charge or encumbrance; and

(i)   the paying and collecting arrangements applied in relation to any Securities prior to their transfer from that party to the other under this Agreement will not have resulted in the payment of any Income in respect of such Securities to the party transferring such Securities under deduction or withholding for or on account of UK tax.

On the date on which any Transaction is entered into pursuant hereto, and on each day on which Securities, Equivalent Securities, Margin Securities or Equivalent Margin Securities are to be transferred under any Transaction, Buyer and Seller shall each be deemed to repeat all the foregoing representations. For the avoidance of doubt and notwithstanding any arrangements which Seller or Buyer may have with any third party, each party will be liable as a principal for its obligations under this Agreement and each Transaction.

## 10. Events of Default

(a)  If any of the following events (each an *"Event of Default"*) occurs in relation to either party (the *"Defaulting Party"*, the other party being the *"non-Defaulting Party"*) whether acting as Seller or Buyer—

   (i)   Buyer fails to pay the Purchase Price upon the applicable Purchase Date or Seller fails to pay the Repurchase Price upon the applicable Repurchase Date, and the non-Defaulting Party serves a Default Notice on the Defaulting Party; or

   (ii)   Seller or Buyer fails to comply with paragraph 4 and the non-Defaulting Party serves a Default Notice on the Defaulting Party; or

   (iii)   Seller or Buyer fails to comply with paragraph 5 and the non-Defaulting Party serves a Default Notice on the Defaulting Party; or

   (iv)   an Act of Insolvency occurs with respect to Seller or Buyer and (except in the case of an Act of Insolvency which is the presentation of a petition for winding-up or any analogous proceeding or the appointment of a liquidator or analogous officer of the Defaulting Party in which case no such notice shall be required) the non-Defaulting Party serves a Default Notice on the Defaulting Party; or

   (v)   any representations made by Seller or Buyer are incorrect or untrue in any material respect when made or repeated or deemed to have been made or repeated, and the non-Defaulting Party serves a Default Notice on the Defaulting Party; or

   (vi)   Seller or Buyer admits to the other that it is unable to, or intends not to, perform any of its obligations hereunder and/or in respect of any Transaction and the non-Defaulting Party serves a Default Notice on the Defaulting Party; or

   (vii)   Seller or Buyer is suspended or expelled from membership of or participation in any securities exchange or association or other self regulating organisation, or suspended from dealing in securities by any government agency, or any of the assets of either Seller or Buyer or the assets of investors held by, or to the order of, Seller or Buyer are transferred or ordered to be transferred to a trustee by a regulatory authority pursuant to any securities regulating legislation and the non-Defaulting Party serves a Default Notice on the Defaulting Party; or

   (viii)   Seller or Buyer fails to perform any other of its obligations hereunder and does not remedy such failure within 30 days after notice is given by the non-Defaulting Party requiring it to do so, and the non-Defaulting Party serves a Default Notice on the Defaulting Party;

then sub-paragraphs (b) to (d) below shall apply.

(b)  The Repurchase Date for each Transaction hereunder shall be deemed immediately to occur and, subject to the following provisions, all Cash Margin (including interest accrued) shall be immediately repayable and Equivalent Margin Securities shall be immediately deliverable (and so that, where this sub-paragraph applies, performance of the respective obligations of the parties with respect to the delivery of Securities, the payment of the Repurchase Prices for any Equivalent Securities and the repayment of any Cash Margin shall be effected only in accordance with the provisions of sub-paragraph (c) below).

(c)   (i)   The Default Market Values of the Equivalent Securities and any Equivalent Margin Securities to be transferred, the amount of any Cash Margin (including the amount of interest accrued) to be transferred and the Repurchase Prices to be paid by each party shall be established by the non-Defaulting Party for all Transactions as at the Repurchase Date; and

   (ii)   on the basis of the sums so established, an account shall be taken (as at the Repurchase Date) of what is due from each party to the other under this Agreement (on the basis that each party's claim against the other in respect of the transfer to it of Equivalent Securities or Equivalent Margin Securities under this Agreement equals the Default Market Value therefor) and the sums due from one party shall be set off against the sums due from the other and only the balance of the account shall be payable (by the party having the claim valued at the lower amount pursuant to the foregoing) and such balance shall be due and payable on the next following Business Day. For the purposes of this calculation, all sums not denominated in the Base Currency shall be converted into the Base Currency on the relevant date at the Spot Rate prevailing at the relevant time.

(d) The Defaulting Party shall be liable to the non-Defaulting Party for the amount of all reasonable legal and other professional expenses incurred by the non-Defaulting Party in connection with or as a consequence of an Event of Default, together with interest thereon at LIBOR or, in the case of an expense attributable to a particular Transaction, the Pricing Rate for the relevant Transaction if that Pricing Rate is greater than LIBOR.

(e) If Seller fails to deliver Purchased Securities to Buyer on the applicable Purchase Date Buyer may—

(i) if it has paid the Purchase Price to Seller, require Seller immediately to repay the sum so paid;

(ii) if Buyer has a Transaction Exposure to Seller in respect of the relevant Transaction, require Seller from time to time to pay Cash Margin at least equal to such Transaction Exposure;

(iii) at any time while such failure continues, terminate the Transaction by giving written notice to Seller. On such termination the obligations of Seller and Buyer with respect to delivery of Purchased Securities and Equivalent Securities shall terminate and Seller shall pay to Buyer an amount equal to the excess of the Repurchase Price at the date of Termination over the Purchase Price.

(f) If Buyer fails to deliver Equivalent Securities to Seller on the applicable Repurchase Date Seller may—

(i) if it has paid the Repurchase Price to Buyer, require Buyer immediately to repay the sum so paid;

(ii) if Seller has a Transaction Exposure to Buyer in respect of the relevant Transaction, require Buyer from time to time to pay Cash Margin at least equal to such Transaction Exposure;

(iii) at any time while such failure continues, by written notice to Buyer declare that that Transaction (but only that Transaction) shall be terminated immediately in accordance with sub-paragraph (c) above (disregarding for this purpose references in that sub-paragraph to transfer of Cash Margin and delivery of Equivalent Margin Securities).

(g) The provisions of this Agreement constitute a complete statement of the remedies available to each party in respect of any Event of Default.

(h) Neither party may claim any sum by way of consequential loss or damage in the event of a failure by the other party to perform any of its obligations under this Agreement.

(i) Each party shall immediately notify the other if an Event of Default, or an event which, upon the serving of a Default Notice, would be an Event of Default, occurs in relation to it.

## 11. Tax Event

(a) This paragraph shall apply if either party notifies the other that—

(i) any action taken by a taxing authority or brought in a court of competent jurisdiction (regardless of whether such action is taken or brought with respect to a party to this Agreement); or

(ii) a change in the fiscal or regulatory regime (including, but not limited to, a change in law or in the general interpretation of law but excluding any change in any rate of tax) has or will, in the notifying party's reasonable opinion, have a material adverse effect on that party in the context of a Transaction.

(b)   If so requested by the other party, the notifying party will furnish the other with an opinion of a suitably qualified adviser that an event referred to in sub-paragraph (a)(i) or (ii) above has occurred and affects the notifying party.

(c)   Where this paragraph applies, the party giving the notice referred to in sub-paragraph (a) may, subject to sub-paragraph (d) below, terminate the Transaction with effect from a date specified in the notice, not being earlier (unless so agreed by the other party) than 30 days after the date of the notice, by nominating that date as the Repurchase Date.

(d)   If the party receiving the notice referred to in sub-paragraph (a) so elects, it may override that notice by giving a counter-notice to the other party. If a counter-notice is given, the party which gives the counter-notice will be deemed to have agreed to indemnify the other party against the adverse effect referred to in sub-paragraph (a) so far as relates to the relevant Transaction and the original Repurchase Date will continue to apply.

(e)   Where a Transaction is terminated as described in this paragraph, the party which has given the notice to terminate shall indemnify the other party against any reasonable legal and other professional expenses incurred by the other party by reason of the termination, but the other party may not claim any sum by way of consequential loss or damage in respect of a termination in accordance with this paragraph.

(f)   This paragraph is without prejudice to paragraph 6(b) (obligation to pay additional amounts if withholding or deduction required); but an obligation to pay such additional amounts may, where appropriate, be a circumstance which causes this paragraph to apply.


## 12.  Interest

To the extent permitted by applicable law, if any sum of money payable hereunder or under any Transaction is not paid when due, interest shall accrue on such unpaid sum as a separate debt at the greater of the Pricing Rate for the Transaction to which such sum relates (where such sum is referable to a Transaction) and LIBOR on a 360 day basis or 365 day basis in accordance with the applicable ISMA convention, for the actual number of days during the period from and including the date on which payment was due to, but excluding, the date of payment.


## 13.  Single Agreement

Each party acknowledges that, and has entered into this Agreement and will enter into each Transaction hereunder in consideration of and in reliance upon the fact that, all Transactions hereunder constitute a single business and contractual relationship and are made in consideration of each other. Accordingly, each party agrees (i) to perform all of its obligations in respect of each Transaction hereunder, and that a default in the performance of any such obligations shall constitute a default by it in respect of all Transactions hereunder, and (ii) that payments, deliveries and other transfers made by either of them in respect of any Transaction shall be deemed to have been made in consideration of payments, deliveries and other transfers in respect of any other Transactions hereunder.


## 14.  Notices and Other Communications

(a)   Any notice or other communication to be given under this Agreement—

   (i)    shall be in the English language and, except where expressly otherwise provided in this Agreement, shall be in writing;

   (ii)   may be given in any manner described in sub-paragraph (b) below;

   (iii)  shall be sent to the party to whom it is to be given at the address or number, or in accordance with the electronic messaging details, set out in Annex V.

(b)   Any such notice or other communication shall be effective—

   (i)    if in writing and delivered in person or by courier, at the time when it is delivered;

(ii)   if sent by telex, at the time when the recipient's answerback is received;

(iii)   if sent by facsimile transmission, at the time when the transmission is received by a responsible employee of the recipient in legible form (it being agreed that the burden of proving receipt will be on the sender and will not be met by a transmission report generated by the sender's facsimile machine);

(iv)   if sent by certified or registered mail (airmail, if overseas) or the equivalent (return receipt requested), at the time when that mail is delivered or its delivery is attempted;

(v)   if sent by electronic messaging system, at the time that electronic message is received;

except that any notice or communication which is received, or delivery of which is attempted, after close of business on the date of receipt or attempted delivery or on a day which is not a day on which commercial banks are open for business in the place where that notice or other communication is to be given shall be treated as given at the opening of business on the next following day which is such a day.

(c)   Either party may by notice to the other change the address, telex or facsimile number or electronic messaging system details at which notices or other communications are to be given to it.

## 15.  Entire Agreement; Severability

This Agreement shall supersede any existing agreements between the parties containing general terms and conditions for Transactions. Each provision and agreement herein shall be treated as separate from any other provision or agreement herein and shall be enforceable notwithstanding the unenforceability of any such other provision or agreement.

## 16.  Non-assignability; Termination

(a)   Subject to sub-paragraph (b) below, the rights and obligations of the parties under this Agreement and under any Transaction shall not be assigned, charged or otherwise dealt with by either party without the prior written consent of the other party. Subject to the foregoing, this Agreement and any Transactions shall be binding upon and shall inure to the benefit of the parties and their respective successors and assigns.

(b)   Sub-paragraph (a) above shall not preclude a party from assigning, charging, or otherwise dealing with all or any part of its interest in any sum payable to it under paragraph 10(c) or (d) above.

(c)   Either party may terminate this Agreement by giving written notice to the other, except that this Agreement shall, notwithstanding such notice, remain applicable to any Transactions then outstanding.

(d)   All remedies hereunder shall survive Termination in respect of the relevant Transaction and termination of this Agreement.

## 17.  Governing Law

This Agreement shall be governed by and construed in accordance with the laws of England. Buyer and Seller hereby irrevocably submit for all purposes of or in connection with this Agreement and each Transaction to the jurisdiction of the Courts of England.

Party A hereby appoints the person identified in Annex VI hereto as its agent to receive on its behalf service of process in such courts. If such agent ceases to be its agent, Party A shall promptly appoint, and notify Party B of the identity of, a new agent in England.

Party B hereby appoints the person identified in Annex VII hereto as its agent to receive on its behalf service of process in such courts. If such agent ceases to be its agent, Party B shall promptly appoint, and notify Party A of the identity of, a new agent in England.

Nothing in this paragraph shall limit the right of any party to take proceedings in the courts of any other country of competent jurisdiction.

## 18.  No Waivers, etc.

No express or implied waiver of any Event of Default by either party shall constitute a waiver of any other Event of Default and no exercise of any remedy hereunder by any party shall constitute a waiver of its right to exercise any other remedy hereunder. No modification or waiver of any provision of this Agreement and no consent by any party to a departure herefrom shall be effective unless and until such modification, waiver or consent shall be in writing and duly executed by both of the parties hereto. Without limitation on any of the foregoing, the failure to give a notice pursuant to sub-paragraph 4(a) hereof will not constitute a waiver of any right to do so at a later date.

### 19. Waiver of Immunity

Each party hereto hereby waives, to the fullest extent permitted by applicable law, all immunity (whether on the basis of sovereignty or otherwise) from jurisdiction, attachment (both before and after judgment) and execution to which it might otherwise be entitled in any action or proceeding in the Courts of England or of any other country or jurisdiction, relating in any way to this Agreement or any Transaction, and agrees that it will not raise, claim or cause to be pleaded any such immunity at or in respect of any such action or proceeding.

### 20. Recording

The parties agree that each may electronically record all telephone conversations between them.

[Name of Party]                          [Name of Party]

By_____            By_____

Title_____           Title_____

Date_____            Date_____

# ANNEX I

## Supplemental Terms or Conditions

Paragraph references are to paragraphs in the Agreement.

1. The following elections shall apply:

[(a) paragraph 1. Buy/Sell Back Transactions may be effected under this Agreement, and accordingly Annex III will apply.]*

[(b) paragraph 1. Agency Transactions may be effected under this Agreement, and accordingly Annex IV will apply.]*

(c) paragraph 2(c). The Base Currency shall be_____;

(d) paragraph 2(l). [list Buyer's and Seller's Designated Offices]

[(e) paragraph 2(s). For the avoidance of doubt, if Securities in any Transaction include Italian government bonds, the Income in respect of such Italian government bonds shall exclude any amount deducted for or on account of tax at source and any tax credits or refunds in respect of Distributions (if any) on such Italian government bonds.]*

(f) paragraph 2(y). The pricing source for calculation of Market Value shall be: _____.

(g) paragraph 2(kk). Spot Rate to be:_____.

(h) paragraph 3(b). [Seller/Buyer/both Seller and Buyer]* to deliver Confirmation.

(i) paragraph 4(f). Interest rate on Cash Margin to be [  ]% for_____currency
[  ]% for_____currency

Interest to be payable [payment intervals and dates]

(j) paragraph 4(g). Delivery period for margin calls to be:_____

2. The following Supplemental Terms and Conditions shall apply

---

*Delete as appropriate.

# ANNEX II

## Form of Confirmation

To:_____

From:_____

Date:_____

Subject: [Repurchase] [Buy/Sell]* Transaction
      (Reference Number:      )

Dear Sirs,

The purpose of this [letter]/[facsimile]/[telex] is to set forth the terms and conditions of the above repurchase transaction entered into between us on the Contract Date referred to below.

This confirmation supplements and forms part of, and is subject to, the Global Master Repurchase Agreement as entered into between us as of [ ] as the same may be amended from time to time (the *Agreement*). All provisions contained in the Agreement govern this confirmation except as expressly modified below. Words and phrases defined in the Agreement and used in this confirmation shall have the same meaning herein as in the Agreement.

1. Contract Date:

2. Purchased Securities [state type[s] and nominal value[s]]:

3. CUSIP, CINS or other identifying number[s]:

4. Buyer:

5. Seller:

6. Purchase Date:

7. Purchase Price:

8. Contractual Currency:

[9. Repurchase Date]:*

[10. Terminable on demand]*

11. Pricing Rate:

[12. Sell Back Price:]

13. Buyer's Bank Account[s] Details:

14. Seller's Bank Account[s] Details:

[15. The Transaction is an Agency Transaction. [Name of Agent] is acting as agent for [name or identifier of Principal]]*

[16. Additional Terms]:

Yours faithfully,

---

*Delete as appropriate.

# ANNEX III

## Buy/Sell Back Transactions

1.  In the event of any conflict between the terms of this Annex III and any other term of the Agreement, the terms in this Annex shall prevail.

2.  Each Transaction shall be identified at the time it is entered into and in the Confirmation relating to it as either a Repurchase Transaction or a Buy/Sell Back Transaction.

3.  In the case of a Buy/Sell Back Transaction the Confirmation delivered in accordance with paragraph 3 of the Agreement may consist of a single document in respect of both of the transactions which together form the Buy/Sell Back Transaction or separate Confirmations may be delivered in respect of each such transaction. Such Confirmations may be in the form of Annex II to the Agreement except that, subject to paragraph 5 below, such Confirmations shall not include the item specified in paragraph 10 of Annex II.

4.  The following definitions shall apply to Buy/Sell Back Transactions:

    (i)   *"Accrued Interest"*, with respect to any Purchased Securities subject to a Buy/Sell Back Transaction, unpaid Income that has accrued during the period from (and including) the issue date or the last Income Payment Date (whichever is the later) in respect of such Purchased Securities to (but excluding) the date of calculation. For these purposes unpaid Income shall be deemed to accrue on a daily basis from (and including) the issue date or the last Income Payment Date (as the case may be) to (but excluding) the next Income Payment Date or the maturity date (whichever is the earlier);

    (ii)  *"Sell Back Differential"*, with respect to any Buy/Sell Back Transaction as of any date, the aggregate amount obtained by daily application of the Pricing Rate for such Buy/Sell Back Transaction (on a 360 day basis or 365 day basis in accordance with the applicable ISMA convention, unless otherwise agreed between the parties for the Transaction) to the sum of (a) the Purchase Price and (b) Accrued Interest paid on the Purchase Date for such Transaction for the actual number of days during the period commencing on (and including) the Purchase Date for such Buy/Sell Back Transaction and ending on (but excluding) the date of calculation;

    (iii) *"Sell Back Price"*, with respect to any Buy/Sell Back Transaction, means:

          (x)  in relation to the date originally specified by the parties as the Repurchase Date pursuant to paragraph 3(b)(iii) of the Agreement, the price agreed by the Parties in relation to that Buy/Sell Back Transaction, and

          (y)  in any other case (including for the purposes of the application of paragraph 4 (margin maintenance) or paragraph 10 (Events of Default)) of the Agreement, the product of the formula (P + AI + D) - (IR + C), where -

               P =   the Purchase Price

               AI =  the amount, equal to Accrued Interest at the Purchase Date, paid under paragraph 8 of this Annex

               D =   the Sell Back Differential

               IR =  the amount of any Income in respect of the Purchased Securities payable by the issuer on or, in the case of registered Securities, by reference to, any date falling between the Purchase Date and the Repurchase Date

               C =   the aggregate amount obtained by daily application of the Pricing Rate for such Buy/Sell Back Transaction to any such Income from (and including) the date of payment by the issuer to (but excluding) the date of calculation

5.  When entering into a Buy/Sell Back Transaction the parties shall also agree the Sell Back Price and the Pricing Rate to apply in relation to that Transaction on the scheduled Repurchase Date. The parties shall record the Pricing Rate in at least one Confirmation applicable to that Buy/Sell Back Transaction.

6.  Buy/Sell Back Transactions shall not be terminable on demand.

7.  In the case of a Buy/Sell Back Transaction, the Purchase Price shall be quoted exclusive of Accrued Interest to the Purchase Date on the Purchased Securities and the Sell Back Price shall be quoted exclusive of Accrued Interest.

8.  For the purposes of paragraph 3(c) of the Agreement, in the case of a Buy/Sell Back Transaction, the Purchased Securities shall be transferred to Buyer or its agent against the payment of the Purchase Price plus an amount equal to Accrued Interest to the Purchase Date on such Purchased Securities.

9.  In the case of a Buy/Sell Back Transaction, paragraph 3(f) of the Agreement shall not apply. Termination of such a Transaction will be effected on the Repurchase Date by transfer to Seller or its agent of Equivalent Securities against the payment by Seller of (i) in a case where the Repurchase Date is the date originally scheduled by the parties pursuant to paragraph 3(b)(iii) of the Agreement, the Sell Back Price referred to in paragraph 4(iii)(x) of this Annex plus an amount equal to Accrued Interest to the Repurchase Date; and (ii) in any other case, the Sell Back Price referred to in paragraph 4(iii)(y) of this Annex.

10.  If the parties agree that a Buy/Sell Back Transaction is to be repriced in accordance with paragraph 4(i) of the Agreement, they shall at the time of such repricing agree the Purchase Price, the Sell Back Price and the Pricing Rate applicable to the Repriced Transaction.

11.  Paragraph 5 of the Agreement (relating to Income payments) shall not apply to Buy/Sell Back Transactions.

12.  References to "Repurchase Price" throughout the Agreement shall be construed as references to "Repurchase Price or the Sell Back Price, as the case may be".

13.  In Paragraph 10(c)(i) of the Agreement (relating to Events of Default), the reference to the "Repurchase Prices" shall be construed as a reference to "Repurchase Prices and Sell Back Prices".

# ANNEX IV

## Transactions entered into as agent

1. Subject to the following provisions of this Annex, either party may enter into Transactions as agent for a third person (a "*Principal*"), whether as custodian or investment manager or otherwise (a Transaction so entered into being an "*Agency Transaction*"). In this Annex the party entering into an Agency Transaction as agent is referred to as the "*Agent*" and the other party is referred to as the "*other party*".

2. A party may enter into an Agency Transaction if, but only if—

(a) it specifies that Transaction as an Agency Transaction at the time when it enters into it and in the Confirmation;

(b) it enters into that Transaction on behalf of a single Principal whose identity is disclosed to the other party (whether by name or by reference to a code or identifier which the parties have agreed will be used to refer to a specified Principal) at the time when it enters into the Transaction; and

(c) it has at the time when the Transaction is entered into actual authority to enter into the Transaction on behalf of that Principal and to perform on behalf of that Principal all of that Principal's obligations under the Agreement.

3. A transaction shall not be entered into under the Agreement and this Annex if both parties specify that they propose to enter into that transaction as an agent.

4. Each party undertakes that, if it enters as agent into an Agency Transaction, forthwith upon becoming aware—

(a) of any event which constitutes an Act of Insolvency with respect to the relevant Principal; or

(b) of any breach of any of the warranties given in paragraph 8 below or of any event or circumstance which has the result that any such warranty would be untrue if repeated by reference to the current facts;

it will inform the other party of that fact and will, if so required by the other party, furnish the other party with such additional information as the other party may reasonably request.

5. (a) Each Agency Transaction shall be a transaction between the relevant Principal and the other party and no person other than the relevant Principal and the other party shall be a party to or have any rights or obligations under an Agency Transaction. Without limiting the foregoing, the Agent shall not be liable as principal for the performance of an Agency Transaction, but this is without prejudice to any liability of the Agent under any other provision of this Annex.

(b) All the provisions of the Agreement shall apply separately as between the other party and each Principal for whom the Agent has entered into an Agency Transaction or Agency Transactions as if each such Principal were a party to a separate agreement with the other party in all respects identical with the Agreement as supplemented by the provisions of this Annex other than this paragraph, but with the following additions and modifications—

    (i) if there occurs in relation to the Agent an Event of Default or an event which would constitute an Event of Default if the other party served a Default Notice or other written notice under any sub-paragraph of paragraph 10 of the Agreement, the other party shall be entitled by giving written notice to the Principal (which notice shall be validly given if given to the Agent in accordance with paragraph 14 of the Agreement) to declare that by reason of that event an Event of Default is to be treated as occurring in relation to the Principal. If the other party gives such a notice then an Event of Default shall be treated as occurring in relation to the Principal at the time when the notice is deemed to be given in accordance with paragraph 14 of the Agreement;

    (ii) if the Principal is neither incorporated nor has established a place of business in Great Britain, the Principal shall for the purposes of paragraph 17 of the Agreement as so applicable be deemed to have appointed as its agent to receive on its behalf service of process in the Courts of England the Agent, or if the Agent is neither incorporated nor has established a place of business in the United Kingdom, the person appointed by the Agent under paragraph 17 of the Agreement, or such other person as the Principal may from time to time specify in a written notice given to the other party.

(c)   The Agent shall do all such things and provide the other party with all such information as may be necessary to identify any Transaction Exposure which may arise in respect of any Principal.

(d)   The foregoing provisions do not affect the operation of the Agreement as between the other party and the Agent in respect of any Transactions into which the Agent may enter on its own account as a principal.

6.   Paragraph 9(b) of the Agreement shall be deleted and replaced by the following—

"(b)   it will engage in this Agreement and the Transactions contemplated hereunder as principal or, subject to and in accordance with of Annex IV, as agent and the conditions referred to in Annex IV will be fulfilled in respect of each Transaction into which it enters as an agent;".

7.   At the beginning of the last sentence of paragraph 9 of the Agreement there shall be added the words "Subject to Annex IV,".

8.   Each party warrants to the other that it will, on every occasion on which it enters or purports to enter into a transaction as an Agency Transaction, be duly authorised to enter into that transaction on behalf of the person whom it specifies as the Principal in respect of that transaction and to perform on behalf of that person all the obligations of that person under the Agreement.

## ANNEX V

## Names, Addresses and other details for Communication Between Parties

1. Part A

2. Party B

# ANNEX VI

## Name and Address of Party A's Agent for Service of process

# ANNEX VII

## Name and Address of Party B's Agent for Service of Process

ab